CITIZENS
WITHOUT A CITY

CITIZENS WITHOUT A CITY

Destruction and Despair after the L'Aquila Earthquake

—⁂—

JAN-JONATHAN BOCK

INDIANA UNIVERSITY PRESS

This book is a publication of

Indiana University Press
Office of Scholarly Publishing
Herman B Wells Library 350
1320 East 10th Street
Bloomington, Indiana 47405 USA

iupress.org

Manufactured in the United States of America

First printing 2022

Cataloging information is available from the Library of Congress.

ISBN 978-0-253-05885-0 (hardback)
ISBN 978-0-253-05886-7 (paperback)
ISBN 978-0-253-05887-4 (ebook)

A Camilla Pietropaoli
Ci hai lasciato troppo presto

CONTENTS

ACKNOWLEDGMENTS

MANY PEOPLE SUPPORTED ME IN the process of researching for and writing this book, and I am very grateful for their belief in my work. The text is based on the research I conducted for my doctoral dissertation in social anthropology, and I remain grateful to my PhD supervisor, Susan Bayly, at the University of Cambridge for her guidance throughout the writing process and enthusiasm for this project. My faculty advisor, Paola Filippucci, also read many drafts of the dissertation and provided invaluable Italian perspectives on my analyses. Mattei Candea and Mark-Anthony Falzon examined the dissertation and gave me generous and supportive feedback, which helped me in the process of writing this monograph. I would also like to thank Caroline Humphrey, Michael Herzfeld, Nick Long, and David Nugent for reading early drafts and helping me to develop my ideas further.

The Division of Social Anthropology at the University of Cambridge was an inspiring environment throughout the conception and completion of my research. I would like to thank, in particular, Andrea Grant, Jonas Tinius, John Fahy, Alex Orona, Alex Flynn, Lys Alcanya-Stevens, Sazana Jayadeva, Falk Para Witte, Johannes Lenhard, Steve Schiffer, James Laidlaw, Sian Lazar, Max Watson, Tom White, Paolo Heywood, Jo Cook, Sertaç Sehlikoglu, Maja Petrović-Šteger, Hildegard Diemberger, Joel Robbins, Yu Qiu, Holly High, Richard Irvine, Fiona Wright, Henrietta Moore, Felix Ringel, and Michał Muraswki for many engaging and inspiring conversations.

My college, Peterhouse, supported my PhD research financially, as did the German Business Foundation (SDW). During the doctorate, I made brilliant friends in Peterhouse, Cambridge, and the SDW, and my exchanges with them about the L'Aquila earthquake and its aftermath helped me refine my thinking, especially with Jack Clearman, Julien Domercq, Jennifer Wallace, Mari Jones, Steven Connor, Stephen Hampton, Magnus Ryan, Brendan Simms, Tim Crane, Saskia Murk-Janssen, Bridget Kendall, Daisy Dixon, Alon Margolin, Giovanni Zappia, Cornelius Riethdorf, Anna Savoie, Fionnbarra de Lása, Michael Burke, Yi-Shan Tsai, Will Anderson, Stevan Veljkovic, Thomas Probert, Sami Everett, Patrick Wollner, Lucia Rubinelli, Federico Brandmayr, Elisabeth von Hammerstein, David Hohenschurz-Schmidt, Lukas Obholzer, Carlos Dastis, Tina Miedtank, Vicky Pelka, Judith Dada, Natalie Pilling, Jana Höffken, Rike Franke, and Ignacio Pérez Hallerbach. I had further illuminating exchanges about this project with Becky Mantel, Nick Dines, David Alexander, Hannah Mayer and her family, Ted Randolph, Austin Tiffany, Dunya Habash, Kitty O'Lone, Ed Newell, Ulla Braumann, Lea Taragin-Zeller, Rodrigo Garcia-Velasco Bernal, Sharon Macdonald, Piero Vereni, Stefano Portelli, Jonathan White, Cornelia Herzfeld, Andrea Muehlebach, Peter Popham, Miriam Wagner, Shana Cohen, Edwin Cartlidge, Daniel Knight, Stavroula Pipyrou, John Foot, and Robert Gordon.

Above all, however, I want to thank my friends in L'Aquila. I received the warmest of welcomes in a city partly in ruins whose residents had much better things to do than help me practice Italian and understand the ins and outs of local life. Nonetheless, Aquilani were incredibly generous with their hospitality and made my life in the city much easier. I made many new friends and had the most humbling experiences that have shaped me and stayed with me since.

Alessio supported me from day one and became my closest friend, and I remain grateful to Elvira for introducing me to the city. Many others invited me to their homes and into their lives and shared their stories with me. Among them were: Francesco and Diana; Antonello and Sabina; Vittorio and Iuana; Betty; Ilaria and Luca; Marta and Gianni and their families; Vincenzo and Federico; Massimo; Giustino; Renza; Stefano; Giusi; Walter; Antonio; Dario; Massimo; Michela; Daniela; Alessandro the poet; Lorenzo; Mara; Dimitra; Giulia and Isabella; Matteo; Federica; Mattia; Claudia; Laura; Gloria and Andrea; and Sara, Ivano, Patrizio, and Romina. I want to thank everyone at Ju Boss, Lo Zio, and Matteo's. Anna, Marianna, and Lorenza became close friends and helped me make sense of everyday life, as did my friends at VIVIAMO LAq, especially Daniel and Valeria, and their families. I learned about theater and cultural work at E Che Varietà, thanks to Giulio, Irene, Giancarlo, and Tiziana. I want to thank the lawyers involved at the Major Risks Commission trial and the engineers and architects from Renzo Piano's building workshop.

My thanks also go to two anonymous reviewers who helped me improve the manuscript and to Jennika Baines at Indiana University Press, who was patient and supportive throughout the writing and production process, and to the excellent copyeditors. Martin and Regine Daubner also supported my PhD research, and I am grateful for their generosity. Finally, I would like to thank my parents, Uli and Iris, and my sisters, Joana and Rebecca, as well as their partners, for being a wonderful family.

While many people contributed to my process of thinking about politics and crisis in L'Aquila, they share no responsibility for any of this book's short-comings. It is difficult to do justice to the complexity, beauty, challenges, and contradictions of community life, and I hope Aquilani will find their experiences reflected in my work. I have chosen to change most people's names—and mention only their first names above—out of respect for their privacy and their social relations, not because they do not deserve to be named. To the contrary, my friends in L'Aquila changed my view of the world, and I will remain grateful for that.

All translations from Italian sources, interviews, and other material are mine.

Jan-Jonathan Bock
Goslar, 2020

CITIZENS
WITHOUT A CITY

ONE

INTRODUCTION

The L'Aquila Earthquake

THIS IS A BOOK ABOUT political life under exceptional circumstances; it is about disenfranchisement, the struggle to be heard and to shape one's future, and unresponsive government. The stage of the story is the city of L'Aquila, which is situated in the Italian Apennines and is the capital of the Abruzzo region. On April 6, 2009, L'Aquila and large parts of central Italy were rocked by a powerful earthquake. The tremors, which came in the middle of the night, left hundreds dead and thousands injured and led to the displacement of tens of thousands of Abruzzesi—the people of Abruzzo—who had fled damaged neighborhoods, towns, and villages. A large number would not return home for years; many moved away for good, leaving the seismic mountain regions for the safer coastal areas near Rome or Pescara.

In the wake of the disaster, the national, regional, and local authorities, as well as civil society, families, and individuals, transformed the ways in which state institutions interacted with Italian citizens. Through the declaration of a state of emergency, the national government assumed significant powers to shape everyday life in the affected areas, influencing municipal politics, architecture, local cultural expression, participation in public life, social interactions, romantic relationships, work and career choices, and the stories people told one another and outsiders about their lives. This book traces some of the ramifications of the earthquake and its political aftermath, exploring how a lack of responsiveness to local demands on the part of the government created frustration and anger among the displaced population. Affected citizens—now without access to important urban spaces and suffering from a reduced

Figure 1.1. Abruzzo countryside

Figure 1.2. Ruins in L'Aquila's centro storico

INTRODUCTION   3

ability to associate autonomously and self-govern—struggled to recover a sense of ownership over their existence and stories and to influence L'Aquila's future.

This is an account of how the Italian state transformed urban political culture in the wake of a major natural disaster, disenfranchising survivors by excluding them from decision-making processes while imposing policies and projects that would affect local life for years to come. I document the government response as well as local interpretations thereof and describe how some Aquilani reacted to the transformation of their city by demanding transparency and possibilities for participation in different arenas of city life: street protests and elections, theater and literature, material reconstruction and urban design, and court cases identifying guilt and responsibility for tragic suffering and the lives that were lost.

At the same time, the aftermath of the L'Aquila earthquake illustrates that assumptions regarding the existence of a single community of survivors with similar aspirations and visions for the future resulting from a shared experience of catastrophe are simplistic. Envy, misunderstanding, and estrangement among those affected by the earthquake were common, exacerbating a challenging situation and hampering efforts to participate collectively in political life. This book documents the limits and failures of democratic institutions to serve the people living in a disaster zone and explores how Aquilani, in the face of destruction and despair, experimented with different practices of political participation and citizenship in order to regain control over their own lives and their city and to confront anxiety about the future.

THE EARTHQUAKE AND ITS AFTERMATH

In the initial chapters of this book, I show how the state relief effort, masterminded by the then prime minister Silvio Berlusconi, excluded survivors from decision-making processes regarding emergency and recovery. The state intervention dispersed survivors into isolated resettlement sites and curtailed their capacity for political action. Remote rehousing initially disregarded expectations concerning the reconstruction of historical buildings in the old city center. Much of the media coverage praised the emergency support and critical Aquilani who voiced disappointment with government priorities for relocation and demanded heritage repair found themselves accused of ingratitude. Many survivors found that their visions of recovery were dismissed. I therefore examine how the government intervention led to a crisis of citizenship, disabling Aquilani from shaping urban existence, crippling them as political agents, and producing division and envy, with local people viewing each other increasingly as competitors in a fight over restricted opportunities and resources.

In the latter chapters of this book, I trace how groups and individuals confronted division and disenfranchisement. Many Aquilani attempted to provide alternative accounts of their disaster experience to change public perception and find meaning in suffering, and developed an interest in political participation. Emergent political movements, grassroots activism, cultural work, and other initiatives countered popular media depictions of Aquilani as passive and defective citizens. In court cases, some of the relatives of the 309 earthquake victims sought to expose that the national authorities had failed to prepare the city for catastrophe. However, experimenting with new forms of citizenship also led to agony and rivalry, since not all expected results materialized and divisions over how to evaluate the government effort and promote local views ran deep. This is not a story of successful recovery, but an account of frustration, desperation, and resilience. The experiences of L'Aquila's citizens further our understanding of political behavior in urban settings at difficult times. Survivors' stories also reveal the limits of state institutions, which failed to support participatory citizenship during a crisis. Examining post-disaster existence in L'Aquila reveals the inadequacy of a state approach to disaster management that failed to be inclusive and to accommodate grassroots contributions to recovery. This ethnography is also an analysis of the final years of a particular form of populism, berlusconismo, and its effects on Italian lives—a period that began in the mid-1990s and was marked by the dominance of Italian politics by the media tycoon Silvio Berlusconi.

I conducted fieldwork in L'Aquila between January 2012 and May 2013. Almost three years had passed since the earthquake by the time I arrived in the city. The initial emergency phase had transformed into a period of delayed transition toward something Aquilani called *normalità* (normality). The term was fuzzily employed to describe the reversal of changes that my interlocutors found undesirable: traffic queues, relocated shops, struggles to meet friends from remote parts of the city, noise and dust from building sites, the presence of nonlocal construction workers, heaps of rubbish and debris blocking passages, barriers and railings cutting through neighborhoods, abandoned monuments, or condescending comments by outsiders about Aquilani and their supposed passivity. Normality meant different things to different people, but Aquilani agreed that life had become more demanding, less predictable, and harder to manage. The experience of pervasive uncertainty was a commonplace lament.

A desire for normality reflected a wish to overturn such changes. Regaining control over local affairs and over accounts of the earthquake's aftermath was a key aspect of this strategy to confront destruction and displacement. At the same time, different understandings of normality and irreconcilable differences with regard to visions of the future fragmented efforts to lobby collectively and influence political decision-making regarding recovery plans. The disaster and its aftermath did not result in shared experiences. Whereas some had suffered losses in the family, others had little property damage to report. Entire businesses in historic quarters had to be closed down, leading to unemployment and debt for many, while simultaneously, the construction industry and other companies providing necessities flourished. The activities I describe in this book constitute struggles to create a sense of shared fate and solidarity in the face of unevenness, greed, angst, and misunderstanding with regard to the lives lived by others. When survivors had initially claimed that *siamo tutti terremotati*—literally, "we are all earthquaked," a common phrase in Italian—this claim was soon exposed as a short-lived romanticization of post-disaster solidarity that gave way to rivalry and resentment.[1] This book analyzes the effects of disaster management—namely division and uncertainty—on the one hand and illuminates grassroots attempts to confront isolation and bitterness through new forms of associationism and creative storytelling on the other. Ultimately, I show that the latter had limited success.

In many respects, however, local lives were also strangely routine when I lived in L'Aquila in 2012 and 2013, even though the historic areas remained uninhabited, with many inaccessible even for afternoon strolls. Most Aquilani had returned to work in offices located outside the old center; others had reopened temporary business spaces in containers or other buildings dotted throughout the postwar neighborhoods that were undergoing repair or across the wider periphery. The University of L'Aquila departments had reopened, some of them in disused industrial estates. Schools had been relocated to anti-seismic container facilities. People could drive around streets outside the most damaged areas, while buses connected remote resettlement sites with other parts of the urban territory. A few dozen bars and pubs had reopened near the city center. There were supermarkets and department stores on L'Aquila's outskirts, opened before the earthquake, as well as a good number of restaurants, although they had moved from the old town to less damaged, often unattractive makeshift properties elsewhere. A few months after my arrival, even routine municipal elections were held. Local television stations broadcast from the campaign trail daily, while a new edition of *Il Centro*, L'Aquila's main newspaper, appeared in kiosks each morning. There were times when I forgot about the earthquake; however, in other places or conversations with people, the disaster and its aftermath conditioned everything: emotions and future hopes, love and friendships, employment and professional moves, cultural work, political debate, legal proceedings, arguments among friends, urban planning, and chats in bars or restaurants.

L'Aquila was a contradictory place. Pockets of seemingly routine Italian urban life—the evening *passeggiata* and aperitifs with friends—existed alongside exceptional sites of tragedy and decay, where posters hung reminded passersby of the young children who had perished at the spot, and most historic buildings had been dramatically encased to prevent their collapse. Especially in the partly accessible old town, *centro storico*, destruction and abandonment were ubiquitous. The center, previously home to around twenty-four thousand people, remained uninhabited. Red signs and security fences warned Aquilani against entering large parts of the historic quarters. Military vehicles patrolled streets and squares, driving past graffiti telling soldiers to "go home." In semi-collapsed buildings, one could see "happy birthday" banners from early 2009. Laundry left to dry on the afternoon before the earthquake danced in the wind on semi-collapsed balconies. A vermin plague necessitated the installation of rodenticide boxes. Dust-covered and splintered shop windows still advertised 2009 spring-sale offers. Streets were unlit at night, and local youth climbed over barriers to annoy "occupying" soldiers. As a quiet protest against government inaction, Aquilani had tied latchkeys to rusty railings, protesting against their ongoing displacement in state-sponsored resettlement sites. The earthquake and its aftermath—the two had become almost indistinguishable in people's accounts, when they referred to the painful legacy of *il terremoto*—had repercussions in everyday life. Amid patches of ordinary urban existence, the legacies of devastation and public mismanagement gave L'Aquila a new and dominant identity.

The earthquake always lurked in the background as I examined the political actions that had turned the natural disaster into a crisis of citizenship, which survivors were struggling to overcome. Edward Simpson suggests in his analysis of the aftermath of the 2001 Gujarat earthquake in India that as time passes, even destructive and extreme events can blend into a flattened, "domesticated" past; they are increasingly talked about in a matter-of-fact way, tamed through folklore, cultural practice, and amnesia.[2] But how and when does such domestication occur? At the time of my fieldwork in L'Aquila, the disaster had not evolved into a domesticated story. On the contrary, Aquilani were debating the meaning of normality as well as political responsibilities. Rather than recording accounts of a collective history, tamed by cultural practice, I witnessed struggles over interpretations of the past and the future of a city in which everyday life shifted between anxiety and despair on the one hand and new routines to normalize exceptional experience on the other.

Figure 1.3. Fences and barriers in L'Aquila's old center

Figure 1.4. Military security for buildings clad in bracing

To complicate matters, the 2009 earthquake had not been exceptional. In the years of 1349, 1461, and 1703, seismic shocks had devastated past settlements on the same site as modern-day L'Aquila. The area has been routinely depopulated and repopulated in the wake of natural disasters, with hundreds, sometimes thousands, of casualties. At the time of my fieldwork, survivors once more reflected on their exposure to nature's raw power and on how a history of catastrophe had engulfed their present. For many, remaking political agency and autonomous community life emerged as central objectives for recovery. But how had the earthquake aftermath become so political? How did ideas about new forms of political behavior inform desires for restoration? In this book, I examine the conditions under which a natural disaster can morph into a crisis of political participation. Before delving into the 2009 disaster and its aftermath, however, we need to understand the entanglement of L'Aquila's history with episodes of destruction, displacement, despair—and reconstruction.

DOMINATION AND AUTONOMY

In the mid-thirteenth century, dozens of dispersed hamlets, monasteries, and fortresses in a central Apennine valley appealed to Holy Roman Emperor Frederick II to establish a central market town to exchange goods and produce.[3] The emperor's son, Conrad IV, subsequently founded the new marketplace, called Aquila, meaning *eagle*. The bird of prey is a universal symbol of political power still used by the Russian Federation, Germany, and the United States and is found in L'Aquila's coat of arms. It featured in the crest of the House of Hohenstaufen, then at the helm of the Holy Roman Empire of German Nations, which extended from the North Sea to the south of Italy. Since the empire bridged linguistic and cultural traditions, its power base was unstable; the emperor was concerned about the growing influence of the Christian pope in central Italy. Aquila was founded to underline the emperor's authority in the region.[4] Unlike most urban centers in this part of the country, Aquila did not grow organically out of an older settlement but was a purposeful medieval foundation with political intent. In 1294, Pope Celestine V's papal bull granted plenary indulgence to believers praying in Aquila's Collemaggio basilica and also established a Christian presence in, and hold over, the new settlement. Aquila became an important destination for pilgrimage. Two rival powers were vying for authority in central Italy—the emperor and the pope.

According to local lore, ninety-nine hamlets and monasteries founded Aquila, though the historically accurate figure is probably around eighty. Nonetheless, the number has retained symbolic significance. Aquilani tell outsiders that their historic center used to boast ninety-nine churches, ninety-nine squares, and ninety-nine fountains—one from each contributing settlement. The city's landmark is a fountain with ninety-nine spouts. Bars, shops, restaurants, and cultural institutions feature *novantanove* (ninety-nine) in their name. The number offers a glimpse into the city's origin as a place that was founded to serve external powers but that eventually generated a distinctive urban identity for its inhabitants. Over the course of the Middle Ages, Aquila's wealth increased due to the wool trade between northern and southern Italy. Aquila became less dependent on its immediate hinterland.

For a couple of centuries, the monasteries and castles that used Aquila to exchange goods dominated the marketplace. Every settlement had sent residents to populate the new trade hub; Aquila was a duplicate of its medieval surroundings, which were reflected in street names, architecture, customs, and dialects. However, as Aquila became more populous than the monasteries and settlements that had founded and controlled it, its residents sought to cast off external influence. Civic buildings were constructed as expressions of local pride, growing wealth, and autonomy. A local historian, Walter Cavalieri, explained to me that the transition from an externally ruled market town to a city with distinctive civic culture began around 1500.[5] Since Aquila had been internally heterogeneous from its inception, founded by people with diverse dialects and customs, the division between the citizens inside the wall and peripheral peasants became pronounced in the process of creating a robust urban identity; the difference between town dwellers and rural people was emphasized to counter ambiguous loyalties. Walter Cavalieri suggested that this history continues to have repercussions in contemporary closed-mindedness: "There have been three boundaries between Aquilani and the outside world—the mountains, the city walls, and the barriers in their heads."[6]

In the sixteenth century, however, autonomy was again curtailed. The Spanish Crown conquered the Kingdom of Naples, to which Aquila belonged at the time. The wool trade and other economic affairs were placed under Spanish supervision. Aquila was ruled by a foreign power. The Spaniards constructed a monumental castle outside the city walls to control access to the settlement. The Spanish Fortress remains an impressive structure today, with four imposing towers overlooking a deep moat. For Aquilani at the time, it must have been a daunting reminder of external supervision. The fortress was not designed to offer refuge for Aquila's citizens in times of conflict, but to control the citizenry, who had supported France in a previous conflict with Spain. To add insult to injury, the Spanish imposed a punitive tax to fund the fortress's construction. A few centuries later, the Kingdom of Naples became part of the Kingdom of the

Two Sicilies until the foundation of the Italian nation state in 1861. Despite its name, the kingdom included the entire southern half of the Italian peninsula. Naples was its dominant center. In the Kingdom of the Two Sicilies, Aquila was a peripheral place, albeit the second largest settlement. This association with the Kingdom of the Two Sicilies established a widespread imaginary of L'Aquila as a "southern" city, despite its being in the center of Italy, northeast of Rome. This association continues today, and with it comes a host of stereotypes regarding a supposed lack of civic virtue, economic deprivation, state dependence, corruption and clientelism, and passivity and government reliance in the face of challenges.[7]

In 1939, Aquila changed its name to its current form, L'Aquila—*the* eagle. The fascists preferred the more imposing definitive article. Alongside fascist structures that remodeled a part of the old center, the city's borders were redrawn to encompass a string of previously autonomous settlements as part of a large L'Aquila municipality.[8] The 1927 *Grande Aquila* reform had already enshrined the urban center's domination over peripheral villages and towns. It corroborated the reversal of L'Aquila's historical origin as a settlement founded by outsiders to serve their purposes, and subsequently controlled by foreign powers. The relationship between the walled center and its rural periphery still informs local imaginations of the distinction between modern and sophisticated urban *cittadini*—which translates as both *city people* and *citizens*—on the one hand and supposedly rustic and backward *peasants*, or *contadini*, who resent L'Aquila's dominance on the other. After 1945, L'Aquila's population expanded drastically. Beyond the medieval walls, new neighborhoods with modern multistory apartment blocks appeared, complicating the center-periphery division. Many *cittadini* moved from the narrower streets of the centro storico into car-friendly quarters with spacious condominiums.

Before the 2009 earthquake, two-thirds of Aquilani lived in postwar neighborhoods or municipalized villages, but the old centro storico, with its bars, restaurants, coffee shops, public offices, grand squares, churches, and cultural venues, remained the center stage of urban life for Aquilani. The modern quarters never developed significant urban infrastructure for the social lives of their inhabitants. The extensive postwar areas offered few shops, bars, or other amenities that could be reached comfortably by foot. In many areas, construction had been haphazard and unplanned: crooked, narrow streets appeared as if they had been added accidentally in between housing blocks, often without pavements or trees. In one area, the Pettino quarter, tram tracks were laid around the year 2000, and a tram station was built to upgrade connections with the historic center. No trams have ever driven here, however, since the streets were subsequently found to be too narrow, revealing a lack of effective urban planning—and interest—in the postwar neighborhoods. These new parts of L'Aquila were never intended to rival the centro storico; instead they had been designed to provide comfortable, private apartments with ample parking space at a time when indoor plumbing and central heating were rare in old buildings. In the wake of the earthquake, when the historic center became inaccessible, the absence of alternative social, civic, and cultural spaces outside the walled core exacerbated the isolation and fragmentation of citizens. That is one reason why prompt heritage restoration in the old center became a central recovery demand.

In 1952, the University of L'Aquila was founded. It had around twenty-three thousand students in early 2009, out of a city population of just over seventy-two thousand. L'Aquila used to be an attractive place of study for southern Italians; students enjoyed buzzing lives and affordable rents in the center, where some university departments were located. In 1970, L'Aquila became the regional capital of Abruzzo, a central Italian administrative region encompassing Adriatic Sea shores as well as the Apennine Mountains. Bestowing the title of the regional capital on this remote city was recognition of its historical importance for medieval Italy rather than an acknowledgment of the city's current status.[9] Today, the Abruzzo region is known principally for its national parks. For many Italians, this area is an inconspicuous and little-known part of their country, associated with agriculture and hearty cuisine. During the winter months, some ski resorts attract the Roman middle classes. Service-sector employment in the administration of the university or the regional authorities has replaced jobs in manufacturing since the 1970s. Economic power has shifted toward the Abruzzo coastline. The mountain valleys are harder to reach. There are no train connections between L'Aquila and major cities on either side of the peninsula, such as Rome or Pescara. Italians consider the mountainous Apennine areas a picturesque part of their country but also a rustic region lacking extensive tourism infrastructure—especially when compared with Italy's highly developed holiday destinations—and economic opportunities for young people. Aquilani describe each other, and sometimes themselves, as *montanari* (mountain people)—a term with connotations of authenticity, industriousness, and unaffectedness but also of conservatism, resistance to change, and suspicion toward outsiders.[10]

A DISASTER STORY

Catastrophe marked L'Aquila's history throughout the ages. A major earthquake struck Aquila in 1349, only a hundred years after its foundation. It was more powerful than the April 2009 one. Churches and houses collapsed, and eight hundred people perished.[11] In 1456 and 1461, powerful earthquakes flattened dozens of settlements around Aquila, as well as large parts of the town. In subsequent centuries, seismic eruptions and weaker clusters of minor-intensity earthquakes interrupted calm periods. Smaller shocks were common. In 1703, a powerful earthquake razed Aquila to the ground as part of a sequence of otherwise minor-intensity tremors that affected the area for months. On January 14, 1703, a destructive earthquake in this cluster killed about two thousand people in a zone north of L'Aquila, flattening smaller towns such as Accumoli and Amatrice.[12] A few weeks later, on February 2, 1703, the most devastating earthquake in L'Aquila's history killed 2,500 Aquilani and thousands more in the surrounding area. Around eight hundred of them died celebrating mass in the St. Domenico church, when the roof, apse, and transept collapsed on Christians in prayer. Survivors sought to leave Aquila's ruins and settle elsewhere, but a commissioner appointed by the king exempted those who stayed from paying tax. With houses and monuments flattened, the event marked the end of medieval Aquila. Rural Abruzzesi from the hinterland—often vagabonds, prostitutes, and beggars—built and repopulated a new Aquila in the following decades, turning poor country dwellers into Aquilani.[13]

The 1703 earthquake had a profound effect on local identity. In its wake, the white and red colors of Aquila's flag, dating back to the city's foundation by the Holy Roman emperor, were replaced with black and green to symbolize despair and hope. These colors have remained since. Carnival celebrations were shortened for a long mourning period. After 1703, they have never begun before February 2. Aquilani tell visitors that their city still celebrates the world's shortest carnival. In the eighteenth century, disaster survivors and other people in nearby areas started to venerate Saint Emygdius, attributing the sparing of a nearby town, Ascoli Piceno, to his protective powers. This cult has continued until the present day. The few medieval buildings that withstood the disaster were decorated with metal lilies as a reminder of catastrophe and resistance for posterity. A new Aquila, a showpiece of central Italian baroque and renaissance architecture, was built on the ruins of the medieval settlement. It featured picturesque fountains, piazzas, and cobbled alleys lined with splendid buildings arranged around elegant courtyards along grand streets and smaller, lower, and darker houses in poorer quarters.

Although no major seismic event hit the city between 1703 and 2009, destructive earthquakes affected Italy from Sicily to the Alps.[14] The Apennine Mountains, at the heart of which L'Aquila is situated, are among the most seismically active areas of Europe. In 1915, a powerful earthquake razed a nearby town, Avezzano, to the ground. Only one building remained standing.

According to estimates, the disaster killed up to thirty thousand people in the area. Out of thirteen thousand inhabitants in Avezzano, around eleven thousand lost their lives.[15] In 2016, a number of settlements in an area north of L'Aquila were wiped out by a series of tremors that killed hundreds. Earthquakes regularly affect Aquilani, who live in a seismic hot spot. They know that their past is a history of death and destruction. Nonetheless, L'Aquila still exists. Devastation and despair were followed by acts of resilience, demonstrating determination, or simple pragmatism, to rebuild and start again.

THE 2009 EARTHQUAKE

In autumn 2008, seismologists noticed an intensification of seismic activity in the area surrounding L'Aquila (the so-called Aquilano). The sequence of smaller shocks was labeled an earthquake cluster (*sciame sismico*). Such clusters of minor-intensity tremors are common and usually nondestructive. Most such tremors are not even perceived by the population and are only registered by sensitive instruments. However, over the months, tremor frequency and individual intensities increased. The Abruzzo newspaper *Il Centro* reported on the phenomena in December 2008. There was no sign of panic or concern.

The sequence continued in the new year, but most Aquilani did not notice tremors as they went about their daily lives. In February 2009, the first stronger quake of the sequence occurred. Although some schools were evacuated, no major damage was reported. On February 14, *Il Centro* cited seismologists who explained that the tremors were of very low intensity, which they described as normal for the area. A few days later, the same newspaper published an extensive documentation of the earthquake cluster, with maps showing the epicenters of the tremors from the past six weeks. An increase in individual magnitudes was also noted. Four weeks later, in mid-March, many Aquilani could feel several stronger shocks in one day. Over the course of three months, since December 2008, instruments registered 160 minor-intensity earthquakes in the Aquilano area. Aquilani had felt thirty-eight of them. On March 30, seven tremors rocked L'Aquila, as magnitudes increased. People ran into the streets, fearing building collapse; some offices were evacuated. Cracks appeared at the De Amicis school, which was closed alongside other educational institutions and would not reopen. Clocks fell off the walls, and vases toppled over. The next day, L'Aquila's archbishop celebrated a mass in honor of Saint Emygdius—the saint who was believed to have spared a nearby town from destruction in the 1703 earthquake. Aquilani discussed the tremors with friends, family, and colleagues. Local papers published scientific interpretations.

At the time, an amateur seismologist, Giampaolo Giuliani, claimed to have invented an innovative method for earthquake prediction based on radon gas emissions, which he measured with lay instruments. Giuliani predicted that a powerful quake was imminent in the town of Sulmona, one hour south of L'Aquila, which led Sulmona's mayor to warn residents with loudspeaker vans. Giuliani's prediction was false. Nonetheless, in response to growing concerns, Italy's Civil Protection Agency convened a special panel of scientific experts, the Major Risks Commission (Commissione Grandi Rischi), charged with assessing whether the situation should be considered a matter of serious danger to the local population. The government did not want to allow hobby scientists to influence public opinion and create a panic; Giuliani received notice that he was under police investigation for raising a false alarm. In L'Aquila, the Major Risks Commission met to evaluate the evidence. The media subsequently reported that there was no significant risk of a seismic occurrence; the earthquake cluster was described as normal, rather than as a precursor for a dangerous event. The deputy head of the Civil Protection Agency, Bernardo De Bernardinis, chaired the expert meeting. He told a regional television station that the continuous discharge of seismic tension through minor-intensity tremors, rather than a single large earthquake, rendered the territory safer. For many Aquilani, those were reassuring statements.

The Civil Protection Agency did not receive notification from the experts to set up evacuation areas, erect night shelters, or put in place other precautionary measures. Many residents interpreted the absence of government activity as a positive sign. During the days that followed the expert meeting, tremors continued. By Palm Sunday, April 5, 2009, Aquilani had sustained months of seismic events. The mayor announced that a number of schools and public buildings would not open the next morning, as inspections were needed to assess their stability. Later that night, the earth shook twice, perceptibly but not destructively. Exhausted, Aquilani fell asleep. Then, at 3:32 a.m., the country's most powerful earthquake since 1980 struck central Italy. It measured 6.3 on the moment magnitude scale and lasted for more than twenty seconds, combining horizontal and vertical movements. Thousands of buildings sustained damage, often serious. Many collapsed completely or partially, burying thousands of Aquilani in their beds; 309 people died, and 1,500 were injured.

In just a few seconds, most of the area's distinctive historic architecture—concentrated in L'Aquila's walled center and in peripheral towns and villages—was left in a semi-ruined state. Outside the historic quarters, postwar condominiums collapsed. Investigators later found that they had not been earthquake-proof.[16] Even in Rome, one hour's drive away, people awoke from the tremors. When the earth stopped shaking, a cloud of dust and powder from collapsed buildings engulfed the area. The smell of gas, leaking from fractured pipes, permeated the air. Since no precautions had been taken, it took the national emergency services hours to arrive in the city. Aquilani helped each other, digging through the rubble and waiting for the morning, withstanding a series of aftershocks. The seismic sequence became known as the 2009 L'Aquila earthquake.

THE STATE RELIEF EFFORT

In the early hours of April 6, 2009, the Civil Protection Agency arrived in L'Aquila. The national authorities declared most of L'Aquila's neighborhoods unfit for habitation and initiated a large-scale evacuation scheme. Forty-three municipalities in central Italy reported substantial damage.[17] Under the leadership of Berlusconi, the Italian government launched a widely acclaimed emergency relief operation. Sixty-seven thousand people were removed from their homes. They were given the choice either to relocate to one of 170 camps that were quickly erected on sports grounds and other open spaces across the L'Aquila municipality by the Civil Protection Agency and volunteer organizations (one-third chose this) or to move into free-of-charge hotel rooms along the Adriatic Coast, one hour east of the city (another third); the remaining survivors found accommodation with friends or relatives. Along with thousands of helpers and volunteers from all over Italy who delivered donations in their private vans, looters arrived in the ruined region; they looked for cash, jewelry, and other precious items in abandoned buildings as they pretended to dig for survivors or remove rubble.[18] Italians call them *sciacalli* (jackals). Police and military personnel were deployed to find and arrest them, often unsuccessfully. Many Aquilani would blame outsiders—southern Italians, Neapolitans in particular, and foreigners—for the thefts. Among the chaos of a catastrophe that had wreaked havoc across an extensive territory, they were hard to spot.

A state of emergency was declared, which imposed an access ban to damaged neighborhoods and curtailed citizens' rights. The army and police forces arrived in the devastated territory. The national government superseded the municipal, provincial, and regional authorities. Various forms of state power were centralized in the hands of the government in Rome, coordinated by Guido Bertolaso, then head of the Civil Protection Agency and Berlusconi's right-hand man.[19] L'Aquila's historic center—an extensive assemblage of historical architecture, listed buildings, and century-old monuments—was transformed into an inaccessible red zone cordoned off by metal fences and screened by soldiers. Most structures had not collapsed but had sustained large cracks, caved-in roofs, or broken windows. Diggers and excavators assembled heaps of debris after the bodies had been recovered. The center was cut off from urban life. For many survivors, camp existence became the new routine, with shower cabins and regular mealtimes in cramped canteens. Volunteer organizations and state personnel shuffled alongside the world press. Donations arrived, and Italy's best-known singers recorded a song, "Domani" ("Tomorrow"), to raise money for the displaced. On April 23, a special earthquake decree was passed. It regulated the construction of resettlement sites and the hosting of the G8 summit in the city a few months later, allocated around eight billion euros to the emergency, which was later reduced to 5.8 billion euros to be spent until 2032, introduced tax breaks for the affected areas, and appointed Bertolaso as Extraordinary Commissioner for the Emergency.

Evacuated to coastal hotel resorts and camps, the earthquake survivors witnessed a debate about relocating the regional government offices and the Abruzzo parliament to the coastal city of Pescara because of the damage sustained by public buildings. Many Aquilani regard Pescara as an unsophisticated upstart that rose to regional supremacy in the twentieth century, hundreds of years after L'Aquila's heyday. Old rivalry shaped fears of surrendering a distinctive feature of their city: that after decades of industrial and economic decline, Abruzzo's political center could also shift to the coast. The possibility of ceding a distinctive element of prestige and power to Pescara—a city that already boasted a seaport, tourism infrastructure, the only Abruzzo airport, and railway connections to major Italian cities—added insult to injury for displaced Aquilani. In the end, the Italian government did not pursue its capital-relocation plan. However, the battle to retain the regional administration was only the first in a sequence of struggles to maintain a distinctive identity as an urban and political center.

The national government branded its emergency response unprecedented. Merely days after the destruction, Berlusconi unveiled his solution to the extensive damage suffered by historic buildings: Progetto Case, nineteen permanent rehousing sites for almost seventeen thousand people.[20] Berlusconi had initially favored the construction of only one enormous resettlement city—a second L'Aquila—but the local authorities had managed to dissuade him, arguing that it would mean the end of L'Aquila, since the need for swift reconstruction would disappear. Instead, with Progetto Case, clusters of purpose-built rehousing blocks were attached to damaged villages and towns in L'Aquila's periphery. Berlusconi had become a multimillionaire in the construction industry, rising to national fame for building a chic satellite town, Milano Due, in the 1970s in Milan.[21] The prime minister presented the construction scheme as the product of his personal expertise in the building sector and gave Progetto Case the fashionable English name "new towns."[22] In the press—and by Aquilani who approved of the scheme—the relocation sites were also nicknamed *case di Berlusconi* (Berlusconi's houses). This was probably much to the man's approval, who presented the scheme as his personal gift to the city.[23]

Thanks to emergency legislation to fast-track procedures, the first Progetto Case sites were constructed within months of the earthquake, and Aquilani could apply to relocate from the tent camps or hotel rooms that had become their temporary homes. When the new residents entered the first set of completed resettlement apartments alongside television crews on September 29, 2009—which happened to be Berlusconi's birthday—they found a bottle of prosecco in the fully stocked fridge. A note from the prime minister wished them a serene stay in their new home. In television appearances, Berlusconi praised the recovery progress and promised the swift repair of historic houses and monuments.[24] He overrode the municipal authorities, including the center-left mayor, Massimo Cialente, by concentrating state power in his center-right central government in a way that was "not consistent with consolidated practice and the reality of Italian decentralization."[25] Berlusconi presented himself as a generous patron overseeing the recovery effort, as if success depended on his personal commitment rather than on the bureaucratic state apparatus that supported Aquilani as citizens. In a political culture with strong traditions of clientelism, in which the importance of personal contacts is still often seen as key to private success, this approach was criticized by some Aquilani but also espoused by others, since it seemed to produce results.[26] Those who tried to protest against decisions, such as the plan for Progetto Case resettlement sites, were labelled as disruptive and consequently ignored by the government, producing a "democracy deficit" in the eyes of critics.[27] The government intervention was divisive in its use of emergency powers to override local representatives and concerns, which some saw as a necessary measure in the race against time to complete resettlement sites before winter, while others accused Berlusconi of abusing his position to hand out contracts to firms that supported him politically and pushing through a construction project with Progetto Case that would delay reconstruction efforts.

A substantial amount of state money was allocated for repair projects across postwar neighborhoods. In July 2009, the government hosted Italy's G8 summit of world leaders in the devastated city. Originally, the summit had been planned for the Sardinian island of La Maddalena, but Berlusconi decided with short notice that politicians and the press should come to L'Aquila instead to bear witness to local hardship—and promote

Figure 1.5. Onna, a village on the city's outskirts, was razed by the earthquake.

Figure 1.6. Ruins and stabilizers in L'Aquila's historic center

the government's response. Journalists returned to L'Aquila a mere three months after the earthquake. The attention divided survivors. Many considered the summit the wrong priority for the city at the time and criticized what they considered to be "ruin porn." Others welcomed the event as a great coup by their prime minister; they hoped that the world's attention would accelerate recovery by attracting investment and launching new initiatives supported by foreign governments and businesses. The exceptional speed and the apparent effectiveness of initial relief operations led many survivors to assume that they would find their city's reconstruction and their return to normality—in the restored spaces of civic urban life—to be a very prompt process. At no time did the government openly question the importance of reconstructing the old city center and other parts of the municipality with historic buildings. The Progetto Case sites and repair programs in the postwar quarters, the government promised, would be only the first step toward unprecedented and efficient recovery through restoration of L'Aquila's heritage. Nevertheless, the range of local reactions to the government's disaster response, also certainly colored by preexisting views on Berlusconi and his political style, indicated early on that divisions over recovery strategies, priorities, urban design, and the proper balance between administrative efficacy and grassroots involvement would divide the population of earthquake victims.

MY FIELDWORK PERIOD

When I moved to L'Aquila almost three years later, it was clear that promises made in 2009 regarding recovery and restoration had not materialized. Instead of being repaired, most of the damaged historic houses and monuments had been stabilized through bracing. Buttressed and encased in iron and wooden scaffolding, with thick metal chains pulling external walls together, they appeared frozen in time. L'Aquila's old buildings had been secured for potential future repair, which had been postponed due to a lack of funds and political commitment. The city was in limbo; uncertainty and doubt had become the new normal. Before April 2009, over nine hundred businesses had operated in the historic center. Five years later, only twenty-nine had reopened, mainly smaller cafés, shops, or bars whose owners had obtained special permits to use the ground floors of less damaged buildings.[28] While some businesses had relocated to containers or wooden huts in accessible postwar neighborhoods outside the historic city center, the majority had disappeared. Reliance on state welfare benefits in the province of L'Aquila had increased by

800 percent compared with pre-disaster figures.[29] Five years after the destruction, a national newspaper reported that many of L'Aquila's children had never been to a proper school. Emblematic of suspended urban life, some schools had reopened in containers that were accessible through functional plastic doors and crammed with industrial chairs and tables under hospital-style tubular lamps. These containers were located across and between the postwar quarters or resettlement sites in which people lived and could be reached by private transport, causing daily traffic jams in the morning and again in the afternoon. They had been presented as temporary solutions in 2009, but parents wondered how long "temporary" could last and whether L'Aquila was the right environment in which to raise children and have a family. As a journalist wrote at the time: "From postponement to postponement, from promise to promise, those who were children during the earthquake are now teenagers, and those with hopes witnessed them quickly transform into frustration."[30]

Post-disaster life confronted Aquilani with life-changing decisions: Should they stay or move away? Could they trust state institutions to shape their future and respect local views and aspirations? Should L'Aquila be rebuilt as a historic city, with authentic monuments and old buildings, or should it be modernized? What implications would the city's history of destruction have for the future? How could the city population respect the memory of the 309 victims while simultaneously remaking ordinary life and lighthearted urban culture? What authority would Aquilani have to shape recovery plans and priorities? Three to four years after the disaster, broken promises and delays—which survivors variously attributed to a misdirected state emergency operation, the broken Italian political system, inept local elites, corruption, the global economic crisis and its effects on public finances, or the selfishness of fellow Aquilani—conditioned everyday life. The transition from high-flying pledges and relocation projects to stasis in the old center affected everybody. L'Aquila was a city in limbo. Many were stuck in the remote Progetto Case rehousing units, where resettled residents left handwritten notes in the staircases leading from car parks to individual apartments; this was the only social space that they shared with other residents. The Progetto Case resettlement blocks, placed on elevated platforms with anti-seismic pillars, were antisocial; they lacked public spaces, such as schools, bars, street corners, shops, markets, or cultural venues. They were sleep containers, expedient for a short period in the wake of disaster. Three years on, Aquilani struggled to accept them as permanent homes. Other survivors still stayed in faraway hotels on the Abruzzo Coast. Thousands had moved away.

I lived in L'Aquila during a particular period. The activities I followed and the stories I collected must be understood against this backdrop. The year

2012–2013 was an exceptional one, not just for L'Aquila but also for the country. In November 2011, Berlusconi resigned from the office of prime minister. He had not been able to reassure the financial markets that Italy was a safe haven for foreign investment at the height of the euro crisis, which had evolved out of the financial crisis in the early 2010s. The Italian state was facing bankruptcy. European leaders agreed that the best way to stabilize Italy and keep it in the euro was to create a bipartisan expert government committed to structural reforms and spending cuts without Berlusconi. When the financial crisis became acute in 2008, Italy had a public debt of almost 110 percent of GDP. Five years later, in 2013, the figure had risen to over 130 percent, one of the highest in the Western world. The country was struggling to refinance its liabilities and paid high interest rates on its debt. Italy's newspapers reported daily the so-called "spread" (the English term was used)—that is, the difference in interest rates on ten-year German government bonds and their Italian equivalents. Until 2008, the rates had been very close, but with the financial crisis, Italian government bonds were seen as a risky investment. Interest rates shot up in 2012 and reached 7 percent at the same time as the German finance minister paid 2 percent. A default was a much-talked-about scenario.

In November 2011, Mario Monti, an economics professor and former European commissioner, became Italy's twenty-fifth prime minister. There were no elections. A cross-chamber majority of center-left and center-right parties supported the new government, which implemented the structural reforms that previous administrations had shelved because of their unpopularity with the electorate. Monti appointed a cabinet of technocrats and experts to cut public spending and introduce structural reforms. Faced with a national economic and political crisis, L'Aquila was not a government priority, even though the new administration reiterated previous commitments to reconstruction.

In 2012, a series of earthquakes affected the prosperous Emilia-Romagna region in the north of Italy, requiring urgent emergency intervention. Attention had shifted from Abruzzo. In L'Aquila, the sturdy Progetto Case resettlement sites built by the Berlusconi administration had given survivors a roof above their heads. For outsiders at least, it seemed that the need to act swiftly and pour more money into L'Aquila had passed. The emergency was over. Restoring the old buildings of one of thousands of historic centers in Italy, with a price tag of tens of billions of euros, did not appear to rank highly on the agenda of an unelected expert government seeking to prevent financial collapse, even though the Monti administration appointed a minister responsible for the reconstruction of disaster sites, including L'Aquila.

In L'Aquila, the absence of a perspective for the future was crippling. There was anger that the previous government had dispersed survivors across distant relocation sites and remote hotels without access to the urban spaces of civic and cultural life, thereby hampering political opposition and engagement. In response to the forced displacement, I discovered that numerous Aquilani had established new initiatives to reverse passivity, reinstall citizens as active political agents, insert local priorities on the government's agenda, and promote alternative, grassroots views on reconstruction and recovery. New expressions of political agency emerged in L'Aquila in response to isolation, rivalry, and anxiety. This book documents the visions of recovery pursued, and debated, by citizens without a city who attempted to overcome fragmentation and envy.

DISASTER AND CITIZENSHIP

The study of disaster now has a respectable tradition in anthropology and other social science disciplines.[31] Anthropologists have shown that disasters should not be conceptualized as disruptive events after which survivors return to pre-disaster normality. Rather, a disaster and its repercussions are shaped by social, economic, political, and other factors that create uneven vulnerability.[32] Catastrophes are cultural.[33] As a consequence, disaster recovery does not take a straightforward path toward remaking a collectively remembered reality that existed before the event. Instead, rebuilding a local world is a contested process. What emerges from the ruins of the old is influenced by political and economic actors seeking to expand power and is shaped by different ideas about what it means to live well.[34] The legacies of disaster can rework romantic relationships and family life and alter how affected communities confront the state and state power.[35] The loss of trust in a once-familiar environment can have long-term effects for survivors.[36] Disasters do not end when aid arrives and people are rehoused. Transformative processes continue, often revealing otherwise hidden characteristics of social, political, and cultural life. Such revelations can either reinforce existing structures and values, since people realize their importance, or lead to the questioning of traditional ways of life and authority and the promotion of change.

Until the mid-1990s, disaster anthropology focused on non-Western contexts, documenting how interpretations of modernity or statehood transformed in the wake of destructive events.[37] While most anthropological studies continue to explore non-Western countries, the repercussions of disasters in prosperous Western democracies have begun to capture more anthropological attention.[38] A prominent case has been the devastation of New Orleans by Hurricane

Katrina in 2005, which led to a string of studies on its social, political, and economic consequences. Anthropologists have shown that the destruction caused by Katrina had many social and cultural causes.[39] The hurricane illuminated the uneven distribution of exposure to risk, which was conditioned by a lack of government preparedness, economic inequality, and racial injustice.[40] While some authors, such as writer Rebecca Solnit in *A Paradise Built in Hell*, have drawn attention to the emergence of unusual acts of kindness and solidarity in the face of extreme events, others have highlighted how post-Katrina New Orleans revealed stark injustice and exclusion, rather than collective human experience through shared suffering.[41] The uneven distribution of risk, vulnerability, and death in New Orleans had been manufactured through political decisions that restricted protection to certain "white" neighborhoods. Katrina allowed social scientists to examine tensions, contradictions, and inequalities in an urban setting that was exposed as even more segregated and unequal than previously assumed.[42]

The social and economic transformation of New Orleans continued in the wake of the disaster. A prolonged crisis was manufactured through flawed political decisions. The US government's drive toward privatization following Katrina put many small fishing companies out of business.[43] Author Naomi Klein has suggested that the national government, in collaboration with big business, used the shock of the moment and need for investment to transform traditional economic relations and curtail the participatory rights of poorer communities.[44] Business interests shaped the political economy in the aftermath.[45] Katrina revealed the unevenness of US citizenship, exposing racial and economic inequalities, and illustrated the incapacity of the central government to respond adequately to catastrophe in certain parts of the country with their marginalized urban poor.[46] The social repercussions of Katrina illuminated the fact that formal US citizenship did not mean equal access to protection in the face of extreme circumstances. I take inspiration from this approach to conceptualizing disasters by using the earthquake as the point of departure for a study into the longer-term ramifications for L'Aquila and the Aquilani, exploring new challenges as well as grassroots responses.

Following the 2009 earthquake, with the government intervention dominating public life, ordinarily privileged citizens—students, lawyers, schoolteachers and university professors, business owners, and professionals—who had not considered themselves politically marginal suddenly found their autonomy restricted. Decisions were imposed by Rome without the consultation of local citizens or authorities. People were removed from their private property and prohibited from returning. Large urban areas became inaccessible and were placed under army supervision. Resettlement projects that transformed the urban landscape were launched without consultation, and journalists and politicians held almost exclusive power to depict local developments and realities to outsiders and the world.[47] In 2009, social media and alternative reporting were still in their early stages. While Facebook and YouTube provided some fledgling space for critical grassroots information, the mainstream media were still—probably for the last time—the dominant source of accounts regarding a major Italian catastrophe.[48]

Through state-of-emergency provisions, the national authorities restricted protest and the visibility of alternative viewpoints. L'Aquila's survivors were confronted with a government approach that was neither inclusive nor participatory. The activities pursued by active citizens were aimed at reversing the exclusionary emergency response and creating possibilities for participation in decision-making processes. These attempts developed a new kind of civic culture, by which I refer to a set of cultural, social, and political activities aimed at empowering local people to influence the reconstruction and recovery process through political involvement in new movements and associations, by shaping the future of one's community through activism and legal channels, and by having an autonomous voice. This civic culture had a local focus, which developed in response to the disenfranchising government effort and its isolating resettlement policy, the decay of historic urban spaces, and the rivalry, division, and envy that characterized social interactions in the face of uneven access to financial resources and experiences of suffering or displacement.

Following the disintegration of the Soviet Union, a renewed interest emerged in the social and political sciences in citizenship and in exploring how people and new states could be bound together.[49] One important scholarly focus was on the construction of new nations and political cultures that would follow the socialist dictatorships.[50] Another important area of interest concerned the consequences of globalization for the hybrid, transnational, intercultural, and otherwise complicated types of citizenship emerging in Western countries, where minorities continued to demand more representation and inclusion and boundaries with other nations became more fluid.[51] Some authors attested a general decline of community spirit and growing individualism in such diversifying societies.[52] In order to understand experiences of exclusion better, other analysts introduced a distinction between formal and substantive, or legal and social, kinds of citizenship.[53] In such distinctions, straightforward legal status is split from "social citizenship," which requires active engagement in one's community or society through political participation, which, in turn, generates acknowledgement from the community regarding one's status as an insider.[54]

This emphasis also helps illuminate the lives of "noncitizens"—usually immigrants or refugees without a legal status that guarantees political inclusion as voters—whose contributions to society illustrate a different practice of belonging through action and engagement, or social citizenship.[55] The focus of such studies has been on the inclusion of marginalized groups in diverse societies.[56] This distinction between formal membership in a political community through legal status and substantive or social types of citizenship through engagement and political participation has complicated simplistically legalistic approaches to the definition of citizenship.

In post-disaster L'Aquila, this distinction became blurred. When the government declared a state of emergency, the ordinary rights and privileges associated with formal Italian citizenship were temporarily suspended.[57] The state intervention imposed restrictions and limited the agency of evacuees, who were subjected to the powers of the Civil Protection Agency, which installed, as critics argued, "emergency as a style of governance."[58] For the Aquilani who pursued the activities that I document in subsequent chapters, realizing that formal citizenship—their legal membership in the political community of Italians—could be easily curtailed induced reflections on the intersection of the private and the political. This, in turn, gave rise to new types of engagement in the political process through grassroots activism, party politics, or theater and cultural involvement; some Aquilani used legal channels in order to identify culprits for the tragedy and hold state agencies to account. The groups and individuals who responded to the aftereffects of the state of exception described their engagement both as a reaction to the limiting of their possibilities as rights-bearing citizens and as an exercise in more substantive kinds of citizenship by expanding participation in the political process. The experiences of Aquilani as citizens without a city illustrate a culture of citizenship that has as its objective the reversal of disenfranchisement, forced passivity, and fragmentation—and the restoration of urban spaces in which citizens can gather, deliberate, and take action.

Rather than becoming *again* the citizens that they had been before April 2009, Aquilani were rethinking what it means to live an active political life in a way that would confront apathy and division. Such engagements fused the substantive and formal types of citizenship described in other contexts: having experienced the volatility of their legally defined political membership, Aquilani conceptualized active participation as a way of regaining membership in the political community of citizens and protecting their city. Importantly, citizenship in this context was largely urban and local; the aspirations associated with active engagement concerned the future of L'Aquila and would require participation in decision-making processes regarding reconstruction and recovery. Aquilani would also need to overcome the envy and division within the city population and regain some authority over the ways in which the earthquake's aftermath was conceived outside the city. In this process of experimenting with new forms of political and cultural community life, Aquilani considered important questions: What does being an active citizen mean in a semi-ruined urban environment without the traditional places of congregation, deliberation, and protest? Which new initiatives can be launched for inclusive and effective practices of local citizenship? Through which types of activities can civic culture be expressed when large parts of one's city and its public life remain under state control? How can citizens force the state authorities to own up to having committed serious mistakes that disenfranchised survivors and, in turn, guarantee that new administrations learn from past errors and apologize to victims?

In her analysis of practices of citizenship in Berlusconi's Italy, Andrea Muehlebach suggests that the neoliberal retreat of the state from the provision of welfare was accompanied by a new ethics of care, carefully manipulated by officials.[59] This "neoliberal citizenship" is the result of a cynical exploitation of traditional types of grassroots solidarity that have their roots in both Catholic community life and left-wing associationism and enable the state's withdrawal from social services and security.[60] My analysis approaches emergent forms of citizenship from a different angle, not as purposefully engineered by a shrinking state seeking to pull back from the provision of services, but rather as a grassroots strategy in response to an authoritarian, unresponsive, and disenfranchising government. Citizenship studies have often highlighted the imposition of new regimes and political orders in the wake of disasters, producing, for example, "biological citizens" after the nuclear accident at Chernobyl— people marked by new politico-medical categories that regulated access to state aid.[61] I want to go beyond this analysis of state power and explore under which conditions citizenship can become emancipatory.

Expanding Muehlebach's examination of citizenship as complicit in depoliticization, I explore the re-politicization of citizenship toward the end of an era dominated by berlusconismo—a specifically Italian type of populism that turns politics into a cynical game show in order to deflect from the much more problematic conflation of political power with big business and the deleterious effects of serious corruption, abuse, and political ineptitude.[62] The emergent forms of civic engagement in L'Aquila provide a prism for the wider political situation in crisis-ridden Italy—and other contexts as well—in which democratic states experiment with authoritarian practices and the affected population struggles to push back effectively, realizing the limits of civil society activism in the face of disinterested, and potentially hostile, public institutions. My analysis explores citizenship as a type of political critique directed against a state that does not want to encourage political involvement and simultaneously as an attempt to reconstitute a sense of community against the selfishness and cynicism that spread in a post-disaster city.

Previous analyses of political culture and citizenship in Italy have tended to emphasize the lack of civic virtues and a commitment to the common good, particularly in the south of the country. Famously, shortly after World War II, sociologist Edward Banfield, of the United States, argued that southern Italians lacked an interest in collective well-being, exhibited distrust toward politicians and the authorities, and were only concerned with the fate of the close family— and therefore would remain incapable of developing the virtues and behaviors that were central to the democratic life that had developed in the United States.[63] Banfield saw economic deprivation as the main cause of a popular ethos that he termed "amoral familism," in which moral commitments and sacrifice are directed solely toward one's close relatives, often at the expense of the wider community and society. He was soon attacked by other commentators on Italian life for depicting "the south" as a homogenous cultural space without internal differences and for supposedly reinforcing simplistic stereotypes regarding Italy's north-south divide.[64]

While Banfield's critics proposed that the dire economic conditions in Italy's south necessitated an attitude of pragmatic selfishness for survival, rather than the other way round, they still largely agreed with his observations.[65] John Davis wrote, "The facts which Banfield describes are, it is generally admitted, true. Nobody denies, I think, that it is hard to get South Italians to cooperate, or that civic improvement associations are rare, and then ineffectual. Middle-class exponents of the working-class interest are often self-seeking, inconsistent, and haughty."[66] Whereas Banfield described a predominantly rural phenomenon that he believed would vanish with modernization and the domestic migration from the countryside into larger cities, social historian Paul Ginsborg reminds us that urbanization and social change could not eradicate its prevalence: "Familism, it emerged, was not just rural and archaic, destined to disappear with American-style modernization, as Banfield envisaged. It was also urban and modern."[67]

As the subsequent chapters illustrate, Aquilani also accused each other of such selfishness, antisocial behavior, disregard for the common good, and a lack of collective responsibility. I avoid the term "amoral familism," but my interlocutors were less hesitant to describe neighbors, acquaintances, and co-citizens as amoral and backward mountain rustics who were unethical, self-seeking, and rapacious. The presence of a narrow view of the social world and of reciprocal responsibilities toward others rendered new types of civic engagement on the part of those who aspired to change post-disaster L'Aquila more difficult; attempts to establish and popularize a civic culture aimed at improving the common good often resulted in frustration. In such an analysis, it would be simplistic to attribute selfishness and inactivity solely to the intervention of a neoliberal government and its disregard for democratic participation.[68] While the state demonstrated little interest in the views of survivors and did not attempt to reduce tensions through coherent strategies for restoration, financial assistance, or local public consultation exercises to involve the citizenry, Aquilani were not only victims in the wake of the disaster, but also actors.

This book documents how different groups sought to cooperate and remake community life, confronting selfishness and isolation, and why such attempts were often unsuccessful when active groups found it difficult to rally the wider population behind causes and initiatives. In 2012 and 2013, as a result of government mismanagement and a widespread inability to overcome petty differences and define a shared vision for recovery and the future, there was no tight-knit community of disaster survivors that shared interpretations and objectives. Instead, I found pockets of activity scattered across a distraught and often bitter population following uneven and divergent recovery paths. This book explores local citizenship as a battle fought by some groups and individuals seeking to combat divisive tendencies and produce a sense of community in the face of inertia or even hostility on the part of the surviving population and an unresponsive and inattentive state.

The struggles over citizenship that took place in post-disaster L'Aquila stand out for one important reason: they were driven by the fear of losing one's city permanently, both as a home and as a space for community life. The threat of perpetual displacement and limbo was real, since previous government responses to disaster had seen temporary resettlement turn into an enduring new normality or eventually forced survivors to relocate to other, supposedly safer, sites. When a landslide damaged the mountain village of Africo in the southern Italian region of Calabria in the early 1950s, the authorities decided to relocate the entire community permanently to a new, purpose-built settlement in a coastal location, with traumatic effects for the survivors who also lost access to their key source of income, agropastoralism. A few years later, more mudslides devastated several communities in the same area of Calabria. Survivors were sent to emergency camps that were often attached to military bases.

Figure 1.7. Progetto Case resettlement site

This included, incidentally, one in L'Aquila, many hours north of Calabria. Many evacuees stayed for years, found new employment in L'Aquila, and never returned to Calabria.[69] The children and grandchildren of those displaced in the 1950s remembered the stories of how what was initially considered a short-term solution transformed into permanent relocation.

Following the 1980 Irpinia earthquake near Naples, supposedly temporary resettlement sites would remain in place for decades. Corruption and mismanagement led to the disappearance of reconstruction funds. The disaster's aftermath became a glaring example of state failure and collusion between the political and state authorities and organized crime and big business, with disregard for the fate of survivors.[70] The horror of supposedly temporary displacement becoming permanent and of the old city center decaying to such a degree that restoration would become impossible was very real for those Aquilani who had studied the history of Italian disaster management and the damaging influence of political profiteering and corruption. Becoming actively involved was a necessity for many survivors in order to confront disinterestedness and exploitation and to save their city from complete and irreversible ruination by calling fellow Aquilani to action to overcome stagnation, cynicism, division, and apathy.

CHAPTER OVERVIEW

Chapter 2 documents how Aquilani recall their experiences of the earthquake and the government-led state of emergency. I suggest that such accounts of the past enable survivors to reconstitute themselves as active citizens, to challenge media depictions of their homogeneous victimhood, and to claim the right to return to their city.

Chapter 3 explores the 2012 municipal elections as an important dimension of efforts to reconfigure political normality. However, seeking to take an informed decision to shape their city's future as voting citizens, many Aquilani reported frustration with the level of political debate. They struggled to attribute responsibilities to politicians or policies and consequently deplored feelings of powerlessness to shape their future. Aquilani found themselves increasingly on disparate recovery paths, which resulted from different experiences with grief, destruction, displacement, and compensation: envy and rivalry led to a "war among the poor" that turned the 2012 municipal elections into a frustrating experience that pitted Aquilani against one another rather than lead to a shared vision for recovery.

Chapter 4 documents conflicts about the future of L'Aquila as an urban space. Throughout my fieldwork, a string of innovative architectural projects were presented and contested in the city. Commentators perceived as outsiders—critics and architects—were rejected by those Aquilani who were dogmatic about an authentic reconstruction "as it was and where it was," whereas other Aquilani saw the disaster as an opportunity to modernize the city and address the perceived imbalance between the old center and other parts of the urban territory.

Having examined three key dimensions of loss and conflict—depictions of the past, political agency in the present, and control over the future of the city as an urban space—I turn to emergent types of political behavior and civic culture in the latter chapters of this book. I explore such practices as parts of the disaster recovery process by which newly active Aquilani, as well as seasoned activists and cultural producers, created alternative public spaces and challenged the state to deliver on its promises to reconstruct heritage and provide justice to the survivors by punishing those who had acted irresponsibly in the run-up to the disaster.

Chapter 5 explores local grassroots movements and political organizations. I examine how post-disaster campaigning gave way to new engagement with institutionalized politics. Many Aquilani actively sought to regain control over local affairs after experiences of disenfranchisement at the hands of state agencies. The relatives of the 309 victims also transformed suffering into political agency through grassroots campaigning and political work. They lobbied for the restoration of L'Aquila as a safe city.

Chapter 6 documents cultural activities, such as writing and acting, that were intended to reconstitute a sense of shared fate among survivors. The divergent trajectories of local lives in the wake of the disaster and the state of emergency had intensified misunderstanding, isolation, and envy among Aquilani. Those involved in cultural work sought to create inclusive narratives of post-disaster experiences in order to confront misrepresentation, counter the lack of shared urban spaces, and lay new foundations for communal solidarity.

Chapter 7 examines a high-profile lawsuit in which the relatives of the deceased sought to prove that they had behaved correctly on the night of the earthquake while the responsible authorities had betrayed them. Desiring a sense of closure and recognition for their struggle, however, bereaved Aquilani involved in the court case as witnesses and plaintiffs faced fragmentation and hostility for what they considered an important civic gesture. Attempts to prove their capacity to act rationally and follow the rule of law did just the opposite, and bereaved survivors felt estranged from their city, misrepresented in hostile media outlets, and powerless in their attempts to write alternative histories of the earthquake and of the political failures that caused suffering.

Chapter 8 concludes the book. Since disaster management efforts had intensified crisis experiences after the earthquake through disenfranchisement, resettlement, uneven support, and broken promises, some Aquilani pursued new types of political behavior and civic culture in order to promote solidarity, confront division, and ensure that their historic city would not be lost forever. Still, at the time of my fieldwork in 2012 and 2013, local society remained fragmented. Isolated without proper access to their city and let down by ineffective public institutions, activists, artists, writers, the families of the victims, and others who attempted to improve post-disaster life and provide a voice to the survivors found combatting cynicism, envy, and self-interest to be a difficult task.

Ten years later, in 2019 and 2020, while repair and restoration activity had accelerated, many Aquilani had left the city and started new lives elsewhere. Over a decade after the 2009 earthquake, the city's future remains uncertain.

NOTES

1. For an account of emergent forms of solidarity in the wake of disaster and other disruptive events, see Rebecca Solnit, *A Paradise Built in Hell—The Extraordinary Communities That Arise in Disaster* (New York: Penguin, 2010).

2. Edward Simpson, *The Political Biography of an Earthquake: Aftermath and Amnesia in Gujarat, India* (London: Hurst, 2013), 53.

3. For a more detailed overview, see Alessandro Clementi, *L'arte della lana in una città del Regno di Napoli (sec. XIV-XVI)* (L'Aquila: Japadre, 1979); Clementi, *Storia dell'Aquila. Dalle origini alla prima guerra mondiale* (Rome: Laterza, 1998); and Luigi Lopez, *L'Aquila: le memorie, i monumenti, il dialetto: guida alla città* (L'Aquila: G. Tazzi, 1988).

4. Clementi and Elio Piroddi, *L'Aquila* (Rome: Laterza, 1986).

5. Most of the names in this text are fictitious, in order to protect the identities of those who shared intimate and personal stories with me. I made exception for those interlocutors who had important public roles in politics or civil society or who otherwise chose to be identified, since I asked each person I interviewed about their preferences.

6. Walter Cavalieri, in discussion with the author, L'Aquila, Italy, July 10, 2012.

7. For a discussion of the cultural and social implications of the notion of "the south" in Italy, see Luciano Cafagna, *Nord e Sud: non fare a pezzi l'unità d'Italia (I grilli)* (Venice: Marsilio, 1994); Gabriella Gribaudi, "Images of the South," in *Italian Cultural Studies*, ed. David Forgacs and Robert Lumley (Oxford: Oxford University Press, 1996), 72–87; and Jane Schneider, ed., *Italy's "Southern Question": Orientalism in One Country* (Oxford: Berg, 1998). See also Lumley and Jonathan Morris, *The New History of the Italian South—The Mezzogiorno Revisited* (Exeter: Exeter University Press, 1997).

8. For an overview of L'Aquila's fascist period, see Enrico Cavalli, *La grande Aquila: politica, territorio ed amministrazione all'Aquila tra le due guerre* (L'Aquila: Colacchi, 2003); and Simonetta Ciranna, "Segni di monumentalità nazionale nell'architettura abruzzese," in *L'architettura nelle città italiane del XX secolo*, ed. Vittorio Franchetti Pardo (Milan: Jaca Book, 2003).

9. This move remains controversial. L'Aquila is not the most populous Abruzzo city; the title goes to Pescara, a coastal town with an important harbor. To wind up their Aquilani friends, nonlocal students at the University of L'Aquila would sing a chant: *L'Aquila non è il capuluogo della mia regione*—"L'Aquila isn't the capital of my region."

10. For more on the cultural associations of mountain people in Italian culture, see Cesare Poppi, "'We Are Mountain People': Tradition and Ethnicity in the Ladin Carnival of the Val di Fassa (Northern Italy)," PhD thesis, Department of Social Anthropology, University of Cambridge (1983).

11. For an overview of L'Aquila's historical earthquakes, see Luigi Mammarella, *L'Abruzzo ballerino. Cronologia dei terremoti in Abruzzo dall'epoca romana al 1915* (L'Aquila: Adelmo Polla Editore, 1990); Orlando Antonini, *I terremoti aquilani* (Todi: Tau Editrice, 2010); or Aleardo Rubini, *I terremoti in Abruzzo. Cronaca, storia, arte, leggenda* (Villamagna: Tinari, 2011).

12. The same towns were again razed to the ground by a series of tremors that rattled central Italy in August 2016, claiming hundreds of lives and illustrating the ongoing seismic hazard of the Apennine Mountains, as well as failures of the construction industry and governance.

13. Francesco Marconi, "L'Aquila: terremoto del 1703, una catastrofe ignorata," InStoria (2009), accessed August 24, 2013, http://www.instoria.it /home/aquila_terremoto_1703.htm.

14. In 1908, one of the worst natural disasters in Europe, an earthquake in the Strait of Messina between the Italian peninsula and Sicily, killed up to 150,000 people across Southern Italy. See Giorgio Boatti, *La terra trema. Messina 28 dicembre 1908. I trenta secondi che cambiarono l'Italia, non gli italiani* (Milan: Mondadori 2004); John Dickie, "Timing, Memory and Disaster: Patriotic Narratives in the Aftermath of the Messina-Reggio Calabria Earthquake, 28 December 1908," *Modern Italy* 11, no. 2 (2006): 147–166; and Dickie, *Una catastrofe patriottica. 1908: il terremoto di Messina*, trans. F. Galimberti (Roma/ Bari: Laterza, 2008). In 1968, the Belice earthquake in Sicily cost 370 lives. See Giacomo Parrinello, *Fault Lines: Earthquakes and Urbanism in Modern Italy* (New York: Berghahn Books, 2015). In 1976, the northern Friuli region suffered a powerful quake, killing 989 people. The most devastating postwar earthquake hit the southern Irpinia province in 1980, resulting in almost three thousand casualties and causing billions of pounds' worth of damage. See Judith Chubb, "Three Earthquakes: Political Response, Reconstruction, and Institutions: Belice 1968, Friuli 1976, Campania 1980," in *Disastro! Disasters in Italy Since 1860: Culture, Politics, Society*, ed. John Dickie, John Foot, and Frank Snowden (New York: Palgrave Macmillan, 2002).

15. For accounts of the Avezzano earthquake, see Emilio Cerasani, *I terremoti registrati nella Marsica in Marruvium e S. Sabina. Memorie storiche di due civiltà* (Pratola Peligna, IT: Grafica Italiana, 1986), and *Storia dei terremoti in Abruzzo: aspetti umani, sociali, economici, tecnici, artistici e culturali* (Sulmona: Accademia Sulmonese degli Agghiacciati, 1990).

16. In one particularly harrowing case, a construction company had fitted an existing building with a heavy concrete roof that could not be supported by the frame. Among the victims who died when the roof caved in and buried the building was the daughter of the responsible technician. He was sentenced in court for criminally negligent manslaughter, bearing a legal responsibility for his daughter's death.

17. David E. Alexander, "The Evolution of Civil Protection in Modern Italy," in *Disastro! Disasters in Italy since 1860: Culture, Politics, Society*, ed. John Dickie, John Foot, and Frank Snowden (New York: Palgrave, 2013): 60.

18. Alfio Mastropaolo, *La mucca pazza della democrazia. Nuove destre, populismo, antipolitica* (Turin: Boringhieri, 2010): 122–124.

19. Alpaslan Özerdem and Gianni Rufini, "L'Aquila's Reconstruction Challenges: Has Italy Learned From Its Previous Earthquake Disasters?," *Disasters* 37, no. 1 (2013): 122f.

20. Progetto Case stands for Complessi Antisismici Sostenibili ed Ecocompatibili, or Anti-Seismic, Sustainable, and Eco-Compatible Complexes. *Case* is also Italian for "houses."

21. Paul Ginsborg, *Silvio Berlusconi: Television, Power and Patrimony* (London: Verso, 2004), chapter 1.

22. Georg Josef Frisch, *L'Aquila. Non si uccide così anche una città?* (Naples: Clean, 2010a); and Frisch, "Un altro terremoto. L'impatto urbanistico del progetto C.a.s.e.," *Meridiana* 65/66 (2010b): 59–84.

23. This was despite the fact that their cost was largely covered by the European Union Solidarity Fund for disaster recovery (European Court of Auditors 2013).

24. Antonello Ciccozzi, "Aiuti e miracoli ai margini del terremoto de L'Aquila," *Meridiana* 65/66 (2010): 227–255.

25. Özerdem and Rufini, "L'Aquila's Reconstruction Challenges," 125.

26. The roles of clientelism and of personal relations in Italian politics have been analyzed, among others, by Jeremy Boissevain, *Friends of Frieds: Networks, Manipulators, and Coalitions* (New York: St. Martin's, 1974); Ernest Gellner and John Waterbury, eds., *Patrons and Clients in Mediterranean Societies* (London: Duckworth, 1977); Amalia Signorelli, *Chi può e chi aspetta: Giovani e clientelismo in un'area interna del Mezzogiorno* (Naples: Liguori, 1983); and Carlo Rossetti, "Constitutionalism and Clientelism in Italy," in *Democracy, Clientelism, and Civil Society*, ed. Luis Roniger and Ayse Günes-Ayata (Boulder, CO: Lynne Rienner, 1994). For a historical comparison between historical and contemporary forms of clientelism, see also Dorothy Louise Zinn, *La Raccomandazione. Clientelismo vecchio e nuovo*, trans. Caterina Dominijanni (Rome: Donzelli Editore, 2001).

27. Lina M. Calandra, "Territorio e democrazia: considerazioni dal post-sisma aquilano," in *Sismografie. Ritornare a L'Aquila mille giorni dopo il sisma*, ed. Fabio Carnelli, Orlando Paris, and Francesco Tommasi (Rome: Edizione Effigi, 2012a).

28. Attilio Bolzoni, "L'Aquila, così il cantiere più grande d'Europa ha partorito una città fantasma," *La Repubblica*, January 14, 2014, accessed August 10, 2017, http://www.repubblica.it/cronaca/2014/01/14/news/l_aquila_tra_negozi _chiusi_e_palazzi_sventrati_il_cantiere_pi_grande_d_europa_ha_partorito _una_citt_fantasma-75873760/.

29. Redattore Sociale, "L'Aquila quattro anni dopo. Almeno 20 mila persone senza lavoro," April 4, 2013, accessed August 10, 2017, http://www .redattoresociale.it/Notiziario/Articolo/430055/L-Aquila-quattro-anni-dopo -Almeno-20-mila-persone-senza-lavoro.

30. Flavia Amabile, "La vita dei bimbi dell'Aquila mai stati in una scuola vera," *La Stampa*, March 26, 2014, accessed November 10, 2017, https://www.lastampa .it/cronaca/2014/03/26/news/la-vita-dei-bimbi-dell-aquila-1.35782160.

31. Anthony Oliver-Smith, "Disasters and Natural Hazards," *Annual Review of Anthropology* 25 (1996): 303–328; and Doug Henry, "Anthropological Contributions to the Study of Disasters," in *Disciplines, Disasters and Emergency Management: The Convergence and Divergence of Concepts, Issues and Trends From the Research Literature*, ed. David A. Mcentire (Emittsburg, MD: Federal Emergency Management Agency, 2005).

32. Greg Bankoff, "Constructing Vulnerability: The Historical, Natural, and Social Generation of Flooding in Metropolitan Manila," *Disasters* 27, no. 3 (2003): 224–238; and Craig E. Colten, "Vulnerability and Place: Flat Land and Uneven Risk in New Orleans," *American Anthropologist* 108, no. 4 (2006b): 731–734.

33. Susanna M. Hoffman and Oliver-Smith, eds., *The Angry Earth: Disaster in Anthropological Perspective* (London: Routledge, 1999); and Hoffman and Oliver-Smith, eds., *Catastrophe and Culture: The Anthropology of Disaster* (Santa Fe: School of American Research Press, 2002).

34. For studies that emphasize the cultural dimension of disasters and their aftermaths, see Barbara Bode, *No Bells to Toll: Destruction and Creation in the Andes* (New York: Scribner, 1989); Adriana Petryna, *Life Exposed: Biological Citizens after Chernobyl* (Princeton, NJ: Princeton University Press, 2002); and Simpson, *The Political Biography of an Earthquake*.

35. For an account of how intimacy is remodeled in the wake of extreme events, see Veena Das, *Life and Worlds: Violence and the Descent into the Ordinary* (Berkeley: University of California Press, 2006). For diverse perspectives on how disasters remake the relationship between citizens and their state, see Elena Poniatowska, *Nothing, Nobody: The Voices of the Mexico City Earthquake*, trans. Aurora Camacho de Schmidt (Philadelphia: Temple University Press, 1995); Paul L. Doughty, "Plan and Pattern in Reaction to Earthquake: Peru, 1970–1998," in *The Angry Earth*, ed. Hoffmann and Oliver-Smith; Sharon Stephens, "Bounding Uncertainty: The Post-Chernobyl Culture of Radiation Experts," in *Catastrophe and Culture*, ed. Hoffmann and Oliver-Smith; and Keir Martin, *The Death of the Big Men and the Rise of the Big Shots: Custom and Conflict in East New Britain* (New York: Berghahn Books, 2013).

36. Frida Hastrup, *Weathering the World. Recovery in the Wake of the Tsunami in a Tamil Fishing Village* (New York: Berghahn Books, 2011).

37. Megan Vaughan, *The Story of an African Famine: Gender and Famine in Twentieth-Century Malawi* (Cambridge: Cambridge University Press, 1987); Oliver-Smith, *The Martyred City: Death and Rebirth in the Peruvian Andes* (Prospect Heights, NY: Waveland, 1992); and Kim Fortun, *Advocacy after*

Bhopal: Environmentalism, Disaster, New Global Orders (Chicago: University of Chicago Press, 2001).

38. See, for example, Kai T. Erikson, *Everything in its Path: Destruction of Community in the Buffalo Creek Flood* (New York: Simon & Schuster, 1976); Anne Allison, *Precarious Japan* (Durham, NC: Duke University Press, 2013); and Daisuke Naito, Ryan Sayre, Heather Swanson, and Satsuki Takahashi, eds., *To See Once More the Stars: Living in a Post-Fukushima World* (Nampa, ID: Pacific, 2014).

39. Diane E. Austin, "Coastal Exploitation, Land Loss, and Hurricanes: A Recipe for Disaster," *American Anthropologist* 108, no. 4 (2006): 671–691.

40. Colten, *An Unnatural Metropolis: Wresting New Orleans from Nature* (Baton Rouge: Louisiana State University Press, 2006a); Colten, "Vulnerability and Place"; and Beverly Wright, "Race, Place, and the Environment in the Aftermath of Katrina," *Anthropology of Work Review* 32, no. 1 (2011): 4–8.

41. Solnit, *A Paradise Built in Hell.*

42. Imanni Sheppard, *Health, Healing and Hurricane Katrina: A Critical Analysis of Psychosomatic Illness in Survivors* (San Diego: Cognella, 2011); Vincanne Adams, *Markets of Sorrow, Labors of Faith—New Orleans in the Wake of Katrina* (Durham, NC: Duke University Press, 2013); and Jessica Warner Pardee, *Surviving Katrina: The Experiences of Low-Income African American Women* (Boulder, CO: First Forum, Lynne Riener, 2014).

43. John Petterson, Laura Stanley, Edward Glazier, and James Philipp, "A Preliminary Assessment of Social and Economic Impacts Associated with Hurricane Katrina," *American Anthropologist* 108, no. 4 (2006): 643–670.

44. Naomi Klein, *The Shock Doctrine* (London: Penguin, 2007).

45. For an analysis of the neoliberal transformation that followed the Hurricane and how it exacerbated exclusion and injustice, see Oliver-Smith and Gregory Button, "Family Resemblances between Disasters and Development-Induced Displacement: Hurricane Katrina as a Comparative Case Study," in *Capitalizing on Catastrophe: Neoliberal Strategies in Disaster Reconstruction*, ed. Nandini Gunewardena and Mark Schuller (Walnut Creek, CA: Alta Mira, 2008); Cedric Johnson, ed., *The Neoliberal Deludge: Hurricane Katrina, Late Capitalism, and the Remaking of New Orleans* (Minneapolis: University of Minnesota Press, 2011); and John Arena, *Driven from New Orleans: How Nonprofits Betray Public Housing and Promote Privatization* (Minneapolis: University of Minnesota Press, 2012).

46. Ted Steinberg, *Acts of God: The Unnatural History of Natural Disasters in America* (Oxford: Oxford University Press, 2006).

47. See, for example, Irene Bono, "Oltre la «mala Protezione civile»: l'emergenza come stile di governo," *Meridiana* 65/66 (2010): 185–205; Domenico Cerasoli, "De L'Aquila non resta che il nome. Racconto di un terremoto,"

Meridiana 65/66 (2010): 35–58; Ciccozzi, "Aiuti e miracoli ai margini del terremoto de L'Aquila"; Ciccozzi, "Catastrofe e C.A.S.E.," in *Il terremoto dell'Aquila. Analisi e riflessioni sull'emergenza*, ed. Università degli Studi Dell'Aquila (L'Aquila: Edizione L'Una, 2011); Frisch, *L'Aquila*; Gian-Luigi Bulsei and Alfio Mastropaolo, eds., *Oltre il terremoto. L'Aquila tra miracoli e scandali* (Rome: Viella, 2011); Calandra, *Territorio e democrazia. Un laboratorio di geografia sociale nel doposisma aquilano* (L'Aquila: L'Una, 2012b); and Carnelli, Paris, and Tommasi, *Sismografie*.

48. For an analysis of the role of social media and social networks in reports from the L'Aquila earthquake, see Manuela Farinosi and Alessandra Micalizzi, eds., *NetQuake. Media digitali e disastri naturali. Dieci ricerche empiriche sul ruolo della rete nel terremoto dell'Aquila* (Milan: FranoAngeli, 2013).

49. Rogers Brubaker, *Citizenship and Nationhood in France and Germany* (Cambridge, MA: Harvard University Press, 1992); and Will Kymlicka and Wayne Norman, "Return of the Citizen: A Survey of Recent Work on Citizenship Theory," *Ethics* 104, no. 2 (1994): 352–381.

50. See, for example, Katherine Verdery, *What Was Socialism, and What Comes Next?* (Princeton, NJ: Princeton University Press, 1996); Verdery, *The Political Lives of Dead Bodies: Reburial and Postsocialist Change, The Harriman Lectures* (New York: Columbia University Press, 1999); Shalom H. Schwartz and Anat Bardi, "Influences of Adaptation to Communist Rule on Value Priorities in Eastern Europe," *Political Psychology* 18, no. 2 (1997): 385–410; Marc Morjé Howard, "The Weakness of Postcommunist Civil Society," *Journal of Democracy* 13, no. 1 (2002): 157–169; William Mishler and Richard Rose, "Learning and Re-Learning Regime Support: The Dynamics of Post-Communist Regimes," *European Journal of Political Research* 41, no. 1 (2002): 5–36; and Caroline Humphrey, *The Unmaking of Soviet Life* (Ithaca, NY: Cornell University Press, 2002).

51. See, for example, Aihwa Ong, "Cultural Citizenship as Subject-Making: Immigrants Negotiate Racial and Cultural Boundaries in the United States," *Current Anthropology* 37, no. 5 (1996): 737–751; Ong, *Flexible Citizenship: The Cultural Logics of Transnationality* (Durham, NC: Duke University Press, 1999); Stephen Castles and Alastair Davidson, *Citizenship and Migration: Globalization and the Politics of Belonging* (New York: Routledge, 2000); Luis Eduardo Guarnizo, "On the Political Participation of Transnational Migrants: Old Practies and New Trends," in *E Pluribus Unum? Contemporary and Historical Perspectives on Immigrant Political Incorporation*, ed. Gary Gerstle and John Mollenkopf (New York: Russel Sage Foundation, 2001); Nina Glick Schiller, "Transborder Citizenship: An Outcome of Legal Pluralism Within Transnational Social Fields," in *Mobile People, Mobile Law. Expanding Legal Relations in a Contracting World*, ed. Franz von Benda-Beckman, Kebbit von Benda-Beckman, and Anne Griffiths (London: Ashgate, 2005); Lok

Siu, *Memories of a Future Home: Diasporic Citizenship of Chinese in Panama* (Stanford: Stanford University Press, 2005); and Emma Tarlo, "Hijab in London: Metamorphosis, Resonance and Effects," *Journal of Material Culture* 12, no. 2 (2007): 131–156.

52. Robert Putnam, *Bowling Alone: The Collapse and Revival of American Community* (New York: Simon & Schuster, 2000).

53. Kymlicka and Norman, "Return of the Citizen"; and Angus Stewart, "Two Conceptions of Citizenship," *The British Journal of Sociology* 46, no. 1 (1995): 63–78.

54. Bryan Turner, "Outline of a Theory of Citizenship," in *Dimensions of Radical Democracy: Pluralism, Citizenship and Community,* ed. Chantal Mouffe (London: Verso, 1992), 33–62.

55. Tomas Hammar, *Democracy and the Nation State* (London: Routledge, 1990); James Holston, ed., *Cities and Citizenship* (Durham, NC: Duke University Press, 1999); Deborah Reed-Danahay and Caroline B. Brettel, eds., *Citizenship, Political Engagement, and Belonging: Immigrants in Europe and the United States* (New Brunswick, NJ: Rutgers University Press, 2008); Carole Blackburn, "Differentiating Indigenous Citizenship: Seeking Multiplicity in Rights, Identity, and Sovereignty in Canada," *American Ethnologist* 36, no. 1 (2009): 66–78; and Damani Partridge, *Hypersexuality and Headscarves: Race, Sex, and Citizenship in the New Germany, New Anthropologies of Europe* (Bloomington: Indiana University Press, 2012).

56. See, for example, Renato Rosaldo, "Cultural Citizenship in San Jose, California," *PoLAR* 17, no. 2 (1994): 57–63; Steven Vertovec, "Multicultural Policies and Modes of Citizenship in European Cities," *International Social Science Journal* 50, no. 156 (1998): 187–199; Ruth Mandel, *Cosmopolitan Anxieties: Turkish Challenges to Citizenship and Belonging in Germany* (Durham, NC: Duke University Press, 2008); and Vertovec and Susanne Wessendorf, eds., *The Multiculturalism Backlash* (Abingdon, VA: Routledge, 2010).

57. For analyses of how emergencies and states of exception can be used to restrict citizens' rights across different political contexts, see Craig Calhoun, "The Idea of Emergency: Humanitarian Action and Global (Dis)Order," in *Contemporary States of Emergency: The Politics of Military and Humanitarian Intervention,* ed. Didier Fassin and Mariella Pandolfi (New York: Zone Books, 2010), 20–53; and Adi Ophir, "The Politics of Catastrophization: Emergency and Exception," in *Contemporary States of Emergency,* ed. Fassin and Pandolfi.

58. Bono, "Oltre la «mala Protezione civile»."

59. Andrea Muehlebach, *The Moral Neoliberal: Welfare and Citizenship in Italy* (Chicago: University of Chicago Press, 2012).

60. For an analysis of the effects of neoliberal labor realities on Italian society, see Noelle J. Molé, *Labor Disorders in Neoliberal Italy: Mobbing, Well-Being, and the Workplace* (Bloomington: Indiana University Press, 2011).

61. Petryna, *Life Exposed*.

62. Oliviero Beha, *Il paziente italiano: da Berlusconi al berlusconismo passando per noi* (Rome: Avagliano, 2008); Norberto Bobbio, *Contro i nuovi dispotismi—Scritti sul berlusconismo* (Bari, IT: Dedalo, 2008); and Giovanna Orsina, *Berlusconism and Italy: A Historical Interpretation* (Basingstoke, UK: Palgrave Macmillan, 2014).

63. Edward Banfield, *The Moral Basis of a Backward Society* (New York: Free Press, 1958).

64. Sydel Silverman, "Agricultural Organization and Social Structure, and Values in Italy: Amoral Familism Reconsidered," *American Anthropologist* 70, no. 1 (1968): 1–20; and Emanuele Ferragina, "The Never-Ending Debate about The Moral Basis of a Backward Society: Banfield and 'Amoral Familism,'" *Journal of the Anthropological Society of Oxford* 1, no. 2 (2009).

65. David I. Kertzer, "Banfield, i suoi critici e la cultura," *Contemporanea* 10, no. 4 (2007): 701–709.

66. John Davis, "Morals and Backwardness," *Comparative Studies in Society and History* 12, no. 3 (1970): 340–353.

67. Ginsborg, *Italy and Its Discontents: Family, Society, State* (New York: Palgrave Macmillan, 2001), 97. John Foot also agrees that "as a portrayer of a key feature of Italian ideology and social life, Banfield remains important." Foot, *Modern Italy* (New York: Palgrave Macmillan, 2003), 53.

68. See Silvia Pitzalis, *Politiche del Disastro—Poteri e contropoteri nel terremoto emiliano* (Verona, IT: ombre corte, 2016).

69. For more detailed accounts of the 1950s landslides in Calabria, see Corado Stajano, *Africo* (Turin: Einaudi, 1979); and Stavroula Pipyrou, "Adrift in Time: Lived and Silenced Pasts in Calabria, South Italy," *History and Anthropology* 27, no. 1 (2016b): 45–59; See also Pipyrou, *The Grecanici of Southern Italy: Governance, Violence, and Minority Politics* (Philadelphia: University of Pennsylvania Press, 2016a), chapter 2.

70. See the chapter on the Irpinia earthquake in Antonello Caporale, *Terremoti Spa. Dall'Irpinia all'Aquila. Così i politici sfruttano le disgrazie e dividono il paese* (Milan: Rizzoli, 2010). See an analysis of the corruption surrounding what Paolo Liguori terms *Irpiniagate* in Liguori, *Il terremoto della ricchezza. Inchiesta sull'Irpiniagate* (Milan: Ugo Mursia, 2009). See Chubb's comparative overview of government approaches to disaster management in very different parts of the country in Chubb, "Three Earthquakes."

TWO

—⸫—

THE STATE OF EMERGENCY

HOW DO LIVES TRANSFORM IN the wake of destructive events? Why do survivors often turn into heroes or victims in popular accounts? Do their own stories and experiences match official or popular media depictions? And how do survivors confront misrepresentation and propaganda?

In this chapter, I document Aquilani's recollections regarding the initial phases of the disaster-relief operation and compare their stories with state intervention depictions by the government and the metropolitan Italian and international media. In emergency situations, the authorities often treat survivors uniformly as helpless victims.[1] Officials routinely assume that catastrophe induces a homogeneous passivity that hampers the capacity for autonomous decision-making and necessitates authoritarian leadership.[2] Declaring a state of emergency or exception limits local political action and curtails participation, even in stable, wealthy democracies, while favoring top-down, effective decision-making processes.[3] The political response can therefore exacerbate a disaster experience through disenfranchisement; victimhood is also politically produced. The ways in which governments respond to a catastrophe indicate to what extent they are willing to use an emergency to impose new rules and administrative structures, often against the will or interests of those affected.[4]

Victim identities are powerful. When they become entangled with political objectives, they can be mobilized by state authorities, as well as by survivors, to give more authority to one's demands on the one hand and to justify intervention on the other.[5] Rather than with such strategic claims to victimhood, I am concerned with how Aquilani constructed accounts about their experiences in the wake of the earthquake. I suggest that the stories Aquilani told about themselves were shaped by the desire to engage with other depictions that highlight their supposedly passive victimhood. Local stories were aimed at complicating the victim-helper dichotomy. A shared feature of the accounts I collected was an emphasis on critical assessment, active involvement, and resilience in the face of destruction and authoritarian governance. I suggest that such storytelling reveals a desire to portray, and thus to reconstitute, personal sovereignty as autonomous political agents; this, in turn, serves to claim the authority to comment on, and therefore influence, the city's future and demand restoration. Through stories, Aquilani portray themselves as critical citizens and capable commentators.

This chapter shows how different groups and individuals experienced the earthquake and lived through its aftermath. The wide-ranging accounts reveal that there was not one earthquake experience, but a range of recollections, interpretations, reactions, and responses. The disaster did not produce a shared history, but fractured biographies and therefore contributed to the rivalries and envies of subsequent recovery phases, described in latter chapters. Several accounts also refute the authorities' claim to have provided efficient help to supposedly passive victims. I explore such recollections as part of a series of struggles to regain a voice and shape local history. In this chapter, I first document individual accounts that highlight active decision-making to pursue personal life choices amid difficult circumstances. I then turn to an important expression of collective civic involvement—the wheelbarrow protest. In February 2010, almost one year after the earthquake, resettled survivors forced their way into the militarily secured historic center to remove debris from squares and streets. In their recollections of those events, participants sketched the wheelbarrow protest as a showcase initiative of collective civic action in response to two connected experiences of loss: the natural disaster and its destruction of shared urban spaces and the depictions of L'Aquila's population as a generic group of dependent and passive victims without any capacity for organized action.

During my stay in the city, over three years after the earthquake, many informants described the government intervention as "the second earthquake" (*il secondo terremoto*); the work of state agencies was depicted as the continuation of a disaster experience that merely began with the destructive tremors. In such narratives, survivors gave emphasis to personal acts of autonomous decision-making, as well as to collective protest action. The wheelbarrow protest became an important marker in post-disaster life and was mentioned by almost all Aquilani to whom I spoke as they shared their accounts of the earthquake and recovery. Amid the chaos and confusion of resettlement, the protest—as recalled by my friends and contacts—had various significant dimensions: it provided a short-lived sense of community and shared purpose by connecting Aquilani across barriers of age, class, and political leanings behind the objective of reclaiming historic urban spaces; it established a sense of continuity with historical earthquakes and local resilience, since survivors had also used wheelbarrows to remove debris and rebuild Aquila three hundred years ago; and it enabled Aquilani to illustrate through civic action that they were determined to have a say in projects for L'Aquila's restoration, rather than conforming to the stereotypes of passive victimhood that many had found wrong, painful, and offensive. Once debris had been removed collectively from the old center, this moment of collective action soon disintegrated into isolation. Factions and divisions reemerged, illustrating that recovery paths were increasingly divergent and that shared narratives were hard to establish.

THE WORLD IN L'AQUILA

In April 2009, for the first time in postwar Italy, a natural disaster devastated an important regional capital. Other earthquakes after 1945 had affected parts of rural Italy, such as the Belice area in Sicily (1968), the Friuli border zone with Austria (1976), and villages in the southern Basilicata and Campania regions (1980), with only minor damage in large urban settlements. In L'Aquila, the national state authorities justified their extensive relief operation with the loss of important administrative functions in the city, affecting municipal, provincial, and regional authority.[6] National and international commentators initially acclaimed the emergency operation championed by the then prime minister Silvio Berlusconi. They compared the effort favorably with the notoriously negative Italian track record in effective disaster management, particularly before the establishment of the Civil Protection Agency (Dipartimento della Protezione Civile) in 1992.[7] Especially in the country's south, government responses had often benefitted networks of corrupt politicians and organized crime syndicates, rather than affected populations.[8] It appeared to many observers, at least initially, as if the Italian state had learned from mistakes. Berlusconi seemed to accept the relief effort as a personal challenge and brought high levels of government attention to the city's plight, as documented by national and international reporters. The prime minister pledged his personal dedication for the emergency period and subsequent restoration and repair phases and established exceptional administrative structures.

The government placed the city of L'Aquila and parts of the Abruzzo region under emergency legislation.[9] Tens of thousands of evacuees were resettled in hotel resorts along the Adriatic Coast, around one hour's drive from L'Aquila, and in 170 emergency camps, erected in public parks and in sports fields across the L'Aquila valley. While the Red Cross and other NGOs managed some camps, the Civil Protection Agency administered most of them. Large parts of L'Aquila's municipal territory, including all historic quarters and villages, were declared off-limits to residents and property owners. Troops were posted to evacuated neighborhoods. They patrolled abandoned streets, prevented access to dangerous areas, and deterred looters who had arrived mere hours after the main tremor. With the Civil Protection Agency, a single authority, managed by one of Berlusconi's closest aides, Guido Bertolaso, superseded ordinary municipal powers, such as the local police, city council, and the mayor. Through special appointment, Bertolaso became Extraordinary Commissioner for the Emergency, coordinating all relevant activities, which critical Aquilani and analysts saw as the main reason for disenfranchisement and even militarization.[10]

As the founder of Italy's largest private television network, Berlusconi used his knowledge of imagery and showmanship. He guaranteed a permanent and enthusiastic media presence for the relief effort that he masterminded with Bertolaso, deploying what social scientists Didier Fassin and Mariella Pandolfi, writing about a global trend, have called "extreme interventionism."[11] Italian television has a wide range of lowbrow talk shows and similar formats that mix semiserious political reporting with kitsch and entertainment. Berlusconi made sure to appear frequently on live television during the initial phases of the emergency operation, talking about recovery promises and plans. A few weeks after the earthquake, Berlusconi came under public scrutiny because his then wife, Veronica Lario, made public her outrage about his extramarital affairs. A few days later, on May 5, 2009, Berlusconi appeared on *Porta a Porta*, arguably then the country's most popular talk show. The show host Bruno Vespa asked Berlusconi whether he was more concerned by gossip about his private life or the possibility of disappointing earthquake survivors. "I came here to talk about Abruzzo," Berlusconi responded confidently and with a broad smile, "because I have good news to share with you." He proceeded to wave a thick pile of documents supposedly containing detailed reconstruction plans and gushed about the admiration other countries and their emergency services had purportedly expressed toward his administration for the exceptional response. Berlusconi proceeded to read from the sheets, praising the provision of tens of thousands of hot meals every day and the quick resettlement of survivors in well-equipped hotels, camps, and other types of accommodation.

"I don't think we have ever seen, in a Western country, a situation that was managed in this way by a state government," he said in praise of himself.

Vespa did not ask critical questions as the prime minister went through a long list of what he called unprecedented, exceptional, and generous provisions for L'Aquila and adjacent territories. Occasionally, dramatic clips of ruined neighborhoods interrupted the monologue, as an authoritative voice explained that the government was providing 150,000 euros for every property that had to be rebuilt and 80,000 euros for homes in need of repair. Details of the millions and billions of euros earmarked for resettlement, tax-exemption schemes, and recovery plans accompanied imagery of destruction.[12] Tragedy, state generosity, and statesmanship based on personal expertise became merged in various shows praising the government's effectiveness in responding to the disaster.[13]

Before the earthquake, Berlusconi had rarely received international approval for his political maneuvers. As social historian Paul Ginsborg has shown, the European press had considered Berlusconi a political lightweight since his first premiership in 1994.[14] He was regularly accused of show politics and of abusing his power to tailor immunity legislation that prevented him, as well as his businesses, from being subject to police investigations.[15]

The predominantly negative coverage changed in the wake of the earthquake. The international press, as well as the metropolitan media, commended the prime minister for his relief intervention. Four days after the city's devastation, British journalist Peter Popham summed it up: "Berlusconi Turns Adversity to Political Advantage After Quake; the Italian Leader's Energetic Reaction to the Disaster Has Been a PR Triumph."[16] The prime minister styled himself as a paternal superhero, with only the occasional gaffe, such as his suggestion that the survivors should see resettlement in hotels and tent camps as a government-sponsored holiday.[17] Berlusconi's signature type of populism, berlusconismo, impressed many observers, since the prime minister appeared with energy, creativity, and verve.[18] His presence at state funerals was praised, as he pledged his personal commitment to the recovery. With hindsight, his attempt to connect death and grief with his own political future might raise eyebrows, but at the time, not even the *New York Times* reported critically: "At a news conference after the funeral, Prime Minister Berlusconi said that 'people have been asking me, "Please don't leave us alone." I made a promise to them in front of their coffins,' he said. 'The government has assumed this responsibility.'"[19]

Besides the international media, metropolitan Italian newspapers and television channels also assessed the relief effort positively, praising Berlusconi for allocating reconstruction funds without much bureaucratic hassle. The dominant impression at home and abroad was that "the emergency effort has been a masterpiece of organization and efficiency, with more than 17,000 of the 28,000 homeless accommodated almost instantly in the sky-blue tents of the Ministry of the Interior."[20]

A key event in the earthquake aftermath—an event Berlusconi presented as a maneuver to bring global attention to suffering and accelerate recovery—was the G8 summit of world leaders, hosted in L'Aquila July 8–10, 2009. Before the earthquake struck the mountain city, the Italian government had chosen the reclusive island of La Maddalena, near Sardinia, to welcome Barack Obama, Angela Merkel, Vladimir Putin, and other heads of government or state. The decision had been taken before Berlusconi assumed office to boost the island's economy. The new prime minister embraced the location initially and even increased the budget by over 50 percent to over three hundred million euros to construct a spectacular glass conference venue suspended over the island's scenic bay.[21]

It is important to recall that Berlusconi had previously hosted one of the most controversial summits in the history of the G8, in Genoa in 2001, which had turned the northern port city into a fortress. Large parts were declared off-limits, with high barriers erected throughout Genoa's center. The city became divided and walled. Many residents left their homes to avoid being trapped; numerous shops and restaurants were closed. After the bursting of the dot-com bubble around the year 2000, the anti-globalization movements reached their peak.[22] Tens of thousands of protesters from all over the world arrived in Genoa to denounce capitalism, global injustice, and the world's leading economies for exploiting the global south.

The violence of the Genoa summit shocked the world. Media companies showed horrific scenes of police brutality, motionless bodies, and blood-ied streets, as the Italian authorities cracked down on protesters in what observers described as the "battle" of Genoa.[23] In the July heat, many demonstrations turned violent, and the violent so-called *black bloc* wreaked havoc in the city: windows were smashed, offices and shops were raided, and bricks and bottles were hurled at the police, who retaliated with tear gas and beatings. The anger was not so much an expression of domestic Italian grief as exasperation with the new US president, George W. Bush, who had refused to sign the Kyoto Protocol to combat global warming and planned the installation of missile shields in central Europe. Street fighting was intense: for the first time in the summit's history, a protester, twenty-three-year-old Carlo Giuliani, was shot and killed by a policeman. Special police forces also raided the Diaz school—which had become the headquarters for anti-globalization protesters—and subjected many of those arrested to what the European Court of Human Rights later described as torture.[24] The escalation shocked many and led to a string of court cases against the

Italian police. Genoa became a byword for police violence, public disorder, and anarchy. Eight years later, Berlusconi was back in power, keen to avoid a repetition of the scandalous Genoa summit that had marred his time in office.

Even though the government had already spent millions of euros on state-of-the-art conference facilities on La Maddalena, the government relocated the meeting to L'Aquila at a few months' notice. The state-of-emergency decree permitted Bertolaso to organize the event without much transparency through the Civil Protection Agency. Bypassing bidding procedures, he handpicked companies to provide the necessary infrastructure, including a new landing strip for airplanes and helicopters.[25] Barracks used to train Italy's military Guardia di Finanza, which had sustained little to no damage, were refitted to become the main summit venue. Three months after the earthquake, Aquilani living in tents watched the world media return. Berlusconi toured the semi-ruined city center with his guests, all equipped with hard hats. L'Aquila's partly collapsed prefect's office featured on front pages around the world, with Berlusconi and Obama walking underneath the crumbling portico, the words Palazzo del Governo ripped in half above them. Germany's chancellor, Angela Merkel, presented an initiative for the reconstruction of a nearby village, Onna, razed to the ground in the earthquake. Members of the Nazi Schutzstaffel (SS) had committed a massacre in the hamlet in 1944, which led the chancellor to assume special responsibility for Onna's recovery. The French government adopted the Santa Maria church in the market square, Piazza Duomo, for restoration. The then Russian president, Dmitry Medvedev, pledged his country's commitment to repairing the grand Palazzo Ardinghelli. Commentators reported local approval regarding Berlusconi's conjoining of international politics with ruination and suffering: "To my surprise earthquake survivors living in local tent camps thought the summit an excellent idea. What better way to draw attention to the fact their lives had been reduced to rubble, than to pull in the likes of George Clooney and other celebrity hangers-on who tend to pitch up at major summits.... In some ways this new 'bare bones' G8 style suits the mood of the moment."[26]

A few years later, I was able to speak to a journalist who had covered the L'Aquila summit. She told me that Berlusconi's relocation from a splendid lagoon to a depopulated and devastated city had prevented criticism. Before the prime minister's decision, she explained, foreign journalists had been expecting to attack Berlusconi, who had only recently been reelected and already come under criticism for sex scandals and his inability to respond adequately to the economic crisis. If the summit had been held at La Maddalena, the luxurious surroundings would have been a fitting backdrop to paint the prime minister as out of touch, irresponsible, and vain. The journalist acknowledged that relocating the event to L'Aquila had been a cunning move: the city's destruction shifted the journalists' focus to suffering—as attractive for the media as political scandal. For the prime minister, the summit served as a shield against attacks and questions about his fitness for office.

Berlusconi avoided derision and criticism. Instead, he used the attention to present a string of recovery initiatives. One of the central projects showcasing his energy was a state-sponsored rehousing scheme for over sixteen thousand people, the Progetto Case; 185 permanent apartment blocks on anti-seismic pillars were spread across nineteen resettlement sites outside the old center, most of them attached to peripheral villages. After past earthquakes in Italy, survivors had often spent years, even decades, in ramshackle accommodations, such as barracks or containers. Berlusconi promised that his recovery initiatives would be different. As the G8 summit was underway, a dozen construction sites illustrated his dedication. The prime minister spent hours on the news explaining his resettlement scheme as unprecedented—physical proof of his commitment. He inaugurated the first rehousing sites two and a half months after the G8 summit, on September 29, 2009, his seventy-third birthday. The event was broadcast live, acclaiming the prime minister's crisis response. Since the destruction in early April, television cameras and government attention had established a continuous presence in the ruined city.

Aquilani were divided about the effects of the emergency operation when I spoke to them three years later. While some considered the government effort a series of self-serving publicity stunts that delayed heritage restoration and return to the center, others defended Berlusconi as the only politician who had allocated billions of euros to emergency and repair projects. A different set of Aquilani assumed that Berlusconi had used their suffering to his advantage but admitted their approval in the hope of benefiting from the attention—a cynical win-win situation. After Berlusconi left office in late 2011, he claimed that the city's disrepair was caused by his successors, and many people in the divided population shared this view. The topic had become toxic for many, since little common ground could be found between those who felt that Berlusconi had exploited their suffering and tragedy and made them worse with vanity projects that disregarded the views and needs of the affected population, and those who continued to assert that if Berlusconi had stayed in office, he would have delivered on his promises to reconstruct the old center with the same efficiency with which he had built the Progetto Case sites. Survivors remembered the initial relief effort, the G8 summit, the frenzied construction activity, and the spectacular and unprecedented media coverage, but whether their recollections were used to evaluate the government work positively or negatively depended on political leanings and the idiosyncratic experiences of destruction and displacement. The political divisions exacerbated other forms of fragmentation and misunderstanding.

In August 2012, a friend drove me past the landing strip that had been built for the summit at a time when some local politicians were still promising that the site could become Rome's third airport and bring tourism to L'Aquila. In his thirties and working as a freelance journalist, Daniele was the opposite of a Berlusconi supporter. He shook his head as he gestured toward the high fence surrounding the now-abandoned landing strip and container terminals, which never saw foreign tourists arrive on their way to Rome:

> Before the earthquake, nobody knew where L'Aquila was, not even Italians. And then everybody came to the city: the pope, Berlusconi, Obama, George Clooney, and even Gaddafi, who brought his camels. We got new roads, new roundabouts, an airport. Everything seemed possible. We were living in tents and hotels, and then this gigantic event happened. It was unreal (*allucinante*). Everyone in the world knew about the earthquake. Of course, we all hoped that the attention would help us recover. Even those who were against Berlusconi and his show that used the city's ruins as a backdrop spoke with the international press to get more coverage for their views and their protest. We all had similar hopes: to use the attention to show our situation to outsiders and help us return to normality. But today, it's hard to say what this circus did for us in the long term: perhaps nothing, perhaps little, perhaps even damage. What matters is that the historic center is still a ruin, and the funds for restoration have disappeared. The future is uncertain.

In 2009, dissenting voices had received little attention. Many survivors—and many of the active citizens I describe in this book—criticized the G8 summit. To them, it distracted from the pressing issues of homelessness and misused funds that had been allocated to the emergency effort and repairs but were spent instead on hosting world leaders. Despite such discontent, it was difficult to coordinate opposition, since emergency legislation curtailed the right to protest.[27] Whenever I initiated a conversation about the summit, it became heated, with other Aquilani joining in to share their views and offer criticism or praise of the prime minister. Central features of the state relief operation remained contested among those most affected by it. In the media, however, positive coverage continued. In November 2009, seven months after the earthquake, a British newspaper praised the prime minister, running the headline, "Silvio Berlusconi Keeps His Promise to the Earthquake Victims of L'Aquila." The article continued:

When Silvio Berlusconi returns to L'Aquila tomorrow for the removal of the tents put up to house the victims of the earthquake that struck the city on 6 April, he can expect a hero's welcome. The Italian Prime Minister may be under pressure over his private life and his attacks on the judges trying him for corruption. But, though his administration is strapped for cash, he has fulfilled a promise to provide decent housing for the highest-priority cases before the winter. In a society where cynicism about the state is ingrained, and where the victims of natural disasters have often been ignored, if not exploited, that is a novelty. It helps explain why, despite scandal and controversy, almost 50% of voters continue to back him.[28]

Outside L'Aquila, positive coverage led people to believe that earthquake survivors had recovered normality quickly. In March 2011, almost two years after the earthquake, the Berlusconi-owned television channel Canale Cinque broadcast another episode of *Forum*, a talk show. Marina Villa, a fifty-year-old Aquilana, spoke about her home city's recovery. "L'Aquila has been reconstructed," she gushed, "and life has begun again. Those who still complain just want to keep eating and sleeping for free." She dismissed criticism as the action of ungrateful scroungers—Aquilani still staged occasional protests in the city or in Rome to draw attention to the ongoing ruination of the old center—and praised her new house and its small garden. Villa also identified the person responsible for the swift return of normality: "We must thank our prime minister," Silvio Berlusconi.[29] Many Aquilani were outraged. Two weeks after the broadcast, Villa was forced to admit that she was not an Aquilana; instead, Canale Cinque had paid her a few hundred euros to praise the government. My friends in the city mentioned the broadcast as an example of how the media had misled Italians about the fate of Aquilani. Many of the survivors who spoke to me lamented a lack of interest by the Italian public about their livelihoods being in limbo. They also attributed the absence of nationwide solidarity to manipulative media coverage, which had endorsed government decisions contested among survivors. As I traveled to different parts of the country during my research, from Milan in the north to the southern region of Puglia, I realized that L'Aquila was of no national importance, and the plight of survivors had been long eclipsed by worries about the country's economy, unemployment, and austerity. With some exceptions, Italians who spoke to me about L'Aquila generally assumed that survivors had been rehoused and the city's crisis resolved.

In the press, Aquilani had often been depicted as passive victims of catastrophe, grateful for state support. Media spectacles need heroes as well as victims.[30] Berlusconi, a businessman-turned-media-tycoon-turned-politician

Figure 2.1. Banner in the old center reading "Let's take our city back"

Figure 2.2. Decay in the centro storico

from northern Italy, could rely on stereotypes regarding the supposed lack of entrepreneurial spirit among backward and state-reliant mountain people. The portrayal of demanding southerners in need of an enterprising northern manager made sense for many Italians. Rather than receiving aid by virtue of being Italian citizens, survivors were deprived of agency as a result of the personalization of the relief effort. Many Aquilani critical of the government later compared the emergency intervention to the ancient Roman strategy of divide and rule; with survivors scattered across hundreds of hotels and tent camps and with the ban on public protest, resistance was almost impossible. Berlusconi remained a highly controversial figure in the city. Frustration with what many considered to be the government's propagandistic distortions of its role in the earthquake aftermath was common. As a consequence, when I asked Aquilani to talk to me about their experiences of the earthquake, an emphasis on agency and autonomy featured in many stories.

AQUILANI AND THEIR RECOLLECTIONS

Tommaso was in his early thirties at the time of my fieldwork; he was working part-time in what he considered a dull office job and living at home with his parents. He had romantic relationships but was not ready to settle down. I met Tommaso at a birthday party, where he first spoke to me about his earthquake experience. He sported a long beard and had a serious demeanor. Intrigued by his story, I asked to meet again, so he invited me to his parents' home on the outskirts of L'Aquila. In his narrative of events in the wake of the earthquake, he emphasized his critical agency; he did not want to be marked by victimhood:

In the earthquake night, the tremors were violent and woke me up. Everything was shaking, but my family home did not collapse; we had only little damage. Everything was still moving when I ran downstairs. I checked that my parents were OK and tried calling my friends, but I couldn't get through and was worried. I turned on the television. The images shocked me: the historic center was ruined. When I heard an ambulance on the street, I ran outside. I waved at the car and asked to go to the center with the doctors to help. We stopped at a collapsed building. There were two fathers, crying. Their sons were buried underneath the rubble. They called their sons' mobile phones, which rang below us, and we knew where to dig. One of the two men couldn't help us; he was just crying. He couldn't move; he was paralyzed. The other one had already made a large hole. He found his own son first, who was dead, and pulled out the body. But he didn't stop. He continued looking for the other one, who wasn't even his own son. I helped him. We finally heard a voice and dug the other son out. He was injured but alive. That incident has marked me more than anything I saw that night. It was beautiful—well, *beautiful* is a difficult word, but you know what I mean.[31]

Tommaso recalled kindness and solidarity in the face of tragedy. In the early hours of April 6, the authorities had not yet appeared in the devastated city; people helped each other. In his account of subsequent developments, Tommaso highlighted how this changed—and how frustrating experiences had transformed his personal life:

A couple of weeks later, I helped a group of Peruvian immigrants who were living in a tent camp. I saw awful things there. In one camp, the Civil Protection Agency supplied food and asked a handful of Aquilani, who had assumed some kind of responsibility for the camp, to distribute it. These self-styled camp leaders refused to give anything to the immigrants. They were plainly racist and didn't want to help non-Italians. I had to smuggle food into the camp for two Peruvian families. The other survivors would have attacked me if they had seen me. The authorities didn't care; they were happy to delegate. There were many who suffered and didn't get any help, especially foreigners who didn't have the right documents. People often say you forget differences when you lose everything. A spirit of solidarity kicks in. But that wasn't always the case, perhaps because people hadn't lost everything. I don't know. But I saw Aquilani bickering at distribution points for donated clothing. "No, I don't like the blue tracksuit, I want the black one." "These shoes? No, give me the other pair, I like the color more." It was difficult for me. I really didn't know how to react; there were humbling selflessness and then egoism and exclusion. These responses and behavior existed side by side, with little in between. And too much of it was ugly, to be honest. That broke me.

You either do a lot or nothing. I stopped hanging out with almost all of my friends after the earthquake. I couldn't be with the same people anymore, after having seen how selfishly many of them had acted during the emergency period. They hadn't shown courage or compassion. They had all been great with words but didn't do anything when it mattered. It was a watershed moment and changed my life.

The government turned the earthquake into a media spectacle. Berlusconi was in crisis, and his government would have collapsed if the earthquake hadn't happened. It helped him forge consensus. The earthquake saved Berlusconi. We knew what was going on. Berlusconi showed up among the Aquilani like a savior, like Jesus Christ. The government said: "We are here. We are doing everything." It was excessive state assistance (*assistenzialismo*).[32] Well-known international NGOs offered help to the

Italian government, but Berlusconi refused. He said that we were a proud country that didn't need help. It was ridiculous.

When we tried to set up grassroots initiatives in the city and protested against the G8 summit, Bertolaso attacked us. He said that the authorities knew better how to handle things and that we should stay out of it. They treated us like inmates of a madhouse: "You are shocked. Don't do anything. Don't think for yourselves." But in such a situation, you have to have a way of reacting. You have to do *something*. You have to find the motivation to get on with life. Otherwise you'll never recover. Instead, the authorities gave people tranquilizers without medical prescription. People turned into vegetables. There was simply nothing to do. Life was so boring. We were infantilized. "The authorities look after you; just behave." We had no power to do anything. The whole situation was crazy, forced into this passive nothingness. So we just drank like animals, every evening. I wasn't sober for months.

Then I stopped. I understood something. Many other Aquilani realized this too, at the same time: life is short. It can end just like this. The shroud had fallen. And so many of us began to do what we had always wanted to do but would never have dared: break out of routines, follow our passions, do whatever renders life worthwhile, live for real. I now work part-time and write poetry in my free time. I sometimes feel I didn't really live before the earthquake. It gives you energy. You feel it in your stomach, this desire to be alive and to live properly when the earth shakes. It's something you cannot describe. You must feel it.[33]

In his story, Tommaso connected the earthquake with the state response and his personal life. He insisted that the disaster had not produced a spirit of solidarity, although he had witnessed instances of mutual support and sacrifice, and that provisions had led to ugly scenes of selfishness, racism, and rivalry. In the face of what might have appeared as a shared tragedy, Tommaso found the behavior of people he used to consider close friends disappointing. He criticized the state response as a publicity stunt and condemned Berlusconi's refusal of support from foreign experts on disaster recovery. He emphasized moments of personal initiative, highlighting occasions that exposed a tension between government claims to a virtuous relief effort and his own experience. The lack of support for foreigners pushed him into action.

Throughout his account, Tommaso constructed himself as a moral and political agent who had not merely recognized suffering but had actively intervened when relief providers behaved objectionably. He recalled being a camp evacuee as an experience of infantilization through state agencies. Tommaso emphasized that many people had sought to be involved right away, setting up grassroots movements to confront the emergency—but the authorities had attempted to disable such initiatives. Tommaso accused the state agencies of turning survivors into victims who were forced into passivity and tranquilized and highlighted instances of initiative and activity. In his narrative, the state relief effort was also the backdrop against which Tommaso decided to reevaluate priorities and change the course of his life. Recovering from disaster did not mean returning to a previously lived life. The disaster was a watershed moment that allowed Tommaso to reflect on and transform his existence. Tommaso grasped the opportunity.

After the earthquake, Giovanni, a computer scientist working at the University of L'Aquila, was moved into a holiday resort on the Adriatic Coast. The government assigned him and his family a single hotel room and paid the bills until December 2009 (eight months total), when they were told they could return to L'Aquila. Their postwar multistory condominium had incurred minor damage and was quickly repaired. Since Giovanni was confined to a wheelchair, the family had chosen a hotel room rather than one of the dozens of nearby tent camps erected in the days after the earthquake. At the time of my fieldwork, Giovanni was involved in politics and was campaigning for a small left-wing party. I met him at an election event, and he invited me to his house to speak. A few months later, I visited him at his home—an apartement on the top floor of a red condominium surrounded by construction sites:

> Before the big earthquake on April 6, the city was divided over how to react to the tremor cluster. I personally noticed the first stronger shock in January 2009, but I got quickly used to the sequence. Most of my friends did too, but we all have a background in natural sciences and knew that there wasn't much we could do anyway. People were talking about earthquakes all the time. My sister was horrified. She reacted very differently and spent many nights in her car, even though her family stayed indoors. Some Aquilani were shrugging their shoulders, and others were frightened by the endless shocks. There was no shared response.
>
> On the tragic night, I was at home. After the first earthquake, around 11:00 p.m., I checked the measurements on the website of the Italian Institute for Geophysics and Volcanology [INGV]. The shock was no stronger than previous ones, so I didn't think about leaving the house. When the next tremor hit at around 1:00 a.m., my son didn't even wake up from it. My wife and I went to sleep. Then, at 3:32 a.m., the big earthquake. It was horrible. You could hear that loud roaring sound coming from below—it is impossible to put into words—and everything was shaking violently. I couldn't get out of bed because of my legs, so I shouted against the noise: "Cover your heads!" I

told my wife to get our son and hide under the kitchen table, but I remained calm, rational. I didn't get what was going on at that moment. When it all stopped, we had to ask a neighbor to carry me down the stairs because we didn't trust the lift. It was only when I sat in our car, and the earth was still moving with aftershocks, that I became worried. But it was in the middle of the night; it was dark and hazy. The air was dusty and glowed. We had no idea about the extent of the damage in other areas with older buildings. It took me a while to realize what was happening.

After the earthquake, social-media use skyrocketed in L'Aquila. For example, across Italy the number of Facebook accounts grew by around 200 percent that year. In L'Aquila, it grew by 500 percent. People were dispersed and wanted to know about each other, and so they went online. Social media was still a novelty then and created a new space for people in camps and hotels without any other form of sociality. I would have preferred staying closer to the city, but because of my disability, we opted for a hotel on the coast, even though it was a long way from L'Aquila. At least we got the funds for repairs without any complication. At first, the government handed out money to anyone who filled in a form. But these initial funds dried up quickly. There was no long-term plan. Our house only had minor damage; it was repaired within months. Friends of mine had much larger bills for their repairs, with entire stories collapsed. It was only because they applied later that they got less money than I did. It didn't make sense. There was no strategy. It wasn't fair or coherent, and this angered many. The government just wanted to make some people happy to get votes.

I didn't have a good time in the hotel. The government paid, but many Aquilani didn't feel welcome there. The hotel staff asked us constantly when we were going to leave because the summer tourists were about to arrive, and they paid more than the government. As if we knew what was going to happen! We had no idea. No one told us anything. The government gave hotel owners fifty euros per person per night, which was a good rate for April, but not for July or August. The hotel owners saw us as an opportunity for profit. As soon as there was someone happy to pay more, they wanted us out. It was unpleasant. We also had to eat our meals in separate rooms from normal tourists. We were second-class citizens. We had to wear identity cards around the neck. Security checked us whenever we entered the hotel. Mealtimes were fixed. I felt like a refugee in my own country, stripped of ordinary rights to influence anything. We could not even complain. We always had to be nice and friendly. We couldn't talk about the negative aspects. After all, we were guests. They accommodated us. We couldn't get annoyed. You had to be grateful because there wasn't anywhere else to go to.[34]

When a major sports competition—the Mediterranean Games—was held in the coastal city of Pescara in the summer of 2009, many displaced Aquilani were forced to change hotels to make space for the athletes. Most survivors switched hotels, or at least rooms, a number of times. That is why Giovanni compared his family's experience to that of stateless refugees: an unstable and precarious existence marked by a dependence on state authorities, with the expectation of gratitude.[35] Giovanni highlighted that he felt he had been stripped of political agency and the ability to be critical toward the authorities, surrendering rights and privileges he associated with his status as an Italian citizen. He contrasted the emergence of new social spaces online with the government attempt to reduce survivors to second-class victims without a voice or representation. Giovanni's account reveals how survivors were led into passive submission. He did not recall active opposition to the emergency management, unlike Tommaso, but nonetheless stressed a capacity to assess critically what had happened to him and his family.

He did not describe himself as an earthquake victim but considered his experience of victimhood an effect of the government's production of second-class citizens. His involvement in politics a few years later was also a result of this experience. Giovanni now sought to influence local affairs, having witnessed how rights and privileges could be suspended and control over one's home city could slip away. Giovanni had benefitted from the generous provisions for homeowners in the aftermath of the earthquake. His account also foreshadows, however, the origins of rivalry: the government had not pursued a coherent and fair distribution of funds, and those who submitted applications later received noticeably less support than the first claimants.

Another Aquilana spoke to me about her experience of displacement in a Civil Protection Agency camp. Anna, a student in the Department of Engineering at the University of L'Aquila, was twenty-three years old when the earthquake struck. She was living with her parents in a historic village within the municipality of L'Aquila, which suffered serious damage in the earthquake. Anna and her family were relocated to a nearby camp. Recalling the emergency period, she highlighted her active contribution to the relief effort and how she believes she improved the way in which the Civil Protection Agency responded to survivors and their needs:

> I created my own kind of existence in the camp because I knew I would have to spend many months there. I had my tent, my bed, my cover, and my table—those were the four things I needed. Before the earthquake, I would never have left my house without makeup or perfume. When I lived in the tent, I didn't mind walking around in my pajamas, not having showered. I

didn't care because I was alive. I had survived. The Civil Protection Agency handed over responsibility to the people in the camp; some of us cleaned, others cooked in the canteen. I set up a small shop, where people could get toilet paper or toothpaste, everyday things, most of them donations. People didn't have to pay, so it wasn't a real shop, but I kept a record of who got what and when and made sure the distribution was fair.

I also became friends with the Civil Protection Agency volunteers. I'm still in touch with some of them. They came from Verona, in northern Italy. Each group of volunteers only stayed for a few weeks. Then, new guys arrived. They had no idea about the camp, and so we helped them figure things out. I was one of the key people they asked, for continuity. I helped them set up the toilet and the shower cabins with my engineering experience, connecting the tubes, water supply, and drainage. One of my university professors saw my work and was very impressed.[36]

Anna portrayed herself as a source of continuity for displaced survivors from her home village. She emphasized that state agents had relied on her and other villagers to manage day-to-day camp life. Through her account, Anna illustrated that the binary distinction between victims and helpers was an illusion—she did not see herself as a passive victim. Anna emphasized the cooperation and support between the Civil Protection Agency personnel from northern Italy and local survivors, since the authorities also relied on evacuees and their expertise. Anna insisted on a capacity for agency, carving out purposeful everyday routine despite displacement. She ascertained her ability to steer recovery processes, rather than being passively subjected to them.

NARRATIVES OF EXTREME EVENTS

The ways in which people remember the past "are themselves events, rather than merely descriptions of events."[37] Memories are not objective images of experienced history but a practice that then reshapes experience in the present.[38] Thus, whenever Aquilani talked to me about their post-disaster lives, they constructed narratives; they situated themselves as active subjects capable of critical assessment, moral agency, and often participation. Many emphasized that they had not seen themselves as victims, or at least not so much as disaster victims, but rather as having been forced into passivity by aspects of the relief effort. I suggest that such accounts responded to dominant depictions of Aquilani as docile aid recipients. Giovanni challenged government claims that it had overseen an unprecedented and successful relief operation, from evacuation to resettlement. His account suggests that the government response had often exacerbated the disaster situation for the survivors by turning them into second-class citizens without a voice or representation and housing them a long way from L'Aquila in coastal hotel resorts. He made it clear that victimhood was a political condition. Anna also challenged assumptions of generic victimhood. She portrayed the relief effort, at least in her camp, as a respectful interaction between survivors and state agents to shape emergency management in cooperation, situating Aquilani as active agents of recovery.

As anthropologist of memory Francesca Cappelletto has shown with regard to Italian wartime massacres, survivors of extreme events have the difficult task of reconciling opposed desires. They "want their narrated memory of the massacre to be a public memory, capable of 'entering into history.' Yet they also dislike the intrusion of anonymous forces from the political world and the larger society into what they call 'our story.'"[39] Aquilani also challenged what they considered intrusions and distorted depictions through autobiographical accounts of active and critical engagement. In her analysis of memory practices in Eastern Europe, historical anthropologist Vieda Skultans argues that "in Soviet Latvia political language redefined autobiography, excluding vast expanses of human experience and specifying rigid areas of definitional relevance."[40] According to Skultans, this exclusion had a devastating effect on people's recollections, because "persistent political intrusion and the condemnation of their lives make it difficult for people to construct a personal past in an active autobiographical voice."[41] I argue that many of my informants constructed autobiographical narratives so as to situate themselves as agents in order to counter depictions of them as passive aid recipients. Crafting accounts constituted an important process of regaining autobiographical authority. In so doing, Aquilani contrasted a type of imposed second-class citizenship with their capacity for personal sovereignty.

Through storytelling, earthquake survivors did not just express emotional needs following bereavement or destruction; they also engaged with the political processes shaping the disaster aftermath. The narratives I collected highlight unexpected—and, in the eyes of many Aquilani, unreported—dimensions of their struggle to control local existence and craft their future in response to what they considered disenfranchisement and misrepresentation. It is beyond the scope of this book to investigate the detailed veracity of each claim to agency; what matters is that this desire to tell stories that were unlike official depictions in the news, government reports, or television talk shows was widespread. It is important to highlight this prevalence to understand the skepticism many Aquilani expressed toward government promises and why aspirations for recovery from the earthquake and its aftermath had important political dimensions, with a focus on citizenship practices.

A particularly painful experience of the post-disaster period was displacement. As I have shown, for many Aquilani, the fear of losing access to their city permanently was real and realistic, given how unreliable previous national governments had been with restoration promises after natural disasters. The initial plan, favored by the Berlusconi administration, to construct only one supposedly temporary resettlement site, a L'Aquila II, had been resisted by the local authorities because they had worried it might render eventual restoration of and return to the old center and historical neighborhoods less likely. At the time of the earthquake, a large number of Aquilani were living outside the city, particularly young students studying at universities across Italy. After the disaster, they faced a particularly difficult conundrum: Should they continue living a relatively normal life in different parts of Italy or return to L'Aquila to experience displacement and the state of exception with their relatives and friends? They also wondered whether their city needed their help pushing back against relocation plans and other decisions they disagreed with. The local population would soon become fractured over claims of who had suffered the most and was entitled to financial compensation and government attention. Those Aquilani who had not been through the earthquake with firsthand experience increasingly felt excluded and were told by those who had run in fear from collapsing buildings that they could never understand what other Aquilani had suffered.

Before the earthquake, Maria had not doubted that she was an Aquilana, given that she had been born and raised in the city. Her father, a winemaker, and her mother, an optometrist, were also from L'Aquila. On the night of the earthquake, however, Maria was in the north of Italy, where she studied theater. She was in her late twenties. Maria returned to Abruzzo within days. The earthquake had spared a second family property in the city's rural hinterland. Maria and other relatives moved there to avoid official camps. Reflecting on her memories of this period, Maria talked about an experience of exclusion. She had to fight her way back into the local community:

> I was the one who couldn't understand, Aquilani told me, because I had
> not been here for the earthquake. I hadn't lived through the tremors, so
> I was suddenly a stranger. When there is a situation that affects an entire
> population, but not you, then they will see you as an outsider despite
> everything that happened previously. It was overnight. "You weren't here, you
> cannot understand, you cannot claim the right to suffering or to being in pain."
> No one acknowledged my suffering. I was anxious, too. I returned to a city

I couldn't live in anymore. It had disappeared, turned into a place I no longer recognized, without any social spaces. Other Aquilani didn't accept the pain I felt; they didn't think it was as real as theirs. But I couldn't leave either. I felt extremely close to my city, much more than before. That is why I chose to return.

I found a part-time job in a petrol station on the outskirts. But I'm mainly managing our vineyards, forty miles away. I get up early in the morning to look after the vines and return to L'Aquila in the afternoon. At weekends, I drive to fairs and markets to sell wine. After the earthquake, I could have chosen to live elsewhere, but I wanted to return to L'Aquila. I wanted to reconnect with my city and to help it recover. I became involved with activists, and we challenged what the government was doing to our city. We set up alternative free camps, outside the control of the Civil Protection Agency. This was my way of showing that L'Aquila was my home and that I wanted to remain a part of it. Today, I feel like I've arrived again. I'm back here and happy. I don't rest much, I'm often tired from work, but I wouldn't want to change anything.[42]

Maria returned to a devastated city, even though she could have continued an easier life studying in northern Italy. She had not lived through the month-long tremor cluster, nor had she escaped from shaking buildings on April 6, 2009. She had not witnessed L'Aquila's destruction firsthand. Yet she returned to a destroyed home and was saddened and shocked by what she found. Her story foreshadows some of the complex fractures that appeared in the wake of the earthquake. Many people accused Maria of not understanding what the earthquake really meant for the people who had experienced it. The local community became more divided, and people like Maria suddenly found themselves excluded from the population of survivors with direct experience. Recovery from disaster, for Maria, therefore meant actively returning, interrupting her studies, taking on menial jobs, joining activist groups and anti-government campaigns, and becoming more involved in the family business—winemaking—which took her on a very different career path from theater. The fear of displacement was real for Maria, who despised Berlusconi and his politics. Staying away from L'Aquila was not an option for her: "The government had no interest in the old center and our heritage. They only wanted to use the earthquake to build more property, which had damaged the urban fabric so much. We wanted our old center back, with its squares and pubs and social spaces, but we had to fight for it."[43] Maria exhibited agency and determination, and she underlined her words with action; returning to L'Aquila and settling in the city were acts of defiance.

As I document such accounts, which frame the disaster experience in the language of personal agency and initiative, I do not wish to romanticize suffering. The earthquake wrecked livelihoods. Bereavement, loneliness, fraught relationships, dispersion, alcoholism, family tensions, depression, sadness, uncertainty, hopelessness, and fear—at least some of these featured in all of the stories I heard. At the same time, Maria, Giovanni, Tommaso and Anna also had other stories. Their accounts illustrated that rather than becoming victims pushed along by disastrous circumstances, Aquilani actively reflected on what was happening to them, on choices and agency. Many of the people I spoke to had accepted the disaster as a challenge and responded, rather than surrendering to something they would otherwise have had to accept: the disaster as a total rupture, leaving them powerless and deprived of identity, except that of victims.

The accounts also document how wide-ranging different post-disaster experiences were. Some people became involved in managing camp life, rising to the challenge with grit, and found the Civil Protection Agency personnel to be supportive. Others witnessed racism, rivalry, and self-seeking even among displaced survivors and changed their social circles as a result. Still others experienced how their superficially comfortable government-sponsored time in coastal holiday resorts turned them into second-class citizens, politically produced victims without a voice. These differences were at the root of how the population of disaster survivors became fragmented, isolated in resettlement sites, camps, and hotel rooms without access to spaces of community or civic associationism. When Aquilani emphasize agency and involvement, they also position their stories in opposition to narratives that saw Berlusconi as the hero and Aquilani as passive victims. While this description might be appropriate for some, many Aquilani refused the label, actively sought involvement in the political process, and attempted to guarantee that their city would be restored to its pre-disaster state, making sure that their temporary relocation would not become permanent.

THE WHEELBARROW PROTEST

Thus far, this chapter has focused on a key concern for many of my interlocutors: using narrative to emphasize personal sovereignty. I now turn to a powerful expression of collective civic action in post-disaster L'Aquila: the wheelbarrow protest.

At a G8 press conference in July 2009, Silvio Berlusconi promised that L'Aquila's historic center would be completely restored before the year 2013.

One month later, Giovanni Chiodi, president of the Abruzzo region and member of Berlusconi's People of Freedom (PdL) party, confirmed that L'Aquila would have such enormous resources that his administration would struggle to spend everything. Berlusconi claimed that he considered buying property in the devastated city to follow the works closely. No politician questioned the restoration of L'Aquila's heritage. In February 2010, ten months after the earthquake, state-of-emergency provisions were eased.[44] Civil Protection Agency personnel left L'Aquila, and some administrative powers were returned to the regional and local administrations. An Extraordinary Commissioner for the Reconstruction, the same Giovanni Chiodi, was appointed to replace Guido Bertolaso as the Extraordinary Commissioner for the Emergency. Many survivors had moved from tent camps into Progetto Case resettlement flats or smaller wooden housing units. Thousands remained in hotel resorts. The historic center was still under army control and was protected by high fences. Large areas of historic neighborhoods in L'Aquila and nearby towns and villages that had sustained similar damage had been turned into inaccessible so-called Red Zones. Barricades and railings were a ubiquitous sight across the cityscape, blocking roads, streets, and squares. Rain and snow fell into abandoned houses through partly collapsed roofs. Expectations that repair of property, churches, and monuments in the historic city center would follow resettlement had been shattered.

L'Aquila's centro storico was cut off from the surrounding urban territory—a territory that had been designed around the old town and its public spaces and sites of urban sociality. Residents could not take an evening stroll among hundreds of bars, shops, and restaurants to celebrate Christmas or New Year's, as four million tons of rubble still covered old town squares in early 2010, ten months after the earthquake. The Civil Protection Agency had overseen the removal of debris and rubble from streets and collapsed buildings onto large squares, where it still waited to be transported out of the city center. Aquilani, as Italian commentators observed cynically at the time, were waiting for their promised miracle.[45] As the first anniversary approached, survivors became melancholic. My landlady, who was living in a family home on the outskirts of L'Aquila, told me later about this period:

> It was a strange period. Christmas was over and the new year had
> begun—2010. But it seemed that nothing was changing. My friends lived in
> resettlement sites or faraway in hotels. The old center remained inaccessible.
> The authorities hadn't told us what was going to happen or when. We wanted
> to return to the center, but you couldn't get past the soldiers. Outsiders
> occupied our city. So what could we have done? We just waited. Stasis.

I had no idea what was going to happen next. Everyone was so far away. It is cold and dark here in the mountains in winter. It was really difficult to meet anyone. We were dispersed. I felt sad and empty.[46]

A scandal then sparked the most important instance of collective activism in post-disaster L'Aquila. During a court case investigating possible corruption concerning subcontracts for the G8 summit in Sardinia, a phone conversation between two construction entrepreneurs was made public. On the afternoon of April 6, 2009, twelve hours after the earthquake, Pierfrancesco Gagliardi, a construction engineer, had called his brother-in-law, Francesco De Vito Piscicelli. The two were euphoric about the prospect of windfalls from construction projects in the devastated city. "It's not like there is an earthquake like this every day," Gagliardi said. Piscicelli agreed: "Absolutely—I was giggling this morning at 3.30 in bed." "Me too," Gagliardi laughed. The recording was played during the trial and found its way into the news.[47] Aquilani reacted with anger. One Aquilano founded a Facebook group called "Those that didn't laugh at 3.32am" (*Quelli che alle 3e32 non ridevano*). Within hours, thirteen thousand people had signed up. They were discussing how to react.

Massimo, a young man in his forties who worked in the management of L'Aquila's hospital and was living in a Progetto Case apartment at the time, later explained to me the impact of the recording: "It was a wake-up call for us. Up to that point, people had not been able to unite, scattered among hotels and tent camps, depressed and lonely. The government pursued this military strategy: divide and rule, dispersing people as much as possible to break up resistance. This had made it difficult to organize protests during the emergency period. But when we heard how these monsters laughed about our suffering, we became angry. Anger united the Aquilani probably for the first time since the earthquake."[48]

On February 14, 2010, Valentine's Day, hundreds of Aquilani met in Piazza Duomo, L'Aquila's market square, which was then one of the few accessible historic spaces at the edge of the historic center. Someone was handing out signs with a slogan: "I didn't laugh at 3.32am." High metal fences and signs warning that this was a military zone prevented the crowd from going further into the old town. Some—then many—started pushing against the barriers. Police and soldiers tried to prevent Aquilani from dismantling the fences, but they were too many to stop. Massimo remembered:

The police and the soldiers saw us pushing against the fences, but they realized that we were just ordinary people, not *black-bloc* troublemakers or something. We weren't hard-core militants, just normal Aquilani, young and old. And we broke through. I don't know how it happened, but someone said: "Let's go to the city hall!" The square in front of our city hall, Piazza Palazzo, has always been an important place for the Aquilani. The market square was relevant for trade, for merchants, but Piazza Palazzo was the place of our civic identity as Aquilani. It was unacceptable that we couldn't go there. Soldiers from random places all over Italy were keeping us out of our city. We belonged there: the city is our space. More and more of us arrived to show their love for L'Aquila on Valentine's Day, and we just walked on. The soldiers tried to stop it, but we were hundreds.

We marched on to Piazza Palazzo. What I saw there shocked me. This used to be heart of L'Aquila's student area, and now it looked like a dump. Rubble and debris covered the entire square, many meters high. It was completely abandoned. They had just piled up bricks and mortar and tiles and broken glass. I couldn't believe it. I began to cry. I was so overwhelmed. Suddenly, someone passed around buckets: "All right, let's clear this up then." The following weeks were just amazing. It was our L'Aquila Spring. There was a great sense of civic engagement. People wanted to do something for their city. Participation was enormous. Those were beautiful days. Coming into the centro storico every weekend was cathartic. We had the feeling that we could really take our lives back into our own hands; we could get our city back.[49]

After that Valentine's Day, a growing number of Aquilani, equipped with wheelbarrows, spades, and buckets, removed collapsed stonewalls and facades, splintered wooden beams and window frames, post-disaster vegetation, and other debris from narrow streets and once-picturesque squares. When the protest reached its peak, tens of thousands of survivors flocked to the old town from remote resettlement sites and faraway hotel resorts to reclaim their city. All of my informants recalled the wheelbarrow initiative as an elating experience during a depressing period. They gushed when they reminisced about clearing streets, passing along buckets of debris, and carting wheelbarrows out of the historic center. Thousands of survivors, representing various age groups and bridging political divides and social classes, participated.

With their action, wheelbarrow protesters illustrated that the government's claim to a successful relief operation was out of kilter with their experience of an ongoing state of exception and decay, displacement and exclusion from the urban spaces that mattered to them. The citizens' removal of debris from the old center, where it had remained for almost one year under state protection, exposed the authorities' failures to restore local heritage and deliver on promises of a swift return to normality in a restored city. Massimo was adamant that L'Aquila did not belong to the government but to Aquilani. He described the wheelbarrow initiative as a conscious effort to reclaim sites invested with local histories and memories. As I was nodding throughout his account, Massimo made sure I understood why he thought the clearing of Piazza Palazzo had been significant:

> When the castles and monasteries in this area founded L'Aquila, they used it as a marketplace for their trade, right? So, the market square was the most important space. But then, when a new local identity developed, another square, Piazza Palazzo, became more important for Aquilani. That is where our ancestors built the city hall—not on the same square as the market—for civic autonomy and emancipation from the settlements that had founded and controlled L'Aquila. That's why it's always been such an important site of local identity, much more than the market square. It's a space that Aquilani built as citizens, and through which they could feel as citizens, not just as marketplace residents. That's why we had to take it back.[50]

In Massimo's narrative, the act of clearing Piazza Palazzo constituted active citizenship with a local scope. The survivors' protest connected them with a century-old history of struggling for autonomy. The wheelbarrow protest did not simply clear city spaces; participants framed the initiative as a continuation of local traditions of emancipation, resilience, and recovery in the wake of disaster. The protest united dispersed Aquilani for a common cause through an act of civil disobedience. Urban spaces and monuments were identified as crucial for local civic identity. Accounts of the wheelbarrow initiative emphasized the intersection of heritage, political belonging, and the concept of *cittadinanza* (citizenship). The spontaneous grassroots action cast the Italian authorities, not the Aquilani, as defective and passive and furthermore contrasted state failure with the creative agency of survivors reclaiming their city.

DRAQUILA

After the disaster, the city's fate became a political battleground, in particular for Berlusconi critics. One year after the earthquake, well-known Italian journalist Sabina Guzzanti presented her documentary film *Draquila*. *Draquila* lambasts the recovery effort and attacks Berlusconi as a sex-obsessed and self-interested megalomaniac with ties to organized crime. Guzzanti suggests that the Civil Protection Agency created a warlike atmosphere across resettlement camps, where meetings were forbidden and Coca-Cola, coffee, and alcohol were banned for being too excitant for mentally unstable survivors. The documentary focuses on the dubious practices of the Civil Protection Agency and the Italian army, which also attempted to prevent Guzzanti's team from filming and activists from protesting against the G8 summit.

Apart from a few exceptions, Guzzanti depicts a desperate population of survivors struggling unsuccessfully against the prime minister's relentless media machine. Given its sympathetic commitment to the Aquilani, whom *Draquila* depicts as having been exploited by leading politicians in a moment of suffering, I was surprised that many survivors criticized the film. While most of my interlocutors agreed that the Civil Protection Agency had enforced rigid controls and intimidated the population in some camps, and some praised Guzzanti for highlighting such practices, others accused the filmmaker of a very selective depiction that used the fate of the city for Berlusconi bashing. One Aquilana, Alessia, a retired schoolteacher, had been interviewed for *Draquila*. When I met her, she lived in one of the resettlement site apartments on the outskirts of the city. She was financially comfortable, paying only a small rent for the flat. Alessia was unhappy with Guzzanti's work:

> Guzzanti came to my flat in the Progetto Case. We talked about everything for about two hours [in the autumn of 2009]. My husband and I had just arrived in the new apartment after having been all over the place for six months, moving in and out of tents, hotel rooms, and so on. So, at that point, we were of course happy that we could finally move into proper and stable accommodation. I didn't think about how much it had cost the taxpayer, whether it could have been done better in another way, whether we should have had containers instead of long-term resettlement sites, and so on. All of these debates came up in her documentary. But for us, it was a different issue. After months of uncertainty and displacement, we were happy that we could move into a new apartment. We were grateful. With time, you realize that many things didn't go the right way and you become more critical. You still wouldn't criticize the place you live in as such, but the choices that were made, or not made, by those in power.
>
> That is why I was disappointed with her film. Guzzanti used only thirty seconds of the material and showed how happy I was with the new flat. And she used this to portray me as a grateful and duped *berlusconiana* [Berlusconi supporter]. Me? A *berlusconiana*? Never! Guzzanti spent months in L'Aquila. She interviewed lots of people. If she used thirty seconds from a two-hour interview, how much else did she cut from other interviews? Lots. And if you cut, then what do you want to achieve? To make your point. *Draquila* was an anti-Berlusconi film through the lens of the L'Aquila earthquake. Her film was not about us, but about Berlusconi. Guzzanti used the earthquake to give more substance to her claim: Berlusconi and berlusconismo were bad for Italy. She could have used any example to attack him. In this case, she simply used us.[51]

Alessia underlined that satisfaction with her new accommodation, following a period of difficult instability, did not mean uncritical support for Berlusconi's politics. She was not a *berlusconiana*. Instead, Alessia distinguished between her personal relief about being able to move into a semipermanent home and her capacity to criticize political choices. Guzzanti disappointed her by failing to make that same distinction, depicting her and others as grateful and overwhelmed. Many of my friends in the city, including those critical of the government, found the documentary biased. While there is acknowledgment of splinter groups that challenge the government, many scenes also show Aquilani exonerating Berlusconi from criticism, to Guzzanti's consternation. In one *Draquila* scene that is painful to watch, Guzzanti asks one Aquilana what she thinks about Berlusconi's recent sex scandals involving underage prostitution. The displaced Aquilana answers firmly: "What's wrong with going after young women? Better than being a *frocio* [a term that is a homophobic slur]." She appears as a backward and unsophisticated rustic uncritically defending her savior.

My friends expressed resentment over being portrayed as simplistic and gullible, even though they would themselves criticize other Aquilani for the traits that Guzzanti singled out as characteristic for the surviving population. Perhaps there was also frustration because Guzzanti had gotten much right. Many Aquilani had acquiesced and accepted the imposition of state power. The most vocal critics of Aquilani were other Aquilani, who accused their fellow survivors of narrow-mindedness and obedience. Sure, they would admit to me, many people had been passive, had resigned under pressure, and had taken tranquilizers, but there had also been pockets of resistance, creativity, agency, and determination to get the city back that were excluded from representation. Furthermore, it was seemingly different when an outsider, such as Guzzanti, twisted local stories to score political points as a privileged filmmaker from a position with little to lose and much to gain financially and for her reputation as a Berlusconi critic. Most of the stories of post-disaster L'Aquila were Berlusconi stories. He was the hero or the villain; Aquilani were stage props and usually victims.

CONFRONTING THE PAST

The accounts I collected contrasted with what survivors considered to be distorted media portrayals of post-disaster life. My conversations were usually marked by an expressed desire to tell a local story, followed by criticism of the government, the media, or even seemingly sympathetic observers, such as

Guzzanti. As a German anthropologist, I was regarded and enlisted as impartial to tell their stories, but the narratives produced for me were nonetheless strategically constructed. People did not react to only the events, but also to the filter that had made these events into stories told and repeated beyond L'Aquila. These filters had removed local life from local control.

The predominance of themes such as agency, civic action, and government critique reveals two crucial aspects of post-disaster life: First, the engagement with external coverage and depictions seen as imbalanced; and second, the importance of reclaiming a voice and agency in order to demand the restoration of the old center. External representations invaded survivors' experiences. The government intervention and accompanying media frenzy showed that Aquilani could not simply concern themselves with reconstruction, mourning, and repair; they also had to respond to how outsiders saw them and their supposed inability to remake their lives so as to make sure that they would be heard.

Documenting survivors' accounts, I have explored how political and personal dimensions of disaster continued to intersect at the time of my fieldwork, years after the earthquake. Narratives are crucial for the process of resituating the self in relation to past events and present identities: "Storytelling, *simply by virtue of its being a shared action of speaking, singing, sitting together, and voicing various viewpoints,* makes possible the momentary semblance of a fusion of disparate and often undisclosed private experiences."[52] Besides this social function of storytelling, I suggest that creating accounts of the past also helped Aquilani to make demands on the future. My interlocutors often described the disaster aftermath as a personal challenge they confronted through initiative and with determination. The wheelbarrow protest was a key manifestation of collective civic action, connecting the 2009 disaster with past catastrophes and an important local history, imagined or otherwise, of emancipation and autonomous recovery.

The disenfranchising state relief operation shaped local responses to the government intervention: resistance and opposition through protest, activism, grassroots movements, arts and culture, politics, and legal proceedings. Not all Aquilani became involved in campaigns or politics, of course, and the stories presented here already indicate how wide-ranging and divergent experiences of the earthquake and its aftermath were, sowing the seeds of division over political responsibilities and the right course of action toward L'Aquila's post-disaster future.

In subsequent chapters, I explore some of the creative projects people pursued in response to experienced misrepresentation and social division as they sought not simply to recover from a natural disaster, but also to overcome a politicized aftermath and rivalry among the surviving population. The next chapter explores the 2012 municipal elections and desires to regain civic normality through a vote that ought to herald a brighter future. In the end, the experience disappointed. No consensus emerged on how visions for the future could be brought together in the pursuit of a common project; divisions and envy intensified over the course of election campaigns and in the aftermath of the vote.

NOTES

1. See Rutherford H. Platt's analysis of how disasters strain democracies and their promise of freedom. Platt, *Disasters and Democracy: The Politics of Extreme Natural Events* (Washington, DC: Island, 1999).

2. See Alexander De Waal, *Famine Crimes: Politics & the Disaster Relief Industry in Africa* (Bloomington: Indiana University Press, 1997); Naomi Klein, *The Shock Doctrine* (London: Penguin, 2007); and Cedric Johnson, ed., *The Neoliberal Deludge: Hurricane Katrina, Late Capitalism, and the Remaking of New Orleans* (Minneapolis: University of Minnesota Press, 2011).

3. Giorgio Agamben, *State of Exception*, trans. Kevin Attell (Chicago: University of Chicago Press, 2005); Craig Calhoun, "The Idea of Emergency: Humanitarian Action and Global (Dis)Order," in *Contemporary States of Emergency: The Politics of Military and Humanitarian Intervention*, ed. Didier Fassin and Mariella Pandolfi (New York: Zone Books, 2010), 20–53; and Silvia Pitzalis, *Politiche del Disastro—Poteri e contropoteri nel terremoto emiliano* (Verona: ombre corte, 2016).

4. Both Gaim Kibread and Barbara Harrell-Bond have shown how victim identities are produced because they are expedient for state institutions seeking to assume greater power and exploit the helplessness they create. See Kibread, "The Myth of Dependency Among Camp Refugees in Somalia: 1979–1989," *Journal of Refugee Studies* 6, no. 4 (1993): 321–349; and Barbara Harrell-Bond, "Creating Marginalised Dependent Minorities: Relief Programs for Refugees in Europe," *Refugee Studies Program Newsletter* 15: (1993), 14–17.

5. Matei Candea and Laura Jeffery, "The Politics of Victimhood," *History and Anthropology* 17, no. 4 (2006): 287–296.

6. Francesco Erbani, *Il disastro: L'Aquila dopo il terremoto—le scelte e le colpe* (Rome: Laterza, 2010).

7. Ian Davis and David Alexander, *Recovery from Disaster* (Abingdon, UK: Routledge, 2016), 11–13. For an overview of the Civil Protection Agency's establishment and its impact on disaster management in Italy, see Alexander, "The Evolution of Civil Protection in Modern Italy," in *Disastro! Disasters in Italy since 1860: Culture, Politics, Society*, ed. John Dickie, John Foot, and Frank Snowden (New York: Palgrave, 2002), 165–185.

8. For an account of the political consequences of the 1980 Irpinia earthquake, see Ino Rossi, *Community Reconstruction After an Earthquake:*

Dialectical Sociology in Action (Westport, CT: Praeger, 1993); and Anna Chairetakis, "The Past in the Present: Community Variation and Earthquake Recovery in the Sele Valley, Southern Italy, 1980–1989," PhD thesis, Department of Anthropology, Columbia University (1991). Francesco Ventura and Frances D'Souza have compared the effects of disaster response initiatives in rural and urban areas affected by the 1980 earthquake, highlighting the detrimental involvement of criminal organizations in reconstruction projects. See Ventura, "The Long-Term Effects of the 1980 Earthquake on the Villages of Southern Italy," *Disasters* 8, no. 1: 9–11; and D'Souza, "Recovery Following the South Italian Earthquake, November 1980: Two Contrasting Examples," *Disasters* 6, no. 2 (1982): 101–109. For analyses of corruption and mismanagement in Italian disaster scenarios, see Mario Caciagli, *Democrazia Cristiana e potere nel Mezzogiorno* (Florence: Guaraldi, 1977); and Giovanni Russo and Corrado Stajano, *Terremoto: le due Italie sulle macerie del Sud, volontari e vittime, camorristi e disoccupati, notabili e razzisti, borghesi e contadini, emigranti e senzatetto* (Milan: Garzanti, 1981).

9. The Italian Parliament passed the relevant decree—"Urgent Interventions to Support the Populations Affected by the Seismic Events in the Abruzzo Region during April 2009 and Additional Urgent Interventions through the Civil Protection Agency"—on April 23, 2009. It introduced a number of provisions for the earthquake aftermath, from suspending certain taxes to the organization of the relocated G8 summit, via details regarding the funding of emergency and subsequent repair operations. Alpaslan Özerdem and Gianni Rufini, "L'Aquila's Reconstruction Challenges: Has Italy Learned from Its Previous Earthquake Disasters?," *Disasters* 37, no. 1 (2013): 124.

10. See Irene Bono, "Oltre la «mala Protezione civile»: l'emergenza come stile di governo," *Meridiana* 65/66 (2010): 185–205; Alfio Mastropaolo, *La mucca pazza della democrazia. Nuove destre, populismo, antipolitica* (Turin: Boringhieri, 2010); and Alfredo Mela, "Emergenza e ricostruzione dopo il terremoto: la resilienza comunitaria e gli interventi di sostegno," *Meridiana* 65/66 (2010): 85–99.

11. Fassin and Pandolfi, *Contemporary States of Emergency*, 22.

12. All quotes from Silvio Berlusconi in *Porta a Porta*, Rai Uno, May 5, 2009.

13. On the significance of the language of miracles in Italian politics, see Antonello Ciccozzi, "Aiuti e miracoli ai margini del terremoto de L'Aquila," *Meridiana* 65/66 (2010): 227–255.

14. Paul Ginsborg, *Silvio Berlusconi: Television, Power and Patrimony* (London: Verso, 2004).

15. See, for example, "Ecco le leggi che hanno aiutato Berlusconi," *La Repubblica*, November 23, 2009, accessed August 10, 2017, http://www.repubblica.it/2009/11/sezioni/politica/giustizia-18/scheda-leggi/scheda-leggi.html.

16. Peter Popham, "Berlusconi Turns Adversity to Political Advantage After Quake; the Italian Leader's Energetic Reaction to the Disaster Has Been a PR Triumph," *The Independent* (2009a), accessed August 10, 2017, http://www.independent.co.uk/news/world/europe/berlusconi-turns-adversity-to-political-advantage-after-quake-1666868.html.

17. In Italy, however, the statement was ambivalently received; some commentators interpreted it positively as an attempt to distract survivors from their difficult circumstances. At the time of my research, there was still much support in L'Aquila for such statements from a number of my interlocutors, which contrasted with the derision Berlusconi had received abroad for the supposedly uncaring and insensitive remarks.

18. For analyses of berlusconismo as a peculiar kind of Italian populism, see Oliviero Beha, *Il paziente italiano: da Berlusconi al berlusconismo passando per noi* (Rome: Avagliano, 2008); and Pierfranco Pellizzetti, *Fenomenologia di Berlusconi* (Rome: Manifestolibri, 2009).

19. Rachel Donadio, "Thousands Mourn Quake Victims at Funeral Mass," *New York Times*, April 10, 2009, accessed August 10, 2017, http://www.nytimes.com/2009/04/11/world/europe/11italy.html?_r=0. (2009).

20. Popham, "Italy's Requiem for Earthquake Victims: As the Mass Funerals Were Held in L'Aquila, a Nation Stopped, Mourned and Wept for Those That Lost Their Lives in the Disaster," *The Independent* (2009b), accessed August 10, 2017, http://www.independent.co.uk/news/world/europe/italys-requiem-for-earthquake-victims-1667295.html.

21. Michele Spanu, "La Maddalena: dopo il mancato G8 è la capitale delle incompiute," *Sardinia Post*, February 27, 2016, accessed August 11, 2017, http://www.sardiniapost.it/cronaca/la-scheda-la-maddalena-dopo-il-mancato-g8-e-la-capitale-delle-incompiute.

22. On the alter-globalization movement, see Klein, *No Logo: Taking Aim at the Brand Bullies* (Toronto: Knopf Canada, 2000); and Geoffrey Pleyers, *Alter-Globalization: Becoming Actors in the Global Age* (Cambridge: Polity, 2010).

23. Carlo Lucarelli, *G8: Cronaca di una battaglia* (Torino: Einaudi, 2009).

24. Roberto Settembre, *Gridavano e piangevano. La tortura in Italia: ciò che ci insegna Bolzaneto* (Torino: Einaudi, 2014).

25. Erstwhile ideas to establish L'Aquila as Rome's third airport came to nothing.

26. Bridget Kendall, "Italy's Minimalist G8 Summit," BBC (2009), accessed August 10, 2017, http://news.bbc.co.uk/1/hi/world/europe/8145847.stm.

27. During the G8 summit, a group of Aquilani critical of the government nonetheless staged a noticeable protest. They wrote "Yes We Camp" in large white letters on a hill near the summit venue, referencing "Yes we can," the

slogan used by the then recently elected American president, Barack Obama, during his campaign.

28. John Hooper, "Silvio Berlusconi Keeps His Promise to the Earthquake Victims of L'Aquila," *The Guardian*, November 27, 2009, accessed August 11, 2017, https://www.theguardian.com/world/2009/nov/27/italy-earthquake-berlusconi -promise-tents.

29. All quotes from *Forum*, Canale Cinque, March 25, 2011.

30. Analyzing the emotional reunion of a Sierra Leone child refugee with her mother on *The Oprah Winfrey Show*, the anthropologist Michael Jackson has shown how media spectacles reduce real-life complexity: "It is in the nature of media spectacles, as it is in the nature of stories, to conjure the illusion of moral closure. And there is always a heroic agent or supernatural helper, like Oprah, who effects the closure, and whose benevolent power makes possible the reunion, the happy ending, the miracle. But such stage-managed moments of truth may easily blind us to the vexed world in which we actually live, and to which we return when the story has been told, the carnival over, and the spectacle done." Jackson, *Life within Limits* (Durham, NC: Duke University Press, 2011), 164–165. People desire closure, and media coverage of superfast resettlement in the Progetto Case sites provided assurance that L'Aquila had been taken care of.

31. Tommaso [pseud.], in discussion with the author, L'Aquila, Italy, May 29, 2012.

32. The term *assistenzialismo* has negative connotations. It most commonly refers to excessive and uncoordinated government spending for poorer parts of southern Italy without a long-term strategy for local development and often in expectation of electoral support in exchange for resource allocation—cash for votes. It also implies that recipients' capacity for agency is increasingly reduced as they become more and more reliant on state assistance.

33. Tommaso [pseud.], in discussion with the author, L'Aquila, Italy, May 29, 2012.

34. Giovanni [pseud.], in discussion with the author, L'Aquila, Italy, July 11, 2012.

35. These recollections contrast with Berlusconi's quip about seeing the displacement experience as a government-sponsored holiday, since people such as Giovanni conceptualized their experience precisely through the difference between their lives as evacuees and those of holidaymakers. Giovanni also located his victimhood status in this difference in status between tourists and refugees. His description of being a second-class citizen was closer to the latter than the former.

36. Anna [pseud.], in discussion with the author, L'Aquila, Italy, December 1, 2012.

37. Francesca Cappelletto, "Long-Term Memory of Extreme Events: From Autobiography to History," *The Journal of the Royal Anthropological Institute* 9, no. 2 (2003): 242.

THE STATE OF EMERGENCY

38. Michael Lambek and Paul Antze, "Introduction: Forecasting Memory," in *Tense Past: Cultural Essays in Trauma and Memory*, ed. Lambek and Antze (London: Routledge, 1996), xiii.

39. Cappelletto, "Long-Term Memory of Extreme Events," 247. See also Sarah Farmer's account of official commemorations of Nazi atrocities in the French village of Oradour-sur-Glane. She describes how the French state appropriated the destroyed site for *national* remembrance and reconciliation initiatives, which often disregarded local memories and the wishes of the few survivors. Farmer, *Martyred Village: Commemorating the 1944 Massacre in Oradour-sur-Glane* (Berkeley: University of California Press, 1999).

40. Vieda Skultans, *Testimony of Lives: Narrative and Memory in post-Soviet Latvia* (London: Routledge, 1998), 68.

41. Skultans, *Testimony of Lives*, 26, 81. Skultans suggests that the neglect of personal memories at odds with official versions of the past "reinforced feelings of loneliness and ultimately made people ill."

42. Maria [pseud.], in discussion with the author, L'Aquila, Italy, January 13, 2013.

43. Maria [pseud.], in discussion with the author, L'Aquila, Italy, January 13, 2013.

44. A decree by Berlusconi's successor, Mario Monti, ended the state of emergency completely on August 31, 2012; see Angelo Jonas Imperiale and Frank Vanclay, "Experiencing Local Community Resilience in Action: Learning from Post-Disaster Communities," *Journal of Rural Studies* 47 (2016): 209.

45. Primo Di Nicola, "L'Aquila aspetta il miracolo," *L'Espresso*, February 11, 2010, accessed August 11, 2017, http://espresso.repubblica.it/palazzo/2010/02/11/news/l-aquila-aspetta-il-miracolo-1.18749?preview=true.

46. Maria [pseud.], in discussion with the author, L'Aquila, Italy, January 13, 2013.

47. Giuliano Di Tanna, "'Il sisma? Stamattina ridevo a letto'," *Il Centro*, February 12, 2010, accessed May 5, 2021, https://www.ilcentro.it/abruzzo/il-sisma-stamattina-ridevo-a-letto-1.411665

48. Massimo [pseud.], in discussion with the author, L'Aquila, Italy, April 29, 2012.

49. Massimo [pseud.], in discussion with the author, L'Aquila, Italy, April 29, 2012.

50. Massimo [pseud.], in discussion with the author, L'Aquila, Italy, April 29, 2012.

51. Alessia [pseud.], in discussion with the author, L'Aquila, Italy, January 15, 2013.

52. Jackson, "Storytelling Events, Violence, and the Appearance of the Past," *Anthropological Quarterly* 78, no. 2 (2005): 355–375. Emphasis in the original.

THREE

—⚏—

DISASTER POLITICS AND THE WAR AMONG THE POOR

THE WHEELBARROW PROTEST WAS SHORT-LIVED. Following the removal of debris from the centro storico, a shared objective across generational, political, socioeconomic, and other groups disappeared. The movement disintegrated. Once piazzas and streets had been cleared of shattered windows, broken bricks, and mortar, Aquilani saw that grassroots action could not reconstruct and render earthquake-proof thousands of buildings and monuments, pave new roads, repair tunnels, and reconnect sewers, water pipes, and telecommunication networks. Aquilani could now wander up and down the main streets in the old city center, which they had cleared with their wheelbarrows, but the buildings lining formerly grand and bustling avenues remained empty, cold, and damp. Railings and fences closed off narrow lanes and smaller squares. Most of the old center continued to be inaccessible. Faced with such violent destruction, civil society association reached its limit. State support, expertise, multiannual funding plans, and coordination beyond the scope of weekend activism were needed. Yet under pressure from an international economic crisis, Aquilani and their semi-ruined historic center slipped down the list of government priorities. The sturdy Progetto Case resettlement scheme had removed the necessity of urgent repair to provide shelter. While building sites sprung up across postwar quarters, the centro storico and other historic villages outside the center not only remained uninhabited, they lacked any construction activity whatsoever. The historical areas wrecked by the earthquake lay deserted for years; monuments had been encased, buttressed, and stabilized, propped up supposedly temporarily until permanent solutions were found.

74

This decay of heritage and once-thronging urban spaces continued when I arrived in the city in January 2012, almost two years after the wheelbarrow protest. Instead of having a clear sense of what the future would hold for them, survivors reported uncertainty about their plans and prospects. In this chapter, I focus on how Aquilani responded when they discovered that the emergency conditions they had considered a short-term nuisance—a state of exception— transformed into enduring limbo, with no end in sight. The need for solutions involving serious politics was apparent, but the necessary political commitment absent. Grassroots engagement or civic movements, however active and committed, could not reverse the material and financial impact of the disaster. Cynicism and political detachment could not guard Aquilani against the stasis induced by the haunting ruination of heritage and historic homes and the isolating effects of dispersal and resettlement. In this climate, many initially embraced the 2012 municipal elections as an opportunity to learn more about the political and bureaucratic mechanisms behind the inaction they witnessed in their city, hold local representatives to account, choose competent crisis managers, and practice democratic normality by selecting or dismissing political visions and personnel through the vote for the first time since L'Aquila's destruction.

Since everything else had disappointed, the election process was a last resort for hope. However, as soon as election campaigns descended into accusations of dishonesty and incompetence regarding the allocation of funds and the feasibility of restoration schemes and their costs, with confusing technical or legal details, this space of hope shrunk, too. The confusing and contradictory claims made during the election campaigns, as well as the eventual reelection of mayor Massimo Cialente, frustrated many survivors seeking signs of a new departure. While Aquilani agreed that political mismanagement had delayed recovery, they were divided over who was at fault—local, regional, or national administrations—as well as over the competence of political parties and the value of different proposals. Disagreements created or revealed social divisions around the vote that seeped into local society and added to misunderstanding. Aquilani could not agree on who ought to be blamed for delays and broken promises, nor on new political strategies, proposals, and personnel to speed up recovery.

During the first months of my fieldwork, political debate and campaigning for the May 2012 elections reached a pinnacle. As I was new to the city, campaign events were insightful for my work. Candidates from a range of parties organized public debates with citizens. Local television stations broadcast a seemingly endless number of cheaply produced electoral adverts and shaky camera interviews, and billboards and walls were covered in slogans and grand promises for a better and more livable L'Aquila. Party stalls became a permanent sight in shopping centers and on the few accessible old town squares and street corners, where Aquilani would take evening strolls among semi-ruined homes and churches cloaked by rugged scaffolding.

Following the state relief operation—when central government had excluded survivors from participating in decision-making processes—the opportunities offered by the electoral process further demoralized many survivors. Regaining the power to control local development in the aftermath of a centralized government relief operation was important for most survivors who talked to me about the elections. Rather than reconnecting Aquilani with their institutions, however, I found that the 2012 elections alienated many from political processes. The failure of electoral politics to inspire local people and create hope seemed to provide more justification for cynicism, withdrawal, and acts of selfishly pursuing one's own interests. Aquilani were told that the municipal elections were perhaps the most important vote the city had ever faced, and many agreed. The proposals discussed during campaigns and the candidates, however, as well as the confusing claims, counterclaims, and accusations that marked the runup to the vote, did not reassure voters that they could influence public affairs in a positive way and put their city on the right track to recovery. The result was dissatisfaction and a widespread sense of entrapment in a state of limbo.

Amid failed promises and increasingly gloomy future prospects, no shared understanding about how to overcome the crisis situation emerged during the course of an important political event. Due to intensifying uncertainty regarding the availability of resources and government support, Aquilani turned on each other.

FIELDWORK IN 2012/2013

When I arrived in L'Aquila in January 2012, a focus of distress and yearning for Aquilani was the state of their thirteenth-century Collemaggio basilica. The earthquake had destroyed the transept ceiling and large dome, and a temporary metal roof spanned the width of the church to shelter it from rain and snow. Thick ropes reinforced the arcade stone columns between the nave and the side aisles, leading to a juxtaposition of medieval Romanesque architecture with the features of a modern-day construction site perched on the edge of a plateau above the L'Aquila Valley. Virtually all monuments in the old city still remained at least partly inaccessible and extensively buttressed.

The Santa Maria church in Piazza Duomo, the central market square, was elaborately encased. A temporary division had been installed between the accessible front and the collapsed choir end of the church. Wire rope penetrated its walls. A large sign outside the church, which overlooked L'Aquila's largest square and was flanked by damaged buildings clad in scaffolding to prevent collapse, announced the French government's G8 Summit commitment to restoring the building. Worn-out Italian and French *tricolori* flew side by side from metal flagpoles. Further along the old town's main avenue, the *corso*, the Italian army controlled the accessible streets leading into the historic center, patrolling night and day in camouflage vehicles and combat uniforms. It was a popular game among youngsters to sneak past soldiers into unlit lanes, pretending to use abandoned doorways as outdoor toilets but then climbing over fences into the supposedly inaccessible parts of the historic center. Young Aquilani enjoyed causing trouble for nonlocal soldiers, who struggled to find their way around dark cobbled streets at night in pursuit of transgressing youth. Both groups saw each other as unlawful intruders.

January and February 2012 were among the coldest months in decades. Snow entered evacuated bedrooms and studies through gaping holes in semi-collapsed roofs in the abandoned centro storico. Even in Rome, a city usually spared from low temperatures, heavy snowfall brought public transport to a standstill. In the far-flung corners of the mountainous L'Aquila province, villages were cut off from the outside world, as unusual heaps of snow blocked plows from clearing steep and winding roads. Helicopters delivered emergency food parcels to remote hamlets. The motorways connecting L'Aquila with Rome and the Adriatic Coast were closed, severing the city from the rest of the country. The news reported that wolves entered Abruzzo villages, roaming for food. Supermarkets ran out of supplies. Temporary container schools, as well as public offices, were closed. Life in L'Aquila became even quieter, interrupted only by the humming of diesel engines in army vehicles patrolling streets and squares hidden under a white blanket, with few footprints to indicate human presence. With urban decay and military control existing side by side, the Italian state was at the same time painfully absent and invasively present.

The harsh winter, a population dispersed into isolated resettlement sites, and my struggle with local accents rendered the start of the research period in January 2012 difficult. Unusual for an Italian city, there were few obvious public spaces to frequent and meet people. Apart from some peripheral shopping centers, bars, and restaurants, social life had withdrawn into the private spaces of Progetto Case resettlement site living rooms or repaired apartment buildings across the outskirts. Hence, I was glad to discover that municipal elections for the mayor and city council would be held in a few months' time.

Candidates arranged meetings with voters in quarters, villages, and neighbor-hoods across the municipality. These *incontri con i cittadini* (meetings with the citizens) became my entry point to local politics. Given L'Aquila's limbo state, the debates I witnessed were not ordinary political wrangling; instead, they illuminated survivors' struggles to understand what had gone wrong in the earthquake aftermath and determine who would be the best person, with the best strategy, to oversee the restoration of heritage and return the city to what was glibly referred to as *normalità* (normality).

During such meetings, survivors clashed while discussing the repercussions of state provisions, particularly regarding connections between the govern-ment's focus on resettlement—pursuing quick and visible projects, with the Progetto Case the most prominent example—and the decay of property and monuments in the centro storico. While some were certain that Berlusconi had crippled the city with his unsubstantial show politics, others exonerated the prime minister as the only politician who had allocated funds for both the emergency period and construction projects.

IMAGINING THE FUTURE

A key argument of this book is that the government response in 2009 had long-term effects on the emotional experiences of earthquake survivors by creating hopes for the future, even among those who were critical of the spectacular emergency operation. When the state failed to deliver on its promises, it cre-ated anxiety and withdrawal into private lives, though it also sparked activism and creativity in politics, society, and culture, which I document in the second half of the book. Months of frantic activity and global attention and a string of high-impact projects produced certain expectations for future initiatives, and this included survivors who disagreed with the authoritarian effort. The gov-ernment had promised to restore historic houses, and for many Aquilani, such pledges had shaped personal expectations that government efficacy, alongside the prime minister's apparent personal agenda, could have positive effects for them. The speed and rigor with which the Progetto Case sites were built and the money allocated to repair projects in postwar quarters seemed to prove state willingness to turn L'Aquila around quickly, even when accompanied by self-promotion and the exclusion of anti-government voices.

Four years after the relief effort, in early 2013, I met Rocco Pollice, a L'Aquila-based psychiatrist and prominent figure in debates about psychological recov-ery. Shortly after the disaster, which had damaged L'Aquila's hospital, in which Pollice used to work, he set up a youth trauma center in a makeshift wooden building on a piece of lawn outside the then-inaccessible clinic. Pollice had listened to hundreds of stories of loss and hopelessness. Aquilani held him in high esteem. His SMILE center—a purposefully happy acronym for Medical Service for Preventive Measures Regarding Mental and Psychological Suffering among Young People—was highly regarded.[1] Numerous contacts in the city suggested I speak to him. When we finally got a chance to meet, Dr. Smile, as he was known around L'Aquila, showed me proudly around his makeshift structure.

The temporary wooden hut looked out of place next to the functional yellow-brick exterior of L'Aquila's San Salvatore clinic on the city's outskirts. Pollice was charming and serious as he outlined the earthquake's psychological legacies: depression levels, the number of patients with anxiety disorders, and mortality rates had risen significantly. The SMILE center was still in use in 2013, even though the main hospital had been repaired and resumed most functions. "I find that hospitals can be a bit sterile and ugly," Pollice noted. "This hut is more comfortable and homely. People are more at ease to speak about anxieties here; it doesn't feel as clinical."[2]

Pollice told me that he and his wife used to live in an apartment in the historic center. Like most Aquilani, they had fled their home in the middle of the night. Pollice was allowed to return a few weeks later, accompanied by firefighters, to rescue key family possessions. The extent of the damage and destruction had shocked him. Nevertheless, he told me four years later, he had believed that he would soon be able to return to his old town apartment:

> I remember clearly how, in September and October 2009, I was reading interior design magazines, choosing how to furnish my apartment following its imminent restoration. I really was certain that I would be able to return home soon. When I think about it today, this wasn't because I was feeling desperate and needed something to hold on to. I was genuinely, completely convinced that the city center's redevelopment was immediate and that our lives would soon be normal again. My wife and I even decided to have a child. We were both convinced that the disaster would only be a short-lived interruption, and not become this permanent crisis. Everything seemed so well organized and planned: the G8 summit, the resettlement sites, really the whole emergency operation. I expected the subsequent stages of the recovery effort to continue with the same speed and efficiency, and so did many other Aquilani, both friends and most of my patients.[3]

The relief effort had left an impression on Pollice and other Aquilani. He did not report cynicism or apathy when he reflected on his experiences of the relief operation and hopes for the future in 2009. Aspirations were generated by the effective response during the emergency phase in 2009. Some months later, however, this impression began to shift:

> Things changed after the last Progetto Case sites had been completed. When evacuees moved into the rehousing blocks, they began to realize that they wouldn't be able to return home soon, since nothing had changed in the historic center. Everyone's focus had been on the resettlement sites, both Aquilani and the media. When we turned our heads to look at the centro storico, we were shocked by the stagnation. My patients reported this: as they moved into the resettlement sites, their concerns shifted as well. Many were anxious about returning to their real homes now. Resettlement was only the first step for them, not the end point. Their anxiety intensified further when the wheelbarrow protest didn't lead to large-scale restoration initiatives either.[4]

Pollice's therapy sessions with hundreds of Aquilani showed that in 2009, many believed in a positive future, despite the tragic circumstances and contested political activities; the relief operation, even though it produced victimhood and excluded survivors from decision-making processes, created expectations of a fast-track recovery. When I arrived in L'Aquila, such expectations had been shattered. The wheelbarrow protest and subsequent stagnation had shown that there would not be a quick fix to the twin problems of dispersal and isolation or the large-scale decay of heritage and historic neighborhoods. Using opportunities provided by election campaign events, survivors deliberated and discussed what had gone wrong: Why had no reconstruction plan been passed? Why did local politicians claim that there was not enough money for heritage repair, while the national government said that the problem was the local administration's incompetence in managing projects? What kind of city did Aquilani want to build? How could survivors become involved in decision-making processes and have their voices heard and visions made known?

THE 2012 MUNICIPAL ELECTIONS

The incumbent mayor's campaign for reelection divided citizens in their assessment of political responsibilities for the paralyzed recovery process. In interviews with the local press and in meetings with the citizenry, Cialente, L'Aquila's mayor, who was from the center-left social democratic party Partito Democratico (PD), interpreted the vote as a referendum on his disaster management. Since delays in the recovery effort were unmistakable, Cialente had to convince voters that he was not responsible for failure, that the situation would be worse without him, and that his expertise guaranteed future restoration.

In February 2010, the Italian government appointed an Extraordinary Commissioner for the Reconstruction, Giovanni Chiodi, the governor of the Abruzzo region and a member of Silvio Berlusconi's center-right People of Freedom (PdL) party. Reconstruction and repair proposals had to be approved by his offices. During the election campaigns, accusations of hampering reconstruction efforts were traded back and forth between L'Aquila's mayor and the commissioner. The technical disputes confused those seeking to understand how responsibilities were divided between the local authorities and the national government via the Extraordinary Commissioner, whose role was designed to connect the local and national administrations. Cialente accused Chiodi of delaying repair and reconstruction initiatives, alleging that Chiodi refused to allocate funds to projects proposed by the municipal authorities. The commissioner refuted the accusations. Chiodi maintained that Cialente's administration had failed to produce proposals in accordance with state regulations and that his offices had no choice but to require revisions. The two accused each other of both ineptitude and point scoring on the backs of the resettled survivors. It was difficult for voters to understand the complex technicalities and the legalese involved in these public discussions and to make informed decisions about public affairs.

At some point in the runup to the elections, nine people had thrown their hats into the ring and announced their candidacy for the office of mayor. As new alliances were formed or dissolved and hopeless campaigns were discontinued, the number fluctuated during the months prior to the vote. "Nine!," my friend Riccardo exclaimed when he saw the number printed on a newspaper cover as we passed a kiosk near his house in early March 2012. Riccardo had become a close contact and informant, a PhD student in a humanities subject who was born and bred in L'Aquila. I asked him why he was surprised. "We have never had that many people run for the office of mayor; usually, you'd have two or three candidates."[5] I asked him why it was different this time. He rubbed his thumb and index finger together: money. Riccardo was certain that restoration and renovation schemes, estimated to bring tens of billions of euros to the city, attracted the attention of people who lacked any obvious qualification to lead the municipal administration but who hoped to use political power for personal benefit. In Italy, a country with a constitution that grants significant powers to regional and local governments, municipal offices have much influence over local affairs. The mayor is not a ribbon-cutting local representative, but an influential figure on a full-time salary who heads the local administration. "They think that the mayor will be able to allocate money to projects and companies. Corruption and embezzlement in Italy have always been connected with the construction business," Riccardo continued.

He was disillusioned. "Most of these candidates have got absolutely no clue; they're only running because they're well connected and promise their cronies a share. The elections are so important for L'Aquila, but we have this bunch of criminal clowns running for office. Their friends will vote for them, and their friends will then expect a piece of the cake. It's often like this in Italy, but so much is at stake here."[6]

Aquilani who talked to me about the elections agreed that they were enormously important for L'Aquila's future. A sense that the inflated number of candidates illustrated expectations to be able to divert funds for private gains exacerbated frustration among those seeking to inform themselves to accelerate recovery. In this context, conspiracy theories were rife. Next to the postwar condominium in which I lived, outside the old center, where repair works had been completed just before my arrival, other buildings were undergoing reconstruction. Every day, trucks reversed down the narrow *senso unico* (one-way street) outside my flat, accompanied by beeping. Men in hard hats and high-visibility vests routinely prevented me from parking my car outside the house in which I lived to allow larger vehicles to pass. Construction noises and drilling interrupted my typing up of fieldwork notes. Opening the window resulted in thick layers of dust on my desk, bed, and bookshelves. I often stopped for a chat with the construction workers, who explained to me why particular buildings had collapsed and others remained standing. One day in April, two weeks before the elections, I asked two of them why little seemed to be moving in the historic center. "The commissioner for the reconstruction, Chiodi, isn't from L'Aquila," one of them offered as an explanation, "but from a town near the coast, Teramo. He doesn't care about our city, and he is using his position to channel money to other projects in his hometown, to please his constituents."

His colleague interrupted to disagree: "Absolutely not—it's our mayor, Cialente. He is inept. He was elected before the earthquake to run a small university town. His job was to look after primary schools and keep pavements clean. This task is too big for him. He's nice enough, but there's a difference between an ordinary provincial official and someone capable of managing a long phase of post-disaster reconstruction. Cialente isn't cut out for this."

His coworker shook his head and maintained that L'Aquila could not recover without Cialente; he praised the mayor's experience from the emergency period and suggested that he knew the right people in Rome. The other man frowned and gestured toward the ruin of a medieval tower visible at the end of the street: "So why hasn't he used his contacts to reconstruct our monuments?" The two disagreed about bureaucratic procedures and legal technicalities, compensation schemes and bidding terms. The jargon confused me, even though I followed the news and debates about reconstruction procedures. Political disagreement is not unusual, but in this case survivors and politicians portrayed the decision between one set of candidates over another as existential, with far-reaching consequences: would the city lose five more years, the length of the mayor's mandate, or see the recovery of private property and heritage in the old town, lifting L'Aquila out of stasis and crisis?

In public meetings, Cialente invoked his local roots to persuade voters; born and raised in L'Aquila, he claimed to care more about the city. Cialente insisted that only he could prevent the city from being occupied, as he called it repeatedly, by outsiders, who lacked an understanding of traditions and local history. The mayor, first elected in 2007, claimed that he alone had prevented the Berlusconi administration from moving the Abruzzo region's offices to Pescara, retaining an important source of regional pride and significance in the battered city. He even compared himself with Hamid Karzai, the former Afghan premier. At one rally, he told enthusiastic supporters: "Like Karzai did with NATO, I will send the Extraordinary Commissioner away. We need to take powers back into our own hands as Aquilani."[7] Cialente invoked a strong sense of local identity to discredit opponents. Such distinctions between insiders and outsiders, Aquilani and non-Aquilani, were common. Surprised by the remark about Karzai, which seemed exaggerated, I asked my friend Riccardo what he thought about the comparison. He considered it a clever statement and outlined the importance of localism in Italian politics, particularly in L'Aquila, with its long history of external domination and emancipation:

> Cialente knows why he talks about the "occupation" [*occupazione*] of L'Aquila. The city's history is about gaining independence from the monasteries and hamlets that founded it. There is a deep-seated fear among Aquilani of having to surrender autonomy to external powers. They are more conservative-minded people, often elderly. And then, more recently, people who disagreed with the heavy-handed government operation, mainly people on the left, often young, attacked the Berlusconi relief effort as an occupation. The soldiers in the historic center today—also an occupation. This is a loaded term. Cialente knows how to manipulate fears of being without control and dominated by outsiders.[8]

Riccardo nonetheless remained skeptical about Cialente's chances. He was unsure about the vote. Despite a preference for left-wing parties, he was disillusioned with Cialente: "He's already been in office for five years. What if things just continue that way? We can't lose more time."[9] Riccardo expressed a widespread sentiment. Aquilani were torn between Cialente's claim that he

Figure 3.1. Sign in the old center reading "Entrance to the construction site" and "POMPEI"

Figure 3.2. Candidates for the office of mayor debating during the election campaign

knew the relevant regulations and ordinances for the reconstruction, as well as the people in Rome—both of which could accelerate renovation and repair processes compared with a newcomer—and the apparent lack of initiatives during his time in office, seemingly belying his claim to be the better choice. "I really don't know who to vote for," Riccardo admitted when we discussed the vote again, now only days before the election, after long and bitter campaigns. He had lost his enthusiasm about the vote. "No decision is right," he closed, as we sat on a small square outside one of the few accessible pubs near the old town, Ju Boss.[10]

THE OUTSIDER

At the height of the election campaign, Giorgio De Matteis, Cialente's only serious contender for the office of mayor, met his supporters in L'Aquila's historical theater. The main room was inaccessible, but a smaller hall within the same building had been restored for gatherings. De Matteis was the vice president of Abruzzo's regional parliament and relied on a broad center-right coalition to challenge Cialente. A few hundred Aquilani across age groups and genders, although middle-aged and elderly men were in the majority, were seated on elegant red chairs. Accompanied by dramatic music in a darkened room, a sequence of short film clips highlighted L'Aquila's abysmal state: abandoned ruins, streets covered in rubbish and debris, vandalism in deserted old town quarters, congestion and traffic jams on the long roads connecting remote resettlement sites with other parts of the overstretched urban territory, and disintegrating container schools. Following each clip, De Matteis outlined his solutions to the difficulty of everyday life that marked urban existence for most residents in this post-disaster city that struggled to recover. He accused the incumbent mayor of inaction: "Cialente promises us to deal with all of these issues if he gets reelected. But why hasn't he tackled them already? It's because he doesn't get on with the commissioner, and so the Aquilani have to suffer from Cialente's inability to swallow his pride and just be professional. His personal antipathy towards Chiodi is delaying L'Aquila's recovery, and this is unacceptable. He's not a *leader* [the last word used in the original English]."[11]

De Matteis invoked a fear that the reconstruction process would remain stalled with Cialente because of his difficult relationship with the Extraordinary Commissioner for the Reconstruction, which was an open secret. Both Cialente and his opponent played on anxieties that the recovery process could be further delayed. Walking back to my car after the campaign event, I chatted with an elderly lady. She was elegantly dressed and spoke high Italian without a local accent. She told me that she was "in the ninth decade" of her life, as she put it.[12] I asked her why she had decided to support De Matteis rather than Cialente. Pointing to the scaffolding cladding houses that flanked the cobbled street, she said she was furious that L'Aquila's mayor was overseeing such decay: "Cialente is running a fear campaign against Chiodi and Berlusconi. Many Aquilani are already scared of the future, so they believe him. He keeps saying that without him L'Aquila will never recover, and he needs these ruins to reinforce his message."[13]

She had supported the Berlusconi administration all the way and told me that the relief operation in 2009 had not been heavy-handed but had simply delivered what was needed in an exceptional situation of destruction. The new technocratic government in Rome, led by a former EU commissioner, Mario Monti, found her disapproval, even though she accepted that Berlusconi had lost the support of other European leaders. "Who has ever done anything for L'Aquila? It was Berlusconi. He is an entrepreneur, he knows business. Look at the Progetto Case sites. They were completed before the summer of 2009 was over. Since Berlusconi's gone, we've been in stasis. De Matteis knows Chiodi, they're from the same political camp; they can work well together. We don't need more delays."[14]

She had parked her car on a small road outside the city center and was heading back to her new apartment in a resettlement site. Before she parted, she explained that Cialente was wrong to complain that the state had not allocated sufficient funds for restoration: "There is enough money. After the earthquake, Berlusconi gave seven billion euros for the emergency effort and heritage restoration. But Cialente doesn't want to use the funds at the moment, because the Extraordinary Commissioner is still in place to oversee how he spends them. Cialente doesn't want to be controlled. He's waiting for the commissioner's offices to be disbanded, so that he can appoint the construction companies that he *knows*."[15]

As she uttered the last word, she pulled down her large sunglasses and glanced at me. I got the message: she was accusing Cialente of corruption, insinuating that the mayor was holding out for more powers to award contracts to companies that would, in turn, offer him financial rewards or well-paid consultant positions. Despite her strong disapproval, she was certain that Cialente was likely to win another term because he had successfully manipulated anxieties. She labeled Cialente a hypocrite: "He always attacks Berlusconi because of the Progetto Case resettlement blocks. Cialente says that they have destroyed the rural periphery and that he wanted to use the funds for restoration projects. But his own administration was involved in designing the project and chose the sites."[16] She shook her head and warned me not to believe the newspapers before driving off in her Lancia.

Discussions about candidates or parties did not just reveal political preferences but exposed fears of the future. In the first round of the elections,
Cialente gained around 40 percent of the vote; De Matteis came second, with
30 percent. All other candidates were eliminated, and Cialente and De Matteis
ran in a second ballot, which the incumbent mayor won with 60 percent of the
vote. His victory did not lead to much public celebration. I knew many people
who admitted to having voted for him without conviction, seeing him merely
as what was often referred to as the lesser evil.

His campaign was marked by hyperbolic and unrealistic claims, such as
the promise to turn the Progetto Case sites, following the reconstruction of
historic homes, into Europe's largest university campus—Italy's equivalent of
Oxford, as the mayor called it—and a plan to convert the landing strip left after
the G8 summit into Rome's third airport. The fact that Cialente received 40
percent of votes in the first round reflected a divided electorate unsure about
the city's future. If the election had been a public referendum on the mayor's
ability as a crisis manager, as Cialente had called the vote, the outcome was
ambivalent at best.

Shortly after the municipal elections, Italy's new expert government, led by
Monti since November 2011, terminated the office of the Extraordinary Commissioner for the Reconstruction. Instead of transferring powers to reelected
Cialente and the local authorities, however, Monti's government created two
special reconstruction offices with three hundred employees. One office was
responsible for the restoration of old L'Aquila proper, and the other for affected
towns and villages in the wider area. The national government continued to
control funds and award contracts.

When Fabrizio Barca, a new government minister responsible for the
recovery of post-disaster sites, presented the plan for the new two offices in
a public assembly in L'Aquila, Cialente accused him of resuscitating the com-
missionership, which, he claimed, had hampered recovery. Cialente warned of
further delays, but the government did not yield. The public assembly where
the two men clashed, held in a marquee in L'Aquila's market square, attracted a
large audience. Tensions between the mayor and Barca were tangible. Buoyed
by his victory, Cialente warned that L'Aquila could not afford to lose more
time. The audience debated whether or not the new administrative structure
would accelerate L'Aquila's reconstruction by providing necessary expertise
or instead delay recovery with unnecessary bureaucratic hurdles. Seemingly
a key step in the recovery of civic normality, the 2012 municipal elections did
not bring an end to a sense of powerlessness and limbo. The 2012 elections
did not constitute a hopeful point of departure for L'Aquila, but instead led

to a continuation of the confusion and shoulder-shrugging that Aquilani had become used to since 2009.

MORE EARTHQUAKES

In May 2012, just after the municipal vote had been held in L'Aquila, seismic shocks hit the prosperous Emilia-Romagna region in the center-north of Italy, famous for its agricultural products, including Parmesan cheese and Parma ham, and a backbone of Italy's economy. Twenty-seven people died, houses and factories were damaged, and tens of thousands of Emiliani left their homes for camps or other emergency accommodation.[17] In L'Aquila, survivors compared the response to the situation in Abruzzo three years previously with the response by the new government. Riccardo suggested that the two cases were completely different: "Look at what's happened since 2009. The government has changed, Berlusconi is gone. Monti is much more level-headed. He won't turn this into a media spectacle and disenfranchise everyone for his own benefit. There isn't enough money either. We have an economic crisis in Italy. The scales are also different. In L'Aquila, the earthquake hit a regional capital, an important center. In Emilia, they have small villages and towns, and factories, which are much easier to repair. They have learned from us, too, from our mistakes. It would not be right to suggest the two scenarios are similar."[18]

When I spoke to Riccardo over a meal at a makeshift restaurant, he highlighted how different the two scenarios were and how difficult to compare. Tommaso— whose narrative of critical involvement in the relief operation I documented in the previous chapter—had overheard our conversation and approached me afterward. He was collecting donations for the evacuees in Emilia-Romagna. Tommaso was also looking for volunteers to accompany him to the area, where he wanted to advise Emiliani on how to interact with state agencies and "avoid our mistakes."[19] Once more, he put stress on his capacity for independent-minded action by supporting disaster victims. Even though they trusted him to deliver their donations, and many gave generously, the Aquilani he approached were reluctant to join Tommaso on his trip north. I volunteered to accompany him and find out how he would talk about post-disaster life to the country's most recent victims of a catastrophe. In early June, we drove to the humid plains of Emilia-Romagna, an important hub of European agriculture. The area is flat and well connected to other parts of the country, unlike the mountainous parts of Abruzzo. Most settlements are smaller towns, dotted around stretches of fields and farms, with important centers, such as Bologna, Parma, or Modena. At night, the moon seems enormous above the flat land, which is sprinkled with churches and state-of-the-art industrial estates. Mosquitoes, rare in L'Aquila, tormented the earthquake evacuees in Emilia-Romagna.

Tommaso had made contact with a nongovernmental organization (NGO) that specialized in distributing donations for development projects in the global south. Its volunteers now collected clothes, food, and everyday necessities—stored in a large warehouse not far from Bologna—for displaced earthquake survivors in the affected areas. A dozen Emiliani evacuees, mainly NGO staff and supporters and their families, spent their nights on camp beds in the storage hall or in campervans parked adjacent to the building. Tommaso and I joined them for a couple of weeks. We cooked together and told stories in the evenings, squeezed on benches around a campfire and sipping wine from plastic cups. We toured the area in Tommaso's car, visiting official camps as much as spontaneous caravan settlements. When Tommaso mentioned that he had come from L'Aquila, people gathered and asked questions. He enjoyed his role as an expert on disaster relief, recalling his experience in authoritative stories. "The situation here is different," he routinely told Emiliani survivors, "because your government wants to support you. In 2009, the government was only interested in exploiting us."[20] The summer nights were warm and humid. Many Emiliani told us they were happy in their campervans, parked in groups with neighbors and friends. The atmosphere was reminiscent of summer festivals. The Civil Protection Agency had assessed buildings and allowed most evacuees to take showers inside. On our tour, we came across other Italians sharing Tommaso's sense of mission: they distributed toothpaste, toilet paper, water bottles, books, camp beds, and torches to survivors. The level of solidarity touched Tommaso: "It is beautiful that so many people want to help. And the Civil Protection Agency is supporting this. That's the main difference to what happened in L'Aquila in 2009."[21]

One day, we visited an official state-run camp administered by the Civil Protection Agency on a sports field on the outskirts of a small town, Cavezzo. In the sweltering heat, a few hundred people were queuing for lunch, served from a large canteen inside a white marquee. The boundary between the camp and its surroundings was not patrolled. On the other side of a low fence, groups of tents were spread across lawns and tarmac surfaces; evacuees living outside ventured inside the Civil Protection Agency compound and joined the lunch queue without checks. They did not want to be part of the camp infrastructure but used the camp amenities on a day-to-day basis. Tommaso identified the camp leader and shared with him his impression that the authorities were pursuing a different, more relaxed approach from what he had seen in L'Aquila. The camp leader, a tall middle-aged man in uniform from northern Italy, confirmed the observation:

What we are doing here is very different. I worked in L'Aquila. Back then, Rome took over all administrative functions. It was a much bigger disaster. Here, we work closely with the mayors and other municipal authorities. We don't issue identity cards. People can leave and come back into the camps as they please. There are many Emiliani who choose not to sleep in the camps, but they still come in to eat or shower. We are trying to cooperate as much as we can with survivors. To be honest, L'Aquila was much harsher, perhaps too harsh. But it was a different time, with different leadership.[22]

Afterward, Tommaso and I joined evacuees in the lunch queue. As we waited for our plastic plates with salad and pasta, Tommaso agonized about what he had just heard, torn between misery and satisfaction:

It's important, and a relief, that he admits that it was necessary to change their approach. That's what we've been demanding all along. But you still won't get anyone to say this officially. I'm glad that survivors here won't have to endure what we had to go through: intimidation and the militarization of state support. But it still makes me angry that the old government turned L'Aquila into a social experiment, and then pretended that everything was perfect and efficient. We are still suffering the consequences. Many Italians believe that everything was and is fine in L'Aquila. And have you read what people have been writing in the papers the last days? "The Emiliani are so much better than the Aquilani. They are so much more civilized. They are going to recover much better." But it's not about Aquilani or Emiliani. The state changed its approach. It's got nothing to do with the Aquilani![23]

Tommaso found the government approach in Emilia-Romagna promising. This contrasted with the stagnation he experienced in L'Aquila, where the mayor had just been reelected as a result of what many considered a lack of better alternatives. Comparisons between the situation in L'Aquila and the northern Italian areas appeared quickly; commentators and pundits asked why there had not been more progress regarding reconstruction in L'Aquila, and many blamed the supposedly passive and inept Aquilani.

Shortly after the first Emilia-Romagna tremors in May 2012, Vittorio Sgarbi— a prominent art historian and television personality from the area—expressed his view that the recovery process in the center-north would be unproblematic. He compared the Emiliani favorably with their L'Aquila counterparts. His comments were widely reported in L'Aquila: "The Emiliani won't just wait around like the Aquilani did. In L'Aquila, there is passiveness. The situation is static. It's still the same today as it was immediately after the earthquake. People wait for the state to do something. They are just complaining and crying."[24]

In a country in which stereotypes about southerners as lazy, government-dependent, and undeserving abound, Sgarbi provoked a strong reaction.[25] Aquilani responded with anger in online discussions and letters to newspapers. Some talked about defamation charges. When Aquilani, such as Riccardo, insisted that the two earthquakes were dissimilar, they also sought to reject the kind of comparison that depicted Abruzzo's survivors generically as defective citizens and passive victims who bore responsibility for their own stagnation—even though many of my friends and contacts in the city would agree that other Aquilani had contributed to the stasis and limbo through greed, selfishness, and a lack of purposeful collective action in the wake of the wheelbarrow protest. Guido Bertolaso's successor as the leader of the Civil Protection Agency, Franco Gabrielli, reached a similar conclusion, which he shared with a prominent national newspaper, *La Repubblica*: "There are always many different causes, but these do include local responsibilities. In Emilia, things have been very different from what I experienced in L'Aquila. It is always easy to blame others, to blame outsiders. But in some communities there is a certain level of activity, a desire to do something. It's something innate. Looking at the historical record, the difference lies not in the money spent on a certain area, but in that area's capacity to plan and to organize. And the Emiliani have reacted better [than the Aquilani]."[26]

While Aquilani would agree, in private and in conversations with one another, that many of their fellow citizens had been passive and indifferent, seeking personal gain rather than pursuing a recovery effort that would benefit the entire community, remarks by outsiders tarring all Aquilani with the same brush were rebutted. The comments by Sgarbi and Gabrielli were typical of comparisons that described Emiliani as northern, organized, and hardworking people and Aquilani as passive, relying on the state and delaying recovery through inaction. Much was at stake when Aquilani rejected such accusations, even though, in private, they would not hold back and would criticize each other for the same character traits and behaviors that outsider commentators also identified—at stake was the fear that, if a narrative of self-responsibility took hold, the Italian state might not come under public pressure to allocate more funds, personnel, and attention to the recovery effort in L'Aquila.

The people with whom I worked in L'Aquila also tended to be very active: they were protesters, campaigners, politicians, artists, cultural producers, journalists, writers, members of associations of the bereaved, and others seeking to turn a corner and promote heritage repair and recognition of their visions for the future. They did not accept being grouped alongside passive Aquilani, whom my activist contacts painted as indifferent, cynical, apathetic, and uninterested

in the common good. Accusations of ineffectiveness and self-responsibility created a conundrum for my interlocutors in L'Aquila: they wanted to keep up the
pressure on other Aquilani to become involved and shed their passivity so the
Italian state would listen to local voices and speed up its recovery efforts, but
they also had to reject portrayals of all Aquilani as passive and at least partly
responsible for the sorry state of their city. They rejected the negative stereo-
typical casting of Aquilani, since this depiction overlooked the role played by
the government intervention, which even Civil Protection Agency personnel
would admit, off the record, had been heavy-handed, and the grassroots activism against stasis and resignation.

The nationwide debate about differences between the earthquakes in
Emilia-Romagna and L'Aquila affected how Italians thought about Aquilani. In
the summer following the 2012 municipal elections, L'Aquila's most important
annual religious and community festival, the Perdonanza, took place in the city.
While waiting for the medieval reenactment of a religious procession, I spoke
to an elderly Aquilano, who introduced himself as Alfredo. He stood near me
in the shade, looking after his young granddaughters, who donned colorful
medieval costumes. We were all sheltering from the scorching sun underneath
ripped scaffolding in a central piazza, close to the damaged city hall building.
Alfredo remembered the August 2009 Perdonanza, which had taken place only
a few months after the April 2009 earthquake, as an important demonstration
of local resilience: "This is our most significant festival, the most important
gathering in our city. In August 2009, most of us still lived in tent camps, but
we staged the Perdonanza as a statement to ourselves and outsiders: we would
not give up. I had tears in my eyes when the *porta santa* was opened in our
Collemaggio basilica, which is almost a thousand years old. It reminded me
of L'Aquila's history: of previous earthquakes and of our strength to recover.
We were proud of it."[27]

When Alfredo talked about the importance of the 2009 event, I asked him
what it meant to participate in the Perdonanza in 2012. He became somber: "It's
different today. I feel sad seeing that nothing has changed in the historic center,
and the basilica's roof is still down. The government and our local authorities
have betrayed us."[28] As he was explaining what he considered shortcomings by
the national and local administrations, a younger woman interrupted Alfredo.
Her accent revealed that she came from the Abruzzo Coast, not from L'Aquila:
"Sorry to jump in, but I just couldn't help listening to you. I'm really sick of
this story of how bad everyone has treated the Aquilani. The poor Aquilani
are always the victims. Berlusconi is bad, Cialente is bad, everyone is bad. But
I know this city's mentality: I can tell you that the Aquilani have brought this

upon themselves. They just sit around and wait for handouts. They are stubborn, resistant to change, rustic. They don't get up and do something. The
government gave you televisions and bicycles and computers. Just get on with
it, like the Emiliani!"[29]

Taken aback, Alfredo shook his head. She eventually stopped and went
away to take photos of a friend in a medieval costume. Alfredo disclosed that
such comments left him humiliated: "I don't want people to feel that we are
ungrateful. Many Italians don't understand how hard this earthquake hit us.
They can't comprehend unless they go through it themselves. Outsiders cannot
understand what it's like to live like this for years, but they always judge us. We
have done so much; we worked so hard. But look around you: the whole city
looks like this. It's a ruin. We need the government to support us."[30]

After May 2012, portrayals of Aquilani as passive and defective—first
encountered in the aftermath of the 2009 disaster—resurfaced. The disappointing municipal elections and the earthquakes in Emilia-Romagna added
to a sense of despair and powerlessness for many of my interlocutors. For most
of the people to whom I spoke, supporting Cialente in the second round of the
ballot had not been based on conviction. Rather, the fear of delaying reconstruction further by losing an established connection to the government in
Rome had motivated people to reelect an unpopular mayor out of pragmatic
considerations and without certainty that this was the better choice. A few
weeks later, reactions to the Emilia-Romagna earthquakes demonstrated that
Aquilani still faced an uphill battle regarding both recovery and the Italian
public's perception of their situation.

WAR AMONG THE POOR

Over three years after the earthquake, in the summer of 2012, the municipal
elections and responses to the tremors in Emilia-Romagna exacerbated fears
that a return to some kind of urban normality was far in the future. Political philosopher Martha Nussbaum wrote that "a sense of common fate, and
a friendship that draws the advantaged and the less advantaged into a single
group, with a common task before it" are the key components of successful
collective action.[31] I struggled to find a robust version of this "sense of common fate" in L'Aquila. Echoes of such an experience existed in recollections
from the wheelbarrow protest, which had taken place in 2011. On April 6, 2012
and 2013, I witnessed thousands of Aquilani coming together to commemorate the city's destruction with a march around the city. At 3:32 a.m., the
names of the earthquake victims were read out in the Piazza Duomo. Such

commemorative events, however, did not create a sense of shared purpose that could have transformed into enduring action; post-disaster experiences varied widely, and attitudes toward the national, regional, and local government added to social divisions, as did envy toward other Aquilani who had supposedly received greater financial compensation, suffered less, or even benefited from the earthquake.

Social scientists have suggested that cynicism and parody can provide the necessary social glue to bind together communities in challenging times, helping them to confront state power or hopelessness when thinking about the future.[32] This especially has been observed within former Socialist societies, where political cynicism often combines with nostalgia for a past shaped—at least in romanticized memory—by a strong sense of community, a clear idea of belonging, and a shared purpose.[33] Anthropologist Daniel Knight has also found that wit and cynicism helped people in Greece confront the economic crisis of the 2010s and produced a sense of collective suffering to challenge austerity more effectively.[34]

In Italy, humor and sarcasm have also helped citizens come to terms with crisis experiences and devise new approaches to solidarity in the face of hardship.[35] In the wake of the frustrating elections and the fallout of the 2012 Emilia-Romagna earthquakes, however, it became apparent that cynicism or detachment could not guard Aquilani seeking recognition and support against outside attacks or the crippling effects of government inaction in their city. Aquilani also noted that the new government responded with more sincerity to the disaster in Emilia-Romagna, and they were bitter about it. Detachment remained an option, and cynical Aquilani used state resources for their own ends without consideration for the wider community. Pockets of solidarity and cooperation emerged, as evidenced by the large number of associations, groups, political movements, artistic initiatives, and the like, but there was no community-wide effort to bring disparate post-disaster experiences into a narrative of collective suffering that could bridge divisions caused by socioeconomic disparity, access to resources, displacement, bereavement, and so on.

Internal divisions split neighbors, friends, and families, since even those involved in grassroots activities had to realize that their locally relevant commitment could not induce the serious recovery that would benefit the whole city: billions of euros in government funding and expertise to remake the old center and tie together remote and isolated resettlement sites. During the final weeks of the election campaigns in 2012, I asked my friend Riccardo whether or not he was optimistic about the future. He expressed a profound sense of hopelessness:

This is a city of now fifty thousand people. Twenty thousand have left since the earthquake. Nobody wants to spend billions of euros here. What are we? Just sheep and mountains and cheese. An unimportant university and pensioners. No economy. We no longer know what to believe. The government in Rome says it'll take ten years to restore the city center; our mayor says it'll be done in five. Bertolaso used to tell Berlusconi it would take thirty. There are funds, says the government; there are no funds, say the local authorities. And the new special reconstruction offices? That's just a way of subsidizing employment for three hundred people. It's always like this with the south. Just *assistenzialismo* [state assistance to stabilize unsustainable economies while expecting votes for the ruling party in return].[36]

Riccardo planned to leave L'Aquila, perhaps even Italy. Even though he was observing politics closely, Riccardo admitted that he no longer knew what to believe—whether there was enough money to rebuild L'Aquila in its entirety or not; whether the reconstruction would take five, ten, or thirty years; and whether the government was genuine about heritage restoration. Riccardo observed contradictory statements and the conspicuous absence of government interest in the city. Powerlessness and skepticism produced anxieties that L'Aquila might never be reconstructed. This fear contributed to social fragmentation.

When I arrived in L'Aquila in January 2012, I was struck by the high quality of some of the recently repaired buildings outside the city center. My friends explained that many homeowners had declared excessive damage and used state funds to renovate attics and basements, which they now rented to students who had lost pre-disaster contracts for flats in historic buildings. Rather than merely repaired, such flats had been upgraded with state-of-the-art interior design. Many of the bedrooms in the apartments I saw while looking for accommodation had two or even three beds in them. "People are trying to make money. They know the students have no choice, because they are poor and there aren't many places to rent," Riccardo explained as we toured properties.[37] While some Aquilani lived in hotel resorts or remote resettlement sites, others made a windfall from state-funded renovations by renting out spare rooms at inflated rents. The earthquake's legacy, in government policies and payments, split survivors into what they themselves described as "winners" and "losers."

Not even one year after his reelection, L'Aquila's mayor faced vocal opposition when his administration forwarded utility bills covering a three-year period to the residents of the nineteen Progetto Case resettlement sites. The authorities had estimated energy consumption based on floor space, rather than collecting figures from flow meters. Many residents claimed to have been particularly frugal and demanded a public meeting with the mayor to pressure him to reverse the decision. The issue was on the front page of local newspapers for days and was widely discussed. Cialente agreed to explain the decision to the citizens in early 2013.

One cold winter evening, hundreds of Aquilani crammed into a makeshift marquee in one of the larger resettlement sites, close to L'Aquila's city center. They challenged the mayor on the *bollette pazze* (crazy bills), as the utility bills had been nicknamed. Almost as many people as had managed to get into the marquee were waiting outside, trying to follow the conversation inside and occasionally interrupting the event by shouting insults. Cialente and other local administrators faced exasperated survivors who accused the administration of theft. The atmosphere was tense. People talked over each other, and yelling was common. A local councillor, whose responsibilities included overseeing the Progetto Case resettlement sites, sought to calm the situation by invoking what he called the "bigger picture": "Let's not just talk about these bills, OK? They aren't even a thousand euros each. Ask yourselves: If someone gives you a flat, rent-free, after a natural disaster, is that generally a good or a bad thing? That's how you should approach this. Don't be so petty-minded."[38]

The crowd reacted with boos and hisses. One man shouted: "But we want our houses back! That's the big question and the 'bigger picture!'"[39] A microphone was passed around the marquee. One Progetto Case resident voiced his frustration:

> The bills are confusing. It seems that we also have to pay for the maintenance of communal areas, like the lawns, car parks, and staircases. But usually this is paid for by the landlord, which, in this case, is the city of L'Aquila, the *comune*. So why do we have to pay now, as tenants? We don't own the apartments we live in. There are no regulations for any of this. It's a gray area. But instead of communicating with us to find a solution, we get these massive bills out of the blue, after three years. And we have to pay within weeks. No landlord could do this legally. It's so much money. I don't have a thousand euros lying around.

Many supported the statement with applause and "bravo." A woman added: "Of course we want to pay for what we have consumed. Nobody wants to cheat. But we want the figures, no guesses or estimates."

Cialente responded by explaining that the local authorities themselves had only just now received utility bills for the resettlement sites from energy providers: "And of course, these bills include, for example, electricity for car parks and streetlamps. These costs have to be shared equally."

A man at the back interrupted him: "But the lights in my staircase never work!"

"Well," Cialente responded, "you should have called our helpline, and we would have fixed it." Before he could finish the sentence, many people started laughing. Cialente seemed frustrated with the apparent hostility. He demanded to be treated with respect: "I am only trying to help because we need to pay Enel [Italy's largest power company] nine million euros over the next weeks. We will produce personalized bills, but it will take months to get them, so you must pay your bills now, and the city administration will refund any overpay."

The suggestion was met with consternation and resentment. Some shouted: "Liar!," "Theft!," or "We'll never see our money again!" One Aquilana got hold of the roaming microphone to elaborate: "If we pay these bills now, aren't we accepting them? What if we never get our money back? We don't trust you, we don't trust the authorities. No one trusts you to keep word. That is the problem. That's why so many of us are hesitant to pay at this stage."

Cialente insisted that, by law, the city administration could no longer anticipate the payment. He threatened to sue whoever failed to comply and pay within the stipulated time frame. When the intimidation failed to produce consent, he began to beg: "I ask you to pay this installment now, please."

"No!," various members of the audience exclaimed. An elderly man shouted without a microphone: "We're still paying council tax for the old houses we no longer have. We're not paying anything for these apartments!" Frustration with the authorities and enmity were apparent, but there were also differences between those who refused to pay outright and those who wanted to cooperate but demanded more transparency. And there were many others in between who were hoping for some kind of compromise and understanding for their financial situation. Someone asked why Cialente could not use the revenue from the solar panels on the Progetto Case resettlement block roofs to pay the bills, but the mayor explained that the panels were not public property: "When the resettlement sites were built, the Civil Protection Agency struck a deal with Enel. They funded the solar panels, so they get the revenue today. There's nothing I can do about it. That deal did not involve the city administration. Blame Berlusconi and Bertolaso."

Many in the audience shook their heads at the attempt to shift the blame. The debate continued. It lasted for over three hours; many Aquilani waited for their chance to say something, but arguments and viewpoints became repetitive. After two hours, participants lost attention. They began to chat to each other instead of listening to the mayor, gossiping with friends or neighbors. Two more statements elicited particularly angry reactions. One Aquilana suggested that there was no need for a discussion: "It was written in the contract when people entered the resettlement sites, so they'll now have to pay. There are more important issues in our city, and it would be great if we could focus on the essentials." Cialente nodded, but others shouted her down and accused her of having been paid to speak up for the mayor and municipal administration.

Another speech divided the crowd. A young man suggested that the bills were fundamentally unfair for another reason: "How about the Aquilani relocated to hotels for years, or those still staying in army barracks? They don't need to pay any bills, so this is just unfair and random. Unless they pay some contribution as well, we shouldn't."

Some people near him patted his shoulder, but others berated the speaker in vociferous disagreement. The mayor also objected: "We shouldn't create such divisions. The earthquake has hit all of us badly."

"But some worse than others!," someone yelled from outside the marquee and received support from some inside the structure. It was past midnight when a visibly tired Cialente got up to leave. He explained that he had started work at 8:00 a.m. in the morning and had to be back at his desk the same time tomorrow. On the way out, more than two dozen Aquilani stopped him to ask more questions, often pushing themselves forward aggressively or shouting from behind other people in front of them. Many of those trying to speak to Cialente gesticulated passionately, anger and exhaustion visible in their faces. They did not just want to talk about the utility bills; they had brought a plethora of issues to the mayor, who stayed another hour to note down the details of individual cases, promise to look into planning permissions, and suggest contacts within the administration to those seeking answers. Often, he had to explain that not the municipal authorities, but the special reconstruction offices, the regional or national administration, or others were the relevant points of call instead. The next morning, I asked my landlady—a born-and-bred Aquilana in her mid-thirties who ran a small family business and had a penchant for left-wing politics—what she thought about the issue, and she responded:

> Why didn't these people contact the city administration earlier to ask about their bills? But no, they waited for three years and hoped that nothing would come. Well, that's tough. My parents have been paying their bills since they moved back into their house, and that was one year after the earthquake. And if the Aquilani had stayed in their former homes, without an earthquake, they would have had to do the same, no? I don't see the problem with paying utility bills.

Why don't they want to pay? They're living for free in resettlement sites. Many of them are simply greedy. I also know a lot of middle-class Aquilani who've been saving big sums of money since the earthquake, living for free in state-sponsored accommodation. They're better off than before. I know doctors, lawyers, and so on, who are making money from this, since 2009. They bought expensive new cars after the earthquake with the money they could save up by staying in government-sponsored accommodation, and the state paid for the overdue restoration of their second or third homes, which they now let to students. Come on.[40]

I also found the evening discussion with Cialente tiring and frustrating and was surprised by how little sympathy I had for the stubborn and aggressive individuals who were refusing to pay standard bills. They had been displaced for years, and many were facing economic hardship, but they also had rent-free accommodation in comfortable new condominiums. Was their recalcitrance justified? Should they be more cooperative? Were they not all in the same boat? My landlady summed it up poignantly when I asked what she thought about the comment from the meeting that those still staying in barracks or hotel rooms had no bills to pay either: "You know what's really sad? This is becoming a war among people who all suffer: a war among the poor [guerra fra i poveri]."[41]

Distrust and envy were common in L'Aquila. The meeting about the utility bills was just a particularly revealing instance of the divisions that fragmented the people who were also spatially scattered across a semi-ruined urban territory. The war among the poor—Aquilani contesting what they considered an uneven distribution of financial compensation and recovery opportunities— raged in public meetings and private conversations. I was told about neighbors who had repainted exterior walls with state aid, unconnected to the earthquake, and about property owners who had ten different apartments refitted thanks to the taxpayer, while other families remained displaced. Such accusations were a constant feature of conversations about how Aquilani framed their own fate as well as that of others in the disaster aftermath. Lacking trust in the authorities to speed up the return to some kind of normality, Aquilani looked after themselves and their families. For many, this was not always a war among the poor, but among winners and losers. They were not united in the face of shared tragedy; by contrast, they denounced the increasingly uneven impact of the catastrophe.

The natural disaster was transforming into individual crisis experiences. Immediately after the earthquake, the state had allocated billions of euros for emergency measures. These included the construction of the Progetto Case and other resettlement sites, hotel bills, subsidies for displaced Aquilani rent-ing privately elsewhere, support for repair work in postwar neighborhoods, and the G8 summit. Soon after, money began to run out. Aquilani had received support for repairs in modern neighborhoods, but property owners in the old town were anxious that the funding would not suffice. Between 2009 and 2014, Italy saw four different governments change the bureaucratic structures for the distribution of resources for repair and reconstruction. Survivors had to acquaint themselves with administrative vocabulary for complicated claims forms.

In early 2013, I visited a friend, Marco, in his home village on the outskirts of L'Aquila. The old center was still completely inaccessible and largely ruined. The survivors had moved into temporary wooden sheds arranged in a small settlement of so-called Temporary Housing Modules (MAP). Dozens of those had been constructed throughout the periphery of L'Aquila, usually adjacent to the villages or other settlements damaged in the earthquake, whose old houses remained uninhabited and often in a serious state of disrepair. Unlike the sturdy Progetto Case blocks, the semidetached wooden units were inad-equate for the harsh local winters. Their thin walls were not made for the cold and damp Abruzzo mountains. Before the earthquake, Marco had lived in the old village in a home his family had owned for generations. The earthquake had killed a number of family members. I asked how the relief effort had changed village life. His response was bleak:

> When you arrived, did you notice the house with the bright orange facade at the corner? For twenty years, that house had been white. Then it was repainted. All the houses that had some damage repair, even if only minor stuff inside, were repainted in bright colors. Initially, the state was dishing out money. Many exploited the earthquake to upgrade their lives: new bathrooms, new basements, renovated attics, and lively colors. That has changed. It's harder for us who had old historic homes, because it takes so long. If you had a detached postwar building before the earthquake, you're probably doing fine now, in a renovated property, ideally with student lodgers for a bit of extra cash.[42]

Such stories were common. L'Aquila's periphery was dotted with houses in bright red, yellow, and orange; it was an urban territory exhibiting the uneven redevelopment and government support that fueled resentment.

The earthquake had hit one village in the periphery of L'Aquila, Onna, par-ticularly badly. Forty people, out of just over two hundred, had been killed. Most houses had been severely damaged or destroyed. The old buildings had been constructed with cheap stone when Onna was a farmers' village without much money, and the earthquake flattened large sections of the picturesque settlement. The German government had accepted special responsibility for the reconstruction of Onna during the 2009 G8 summit, because the German Nazi SS had committed a massacre in the hamlet in 1944. The German government and private German donors subsequently funded the construction of a new community center, inaugurated in 2010, and a museum for Onna's history, as well as the restoration of the picturesque village church. A German-Italian architect presented the first reconstruction plan for any part of the wider Aquilano territory for Onna in 2011. Onna seemed to move much faster in its recovery than other parts of L'Aquila and the surrounding countryside.

When I spoke to other Aquilani about Onna and its special experience of a double tragedy, I often encountered unexpected bitterness. Over the course of my stay in the city, a number of Aquilani told me that it was a shame their particular neighborhoods had not had a Nazi massacre and now a foreign government to take care of them. Onna residents were envied for benefitting from a Nazi atrocity that few of them remembered. The destabilizing uncertainty, combined with the disparate experiences of anxiety and stagnation in some places and of progress and apparent prosperity in others, deepened community divisions. One retired schoolteacher, who became a key interlocutor for me, summed up the feeling of stasis that many reported: "I've been out of my house for three years and four months. I've lived in many types of accommodation. I've not seen any change in the historic city center. I'm depressed. I'm in a situation in which I've got no idea where I'll be in ten years' time. The future is completely uncertain for me. And even if things remain as they are, static, this won't comfort me, because the present itself is so uncertain. I feel the sense of time strongly, how it passes, every day. It weighs me down."[43]

Stagnation had devastating social and psychological effects. Pollice, the founder of the SMILE youth trauma center, had initially believed the government promises for a swift restoration of the city center. He told me that in 2009, he had been certain that his life would soon return to pre-disaster normality. He had chosen a design for the apartment he believed would be repaired soon and had a baby with his wife. However, he soon recognized that the political promises had been unrealistic. His life would remain transformed for an indefinite length of time. Nonetheless, Pollice continued his work for the traumatized population. Then, almost five years after the earthquake, in early 2014, Pollice returned to the apartment he used to inhabit in the old city center. Since the area was still out of bounds to former residents, he climbed over fences and barriers. Inside his old flat, he scribbled *sono un uomo buono* (I am a good man) on the wall before taking his own life. Dr. Smile left behind his wife and two-year-old son. L'Aquila was in shock. Thousands attended the funeral. Having left L'Aquila almost a year previously, I struggled to understand. To me, he had seemed stable, realistic, and proud of his achievements with the SMILE center. An obituary in a local newspaper attempted to explain the inexplicable:

> What struck others was his altruism, his readiness to help, and this very rare ability of his: never to withhold a word of comfort or encouragement. This is often so much more important and efficacious than medication. Even if no one will ever know what led Rocco to this extreme act, the tragic end of a man who knew how to distinguish between depression and the suffering of life, forces us to think more about repairing people's minds, social lives, souls. Our inner worlds. For five years now, institutions have only paid lip service to this. . . .
>
> Rocco's death renders us more fragile, exposed in a moment in which we realize the scope of the earthquake tragedy, worsened by exhaustion, disappointment, the lack of a prospect for the future, and the many uncertainties which have plagued people for at least four years, and which plague them still. . . .
>
> The institute run by Pollice had to confront the most devastating effects of post-disaster life, an aggravated version of the "usual" sickness of modernity: put badly, having to live in a city that has accentuated the pathologies of the mind and the body. But this fact, permeating the city's suffocating air, has been silenced or hidden; as if the institutions were trying to avoid talking straight, admitting, confronting, and dealing with those serious problems. L'Aquila, with a few isolated exceptions, is a fragmented city now, and does not have a very bright future, to use a euphemism that is taking root here.[44]

The author, Berardino Santilli, suggested that Pollice's suicide had been conditioned by shattered hopes, uncertainty, and the lack of prospects for both L'Aquila's and his personal future. Scientific research conducted by Pollice and his colleagues found that up to 12 percent of the survivors suffered from post-traumatic stress disorder, compared with 1 percent among the wider Italian population.[45] Depression was common, affecting two in three Aquilani. Psychological suffering had become a pervasive earthquake legacy—a shared fate that did not serve to create a sense of common purpose or solidarity, but instead triggered feelings of isolation, grief, loneliness, and sometimes envy. I find it difficult to speculate on the reasons for Pollice's decision, but other survivors saw the matter more clearly. A significant number told me that they had contemplated suicide at some point. For many of my friends in the city who continued to blame Berlusconi for their lack of recovery progress, Pollice's act was the result of false promises, institutional failure, and the absence of future prospects almost five years after the disaster. The obituary shared a common accusation that state institutions had abandoned L'Aquila and were ignoring the pressing issues: ruined social lives and empty souls plagued by stagnation and insecurity in what seemed an increasingly fragmented, both socially and materially, mountain city.

LOST HOPE

Anthropologist Michael Jackson wrote: "Perhaps the worst fate that can befall any human being is to be stripped of the power to play any part in deciding the course of his or her life, to be rendered passive before impersonal forces he or she cannot comprehend and with which he or she cannot negotiate. Under such circumstances, some people fight desperately to regain some sense of being in control, while others submit fatalistically to the situation that has overwhelmed them—having recourse to flight, camouflage, or avoidance."[46]

Faced with destruction, displacement, and death, many Aquilani fought to maintain their capacity to shape lives and livelihoods: Pollice set up an institute to support depressed Aquilani; the wheelbarrow protest reclaimed urban spaces; Tommaso toured disaster-stricken areas of Italy to counsel evacuees; and hundreds, often thousands, of Aquilani attended political events to make sense of past mismanagement and make informed decisions to shape the future. At the time of my fieldwork, however, my conversations and observations revealed anxiety and bitterness. The stagnation that induced frustration had social and political dimensions. Public debates for the municipal elections revealed that survivors struggled to agree on how the promises made in 2009 for a swift recovery had transformed into stasis. If the elections were grasped initially as an opportunity to shape the future by influencing public affairs through the democratic process, campaign events illustrated that the reasons for L'Aquila's lack of progress were technical and confusing.

In the wake of the elections, Aquilani deplored their feelings of powerlessness and became more cynical. Disaster politics was not just ineffective in restoring heritage and returning the city to some kind of normality; the apparent unevenness of compensation schemes and injustice in financial outcomes estranged Aquilani from one another, exacerbating geographical isolation into resettlement sites, peripheral rehousing units, semi-repaired postwar neighborhoods, and freestanding new buildings across the city's hinterland.

In post-disaster L'Aquila, Berlusconi's state had expanded the scope of the intervention and sought to control the minutiae of local lives. In so doing, the government extended its reach into the emotional experiences of survivors.

In his analysis of the role of the state in post-Yugoslavia Sarajevo, political anthropologist Stef Jansen explores how the residents of large-scale housing blocks conceptualized normality, hope, and statehood in the late 2000s, a decade after the end of conflict. At the time, Sarajevans struggled to arrange themselves with the present and found comfort in the imagined future of a new normality that reenacted the unavailable socialist past, with its protective state providing infrastructure, social routines, and official forms of solidarity.[47] The yearning for normality was also transforming into a sense of entrapment in L'Aquila at the time of my fieldwork in 2012 and 2013, three to four years after the earthquake. Unlike Sarajevans, however, Aquilani needed the state to escape from stagnation. Hope, as an orientation toward the future, became intertwined with state power, as Pollice explained. Following resettlement, it was the absence of government support that turned expectations into fears.

Hope, but also the limbo and uncertainty that followed after the wheelbar-row protest, were at least coproduced by a particular kind of disaster management that had kick-started recovery with fast-moving projects in 2009 but then ignored the need to develop long-term policy strategies.[48] The Emilia-Romagna earthquakes revealed that outsiders still regarded Aquilani generically as passive citizens, despite local attempts to use grassroots action to influence decision-making processes. It is not surprising that Aquilani were skeptical about their future; state institutions seemed to exhibit little interest in their fate, and the state response to the Emilia-Romagna earthquakes illustrated that L'Aquila was of second-order importance. Actions aimed at improving one's own circumstances amid the general chaos—such as charging students infla-tionary rents for bedrooms in houses renovated with state funding—revealed a lack of solidarity.

This chapter has illustrated how a sense of loss with regard to the capacity to influence public affairs intensified over the course of the 2012 municipal election campaigns and following the Emilia-Romagna earthquakes and the realization that restoration and recovery would be slow, arduous, costly, and exhausting. Envy and a sense of rivalry added social fragmentation to geo-graphical dispersal and to divisive political disagreement. Whereas the last chapter analyzed experiences of loss as a result of the relief operation and biased media coverage, this chapter has shown that experiences of powerlessness and division continued years after the earthquake, with ramifications for trust in the political system and one's community. The next chapter adds to these two dimensions of loss by exploring discussions about the future of the built envi-ronment and L'Aquila's old center. Aquilani experienced loss also with regard to their capacity to shape the future of their city as an urban space. Aquilani struggled to agree on the kind of architecture and urban design that should characterize future L'Aquila and contested visions of how tradition and history should coexist. They argued over the right relationship between old and new in a place that was recovering unevenly from catastrophe and in which many remained skeptical of plans for modernization, fearing the permanent disappearance of their hometown.

NOTES

1. In Italian: *Servizio di Monitoraggio e Intervento precoce per la Lotta agli Esordi della sofferenza mentale e psicologica nei giovani.*
2. Rocco Pollice, in discussion with the author, L'Aquila, Italy, April 9, 2013.
3. Rocco Pollice, in discussion with the author, L'Aquila, Italy, April 9, 2013.
4. Rocco Pollice, in discussion with the author, L'Aquila, Italy, April 9, 2013.
5. Riccardo [pseud.], in discussion with the author, L'Aquila, Italy, March 9, 2012.
6. Riccardo [pseud.], in discussion with the author, L'Aquila, Italy, March 9, 2012.
7. Mayor Massimo Cialente, during a public meeting to discuss reconstruction plans for the city, L'Aquila, Italy, March 13, 2012.
8. Riccardo [pseud.], in discussion with the author, L'Aquila, Italy, March 13, 2012.
9. Riccardo [pseud.], in discussion with the author, L'Aquila, Italy, March 13, 2012.
10. Riccardo [pseud.], in discussion with the author, L'Aquila, Italy, May 2, 2012.
11. Giorgio De Matteis, during a public event for his *ballottaggio* election campaign, L'Aquila, Italy, May 10, 2012.
12. Unknown person, in discussion with the author, L'Aquila, Italy, May 10, 2012.
13. Unknown person, in discussion with the author, L'Aquila, Italy, May 10, 2012.
14. Unknown person, in discussion with the author, L'Aquila, Italy, May 10, 2012.
15. Unknown person, in discussion with the author, L'Aquila, Italy, May 10, 2012.
16. Unknown person, in discussion with the author, L'Aquila, Italy, May 10, 2012.
17. Andrea Hajek, "Learning from L'Aquila: Grassroots Mobilization in Post-Earthquake Emilia-Romagna," *Journal of Modern Italian Studies* 18, no. 5 (2013): 627–643; and Silvia Pitzalis, *Politiche del Disastro—Poteri e contropoteri nel terremoto emiliano* (Verona: ombre corte, 2016).
18. Riccardo [pseud.], in discussion with the author, L'Aquila, Italy, May 23, 2012.
19. Tommaso [pseud.], in discussion with the author, L'Aquila, Italy, May 23, 2012.
20. Tommaso [pseud.], in discussion with displaced people in an earthquake zone, Finale Emilia, Italy, June 8, 2012.
21. Tommaso [pseud.], in discussion with the author, Finale Emilia, Italy, June 9, 2012.
22. Civil Protection Agency leader, in discussion with the author and Tommaso [pseud.], Cavezzo, Italy, June 8, 2012.

23. Tommaso [pseud.], in discussion with the author, Cavezzo, Italy, June 8, 2012.

24. AbruzzoWeb, "Terremoto: Sgarbi, 'In Emilia ricostruzione rapida, all'Aquila si piange adosso,'" May 5, 2012, accessed August 12, 2017, http://www .abruzzoweb.it/contenuti/terremoto-sgarbi-in-emilia-ricostruzione-rapida -allaquila-si-piangono-addosso/477684-302/.

25. For discussions of "the south" in Italy, see Gabriella Gribaudi, "Images of the South," in *Italian Cultural Studies*, ed. David Forgacs and Robert Lumley (Oxford: Oxford University Press, 1996), 72–87; Jane Schneider, ed., *Italy's "Southern Question": Orientalism in One Country* (Oxford: Berg, 1998); Nelson Moe, *The View from Vesuvius: Italian Culture and the Southern Question, Studies on the History of Society and Culture* (Berkeley: University of California Press, 2002); and Franco Cassano, *Tre modi di vedere il sud* (Bologna: Il mulino, 2009).

26. Piera Matteucci, "Gabrielli: 'Emiliani meglio di abruzzesi,' E Cialente attacca il governo," *La Repubblica*, October 16, 2012, accessed August 10, 2017, http://www.repubblica.it/cronaca/2012/10/16/news/gabrielli_emiliani_hanno _reagito_meglio_di_abruzzesi_la_differenza_non_la_fa_la_quantit_di _denaro-44627704/.

27. Alfredo [pseud.], in discussion with the author, L'Aquila, Italy, August 23, 2012.

28. Alfredo [pseud.], in discussion with the author, L'Aquila, Italy, August 23, 2012.

29. Unknown person, in discussion with the author and Alfredo [pseud.], L'Aquila, Italy, August 23, 2012.

30. Alfredo [pseud.], in discussion with the author, L'Aquila, Italy, August 23, 2012.

31. Martha Nussbaum, *Political Emotions: Why Love Matters for Justice* (Cambridge, MA: Harvard University Press, 2013), 345.

32. See, for example, Alexei Yurchak, "The Cynical Reason of Late Socialism: Power, Pretense and the *Anekdot*," *Public Culture* 9: 161–188 (1997); Yurchak, "Soviet Hegemony of Form: Everything Was Forever, Until It Was No More," *Comparative Studies in Society and History* 45, no. 3 (2003): 480–510; Michael Herzfeld, "Irony and Power: Toward a Politics of Mockery in Greece," in *Irony in Action: Anthropology, Practice, and the Moral Imagination*, ed. James W. Fernandez and Mary Taylor Huber (Chicago: University of Chicago Press, 2001); and Gabriel Torres, *The Force of Irony: Power in the Everyday Life of Mexican Tomato Workers* (Oxford: Berg, 1997).

33. Dominic Boyer, "Simply the Best: Parody and Political Sincerity in Iceland," *American Ethnologist* 40, no. 2 (2013): 276–287; and Boyer and Yurchak, "American Stiob: Or, What Late-Socialist Aesthetics of Parody Reveal about

Contemporary Political Culture in the West," *Cultural Anthropology* 25, no. 2 (2010): 179–221.

34. Daniel Knight, "Wit and Greece's Economic Crisis: Ironic Slogans, Food, and Antiausterity Sentiments," *American Ethnologist* 42, no. 2 (2015): 230–246.

35. For an account of irony in Calabria, see Stavroula Pipyrou, "*Cutting* Bella Figura: *Irony, Crisis, and Secondhand Clothes in South Italy,*" *American Ethnologist* 41, no. 3 (2014): 532–546. For an analysis of sarcasm in Berlusconi's Italy, see Noelle J. Molé, "Trusted Puppets, Tarnished Politicians: Humor and Cynicism in Berlusconi's Italy," *American Ethnologist* 40, no. 20 (2013): 288–299.

36. Riccardo [pseud.], in discussion with the author, L'Aquila, Italy, March 23, 2012.

37. Riccardo [pseud.], in discussion with the author, L'Aquila, Italy, January 14, 2012.

38. Local councillor, at a public meeting with the mayor of L'Aquila to discuss utility bills with concerned citizens, L'Aquila, Italy, January 17, 2013.

39. This, and subsequent statements, unknown persons, at a public meeting with the mayor of L'Aquila to discuss utility bills with concerned citizens, L'Aquila, Italy, January 17, 2013. Statements from mayor Massimo Cialente during the meeting are introduced as such.

40. Anna [pseud.], in discussion with the author, L'Aquila, Italy, January 18, 2013.

41. Anna [pseud.], in discussion with the author, L'Aquila, Italy, January 18, 2013.

42. Marco [pseud.], in discussion with the author, L'Aquila, Italy, March 17, 2013.

43. Giovanna [pseud.], in discussion with the author, L'Aquila, Italy, July 16, 2013.

44. Berardino Santilli, "Il suicido di Rocco Pollice: L'Aquila che non pensa a ricostruire le menti," AbruzzoWeb, January 17, 2014, accessed August 11, 2017, http://www.abruzzoweb.it/contenuti/il-suicidio-di-rocco-pollice--laquila-che-non-pensa--a-ricostruire-le-menti/537157-327/.

45. Ranieri Salvadorini, "Il terremoto nell'anima," *Mente—Il mensile di psicologia e neuroscienze* 100 (2013): 24–33.

46. Michael Jackson, *Excursions* (Durham, NC: Duke University Press, 2007), 116.

47. Stef Jansen, *Yearnings in the Meantime: "Normal Lives" and the State in a Sarajevo Apartment Complex* (New York: Berghahn Books, 2015). Interestingly, anthropologist Hirokazu Miyazaki has suggested that ambiguity is an important dimension of hope, rather than experiences that can add to limbo and thus limit orientations toward the future. See Miyazaki, *The Method of*

Hope: Anthropology, Philosophy, and Fijian Knowledge (Stanford: Stanford University Press, 2004).

48. I have developed the argument about the political effects on affective experiences and political subjectivity further in Bock, "The Second Earthquake: How the Italian State Generated Hope and Uncertainty in Post-Disaster L'Aquila," *Journal of the Royal Anthropological Institute* 23, no. 1 (2017): 61–80.

FOUR

—ᴛᴛᴧ—

CONTESTING URBAN RECOVERY

DEBATES ABOUT RECONSTRUCTION AND RESTORATION began immediately after the earthquake ruined L'Aquila's old town and modern quarters,
as well as villages and settlements in the periphery. In 2012 and 2013, with the
old center still largely inaccessible, questions about the interplay between
urban space and reconstruction initiatives on the one hand and local identity
and political participation on the other shaped conversations about L'Aquila's
future as an urban space. At the time of my fieldwork, a number of significant
construction initiatives were launched and debated in the ruined city. The
fragmented townscape provoked clashes involving state authorities, local
administrators, urban planners, leading architects, and ordinary Aquilani in
terms of what ought to be rebuilt authentically, what could be added in contemporary materials and designs, and in what ways public urban spaces should be
restored or transformed into innovative places of civic associationism.

The earthquake and the state relief effort had ruptured the city's urban
fabric. Before 2009, the urban topography had been similar to that of other
Italian cities: a walled medieval center largely refashioned in baroque and
Renaissance styles, surrounded by postwar neighborhoods with their modern
condominiums and commercial and industrial estates, and framed by municipalized villages on the outskirts that blended into the countryside. At the time
of my fieldwork, the city center and most historic villages remained damaged
and, apart from rare exceptions, uninhabited. Repair projects were underway
in some postwar areas. The Progetto Case resettlement sites had eroded the
municipal borders and challenged center-periphery distinctions that had once
shaped local views on identity and belonging. Against this backdrop of uneven

urban recovery, innovative urban revival proposals were divisive. This chapter explores how conflicts emerged over the right balance between heritage
restoration and the addition of new urban design. Many people in the city
regarded modern architecture projects and urban improvement schemes as
inappropriate distractions that ignored a pressing need for authentic repair and
restoration initiatives, expressing a common fear that the earthquake might
become a pretext for construction companies and self-promoting architects to
transform L'Aquila's historical character. Conflicting responses to rival bids
to turn the city into a showcase of innovative architecture and contemporary
urban revival schemes exposed divisions over the relationship between urban
space and civic identity.

Since Italians usually conceptualize their towns and cities according to
center-periphery categories, the historic core, or centro storico, also played
a key role in shaping views of history and identity after the earthquake. This
focus on the importance of old centers, however, is surprisingly recent: the Italian concept of the centro storico dates back to the 1960s, when the Charter of
Gubbio was put forth in an attempt to protect heritage in an age of urban modernization and postwar sprawl.[1] At the time of the charter's publication, urban
improvement schemes accompanied economic success in the boom years of
the 1950s and 1960s, transforming century-old towns and cities by altering
historic quarters in Italy and elsewhere in Europe with car-friendly private
transport infrastructure.[2] The charter was an early revolt, albeit with little initial success, that challenged the modernist broad-avenue onslaught on cobbled
streets, narrow lanes, and crammed medieval buildings without sanitation. The
charter's authors demanded a revaluation of the aesthetically pleasing, as well
as socially and culturally important, traditional street patterns, pedestrianized
areas, smaller units, accessible public space, and heritage.

The charter's aims were similar to the vision put forward in the United States
by urban scholar Jane Jacobs, who pushed back against the postwar destruction of the historic neighborhoods of New York City, which the municipal
authorities sought to replace with oversized condominiums and superhighways
for automobiles. Jacob's *The Death and Life of Great American Cities*, first published in 1961, had a significant impact on the appreciation of organically grown
urban forms across Western societies.[3] However, as geographer Nick Dines has
argued with regard to such debates, renewed appreciation of the centro storico
in Italy, promulgated largely by people associated with Italy's communist party,
PCI, "was infused with essentialist discourses about 'historical identity' and
'civic memory' which, when not fixed in some golden era, were blind to questions of agency and conflict. What the past meant for different people and who

had the power to define it were questions rarely posed by partisans of the centro storico lobby."[4]

Precisely these questions about identity, agency, and conflict separated architectural visions for post-disaster L'Aquila, where urban expansion in the 1960s and '70s had also produced extensive modern neighborhoods, such as Pettino and Torrione. They were characterized by detached multistory condominiums that soon eclipsed the old center in terms of population. The new roomy and bright apartments offered amenities and comfort, including space for cars, that were unavailable in most old-town buildings. The postwar urban sprawl, however, was at best haphazardly planned. New city quarters lacked infrastructure for social life. L'Aquila's urban sprawl and real-estate speculation, particularly in the city's western parts, put city residents at risk. Pettino, the largest postwar quarter, for example, was built on a known seismic fault line, and the 2009 earthquake caused significant damage there.[5]

Despite the postwar urban expansion, the old center nevertheless remained the pivot for socializing, shopping, culture, civic associationism, protest, student life, and public offices. A growing number of university students started to rent old apartments from those who now lived in modern quarters and owned second or third properties in the centro storico. The comfortable new flats in postwar condominiums only made sense because the old center continued to offer the spaces of social, cultural, and political life that were absent in the modern quarters: scenic piazzas, restaurants, bars, cafés, theaters, music halls, markets, churches, university buildings, public offices, banks, and much more. The postwar building boom did not add autonomous urban neighborhoods but created private refuges that had to be complemented with the public social spaces of an urban center. In 2009, L'Aquila's destruction and evacuation ruptured the organic relationship between different areas of the urban territory. The old center that used to connect parts of the city became inaccessible. When uneven experiences with the recovery process, which I documented in the previous chapter, led to different priorities among Aquilani, divergent urban visions for the future added layers of local conflict over the city's recovery.

In descriptions of their city and its material qualities, Aquilani usually distinguished between the centro storico and areas outside the city walls. Their sense of the city reflected what other ethnographers have observed throughout Italy: identities and understandings of *cittadinanza* (citizenship) are closely tied up with belonging in urban space and the use of public squares.[6] As a concept, *cittadinanza*—the term also is derived from *città* (city)—underlines the importance of urban, locally rooted imaginations of political and social belonging.[7]

In the aftermath of their forced relocation, Aquilani had expressed frustration with the lack of progress regarding urban recovery in the old center through the wheelbarrow protest. The initiative had shown that survivors did not see rent-free resettlement as an adequate substitute for their previous access to historic homes, places of congregation, cultural and commercial venues, and public space for civic activity. The wheelbarrow protest demanded the authorities weave the old center back into the urban fabric and social routines.

When I arrived in the city two years later, however, the wheelbarrow initiative had not been followed by heritage restoration. Whereas the state's apparent inaction had initially permitted survivors to rally around a shared cause and clear the center, there was now disagreement on the functions and character of the future centro storico. Various groups disagreed with a dominant conservationist view, which prioritized the restoration of buildings in authentic pre-disaster fashion and renounced modernization as an undesirable imposition. Enthusiasm and skepticism toward new ideas divided people, as some sought to promote innovative urban visions of a polycentric city that would break the dominance of the old center and bestow autonomy and a higher quality of life on other neighborhoods, whereas others defended the center's exceptional status for the urban topography.

This chapter explores recovery initiatives that illuminate how the entanglement of urban space and belonging produced conflict beyond debates about urban planning or architecture; in the destroyed city, proponents and opponents of juxtaposed urban visions saw their own future at stake. Whereas some feared losing the city and lives they had known forever, others were anxious to turn the destruction into a necessary moment of departure—and many Aquilani found their views somewhere in between these poles. The first project I discuss is a strategic vision for L'Aquila's transformation into a smart city proposed by international experts on urban redevelopment; the second one is the construction of a wooden concert hall designed by one of Italy's most prominent architects, Renzo Piano. Proponents praised each initiative as crucial for the acceleration of L'Aquila's revival, while critics considered them irrelevant and superfluous vanities, championed by outsiders and by misguided local supporters who were gambling away L'Aquila's distinctive urban appearance.

A FRAGMENTED URBAN SPACE

When I lived in L'Aquila in 2012 and 2013, the Progetto Case rehousing units had become the sites of restricted private lives for almost seventeen thousand Aquilani. Varying in design, the resettlement blocks shared key features; they were made up of prefabricated, three-story houses on top of car parks featuring anti-seismic pillars. Each building had twenty-five apartments that varied in size between fifty and seventy square meters. In total, the 185 housing units contained 4,625 brand-new and fully furnished apartments. On average, the sites' distance to the old center was a significant 8.1 kilometers, but individual distances varied between 2.6 and 18.3 kilometers. From the outset, the project had been met with skepticism. Italian urban scholar Georg Frisch, for example, suggested that the Progetto Case resettlement scheme would transform L'Aquila's urban character permanently, countering claims that the blocks would be negligible, transient additions.[8] Besides the durable Progetto Case apartment blocks, twenty-seven smaller settlements with a total of 1,273 semi-detached, single-family wooden huts, called MAP (Moduli Abitativi Provvisori, or, Temporary Housing Modules), were constructed for evacuees from damaged villages and settlements in L'Aquila's rural periphery. These MAP villages varied in design and layout; while some were functional settlements without decorative squares or shared spaces, others were enhanced with village greens and flowerbeds, fountains, and small shops, bars, and cafés. Bungalow huts in the more elegant MAP villages were distinguishable from one another by their colors, building material, and decorations; the respective organization funding the construction of a MAP settlement would be able to choose design and material.[9] In total, forty-six MAP and Progetto Case relocation sites were added to the urban fabric, some far away from and others close to existing, damaged parts of the city.

Beyond this, Aquilani were granted exceptional permission to construct small wooden sheds for use as temporary accommodation units in areas previously designated as allotment gardens. Precise numbers are unknown, but local officials estimated that hundreds of such sheds had been built across the hinterland. The extent of new constructions led a friend, who showed me around the territory shortly after my arrival, to compare post-disaster L'Aquila to an infamous Italian case of urban degeneration: "What is happening to the rural periphery of L'Aquila reminds me of the time I lived in Naples: buildings spring up everywhere, without any concept or plan. Things just happen, without a policy or long-term strategy. Everyone just does what seems good for them and their family. No one knows what to do with the Progetto Case buildings after people will have returned to their homes. Our rural periphery will be destroyed forever. We are witnessing across Italy how the country loses its countryside. In L'Aquila, it's simply happening in fast motion."[10]

Contrasting random construction activity with memories of pre-disaster life, Aquilani commonly highlighted the unique role of the centro storico. Most of them did so positively, but some commented critically on the constraining dominance of the old space. Such voices suggested that the focus on the old center contributed to the despair of the post-disaster years: if the city had been more decentralized, the closure of the centro storico would not be as crippling for community life and limit social, political, cultural, and other activities.

Even prior to the earthquake, L'Aquila had witnessed the transfer of certain economic functions to the periphery. Some years before the disaster, for example, two large shopping centers had opened on the outskirts, near populous postwar neighborhoods. The US-style malls were easily accessible by private transport and included large car parks. After the earthquake, they reopened quickly. Entrepreneurial store managers organized bus shuttles for evacuees stranded in camps without belongings. At the time of my fieldwork, some Aquilani described the shopping centers as socially destructive sites of consumer capitalism that undermined the tradition of window-shopping. Others, however, saw them as blessings that provided shared spaces for social routines. Teenagers gathered there to eat ice cream or smoke cigarettes in the car park. On the weekends, families strolled along the sterile corridors to buy clothes and multimedia equipment, sipping coffee and catching up with former neighbors, friends, and relatives. The shopping centers took over limited social functions from the centro storico; some bars and shops from the old city even reopened branches there.

In the old city, soldiers had replaced window-strollers in closed-off neighborhoods. The wheelbarrow protest and metal stabilizers had rendered some major streets accessible for pedestrians, who promenaded in between uninhabited buildings held together by wire rope and bracing. In partly collapsed houses, kitchen floors were still strewn with debris, cutlery, and furniture. "L'Aquila is dead," someone had written on a wall along the semi-ruined main street in the old center. "Your aunt is dead," had been added in dialect (*Zieta è morta!*), which translates as "Piss off!"[11] Across the old town, empty spaces and semi-collapsed ruins had become sites of public and private commemoration. Candles, pictures, poems, toys, and other private belongings adorned security fences in memory of deceased family members and friends. The memory of lost loved ones was kept alive in numerous small memorial sites.

The relatives of the earthquake victims were also lobbying for the construction of a fountain as a memorial to commemorate the 309 deaths, but when I left L'Aquila in 2013, over four years since the disaster, different factions were still in disagreement over the appropriate location. Whenever I walked or drove around the city with Aquilani, they pointed to ruins or gaping holes in the ground to inform me who had lost their lives where, connecting material

Figure 4.1. MAP wooden hut resettlement village near Onna

Figure 4.2. Protest posters in L'Aquila's old city. Berlusconi, July 2009: "L'Aquila will be reconstructed during this term in office. I will rent a house here to follow the works." Bertolaso, May 22, 2009: "We will reconstruct the old center within five years."

Figure 4.3. Ruins in L'Aquila's old center in 2013

destruction with their social relations and my developing network of acquaintances and friends. The earthquake had layered topographies of death and suffering onto L'Aquila's cityscape, and Aquilani had to familiarize themselves
with new sites and negotiate their meaning. They learned to arrange their lives
within the expectations of bereaved relatives regarding appropriate public
behavior in a city with conflicting desires to both commemorate and move
on from the tragedy; whereas some wanted to party and go out again, others
demanded that evening entertainment ought to be restricted near sites of death.

As temperatures soared in the spring of 2012, Aquilani returned to the
centro storico for early evening strolls along accessible, uninhabited streets.
They wandered around what they called a *città fantasma* (ghost town) and
shared a glass of wine in a bar on the Piazza Regina Margherita, a historic
square in the northern part of the old center, where a handful of proprietors
had obtained special temporary permits to open ground-floor venues. The
upper stories, however, remained uninhabited, their fragile facades held
together by steel frames. The piazza featured an enclosed garden with a few
soaring trees and an old fountain. Its water supply had been interrupted.
With parking spaces available in nearby streets, close to the new Humanities Department of the University of L'Aquila, the square was a hub of evening social life. Before the earthquake, the centro storico had provided

distinct spaces and venues for local and nonlocal university students, school pupils, different social classes, left-wingers and right-wingers, and different generations. Now, the restricted urban space necessitated new forms of social contact, and conflict, that had been separated spatially before 2009.

Limited social routines were nonetheless fragile. Bar owners did not know when their temporary licenses would expire. One of them, Luca, had opened a small, one-room bar on Piazza Regina Margherita that was frequented predominantly by students and younger middle-class professionals. While he was glad that some business had returned, uncertainty and limbo frustrated him. Luca revealed that he might have to close again soon for restoration works:

> I'm happy to close for repairs, of course, but I have no idea when it will happen. The authorities first asked me to close two months ago. Then they postponed it to the next month, then to this month—but, as you can see, nothing's happened. "Probably next month," they told me the other day. I've got no idea for how long I will have to close, or where I will go instead. How do they expect me to run a business or plan my future, or to invest, to pay tax? I barely make any money. This isn't a proper life when you have no idea what the next day will look like. Look around you. These old houses have been rotting for years. No one does anything about it. I don't think the government cares about us. L'Aquila is dying a little more each day.
>
> I'm sure they rebuilt the place faster three hundred years ago. We cannot do anything. We have to wait for inspections and funds and permissions. But these are our houses. If I didn't feel so close to this place, I would leave. I'm still young and could start somewhere else, but it's hard to abandon your home during difficult times. I think I would always feel that it's somehow my fault if nothing changes in the future, because I might have been able to make a difference. So I'm trapped, frozen—a bit like these old buildings. Scaffolding and iron chains hold their walls together and so they look kind of fine, just a little worn, but they are falling to pieces inside.[12]

Three months after our conversation, in the autumn of 2012, a series of low-intensity earthquake tremors shook the city. In the old center, roof tiles and parts of scaffolding rained onto deserted streets. The mayor prohibited access to the centro storico temporarily, including Piazza Regina Margherita. Luca had to close his bar. The city administration stipulated that businesses had to renew their temporary licenses and demonstrate building safety. Some, including Luca's, reopened after a few weeks; others remained closed. I asked Luca on a number of occasions whether he had received news about the restoration of buildings in the piazza; he usually answered with a shrug of his shoulders. When I left L'Aquila at the end of my fieldwork, his bar was open again and he still waited for an official notice about permanent restoration, which had been postponed again. Luca casually pointed his chin upward when I asked him about what was coming next, which means "who knows?!" He did not plan ahead anymore, but instead turned to fatalism and short-term expectations, since government regulations, municipal interventions, or a new tremor might thwart plans any day. Like other business owners and entrepreneurs, four years after the earthquake, he lived precariously.

Aquilani struggled to develop new routines in restricted urban spaces that could be closed off at short notice. In the absence of approved regeneration plans, speculation about the future and possible urban redevelopment initiatives was rife. Every week, grassroots groups hosted debates about L'Aquila's urban future and presented their own proposals. Citizens' assemblies, newly formed associations, and local researchers generated a plethora of plans for recovery and alternative urban futures, which were discussed in a lively fashion in a city holding out with growing desperation for recovery.

URBAN BRANDING: L'AQUILA 2030

Conflicts about urban recovery trajectories and heritage matter, since "the negotiation of the form and meaning of spatial representations is illuminating as a public forum in which people work out larger conflicts stemming from the growing impact of globalization, increased tourism, and the struggle by both individuals and the state to maintain a distinct cultural identity."[13] Divergent views about L'Aquila's old center, its future form and character, and its relationship to other parts of the urban territory—postwar neighborhoods, peripheral municipalized villages, and the dozens of post-disaster resettlement sites—exposed conflicting visions with regard to the city's future and to interpretations of its history. Since history resides in architecture, transformative events—destruction resulting from conflict or natural disasters, changes in the economic and industrial circumstances, or major sports competitions and concomitant urban redevelopment—that alter the material fabric can also shift urban identities.[14] The 1992 Olympic Games, for example, transformed Barcelona, Spain's second city, into a popular holiday destination. In the wake of the Franco dictatorship, the Olympics helped relaunch Barcelona by spurring development across its rundown inner city and port areas—globalizing strategies that were also contested by residents who feared losing access to their neighborhoods and community spaces.[15]

The malleability of urban identities permits town planners and architects to deploy urban renewal initiatives to reposition places in public perception.

With globalization, cities have become competing brands in a global market that are vying with one another to attract events, tourists, conferences, offices, industry, employment, and investment.[16] Local, regional, and national authorities are at pains to prevent their city from becoming an ignored "non-place" in the race for distinctiveness.[17] Politicians often employ high-profile architects or urbanists to help them enhance a city's brand through redevelopment projects. Soon after the 2009 L'Aquila earthquake, powerful local figures also began to investigate how high-profile urbanists could support the city's recovery. The hope was to develop a more positive identity for L'Aquila, allowing the city to shed its association with death and disaster.[18]

Two and a half years after the earthquake, the Organization for Economic Cooperation and Development (OECD) and the University of Groningen, in the Netherlands, entered into discussions about possible urban futures for L'Aquila. Fearing the crippling effects of endless stagnation, Italian trade unions and the business and industry association Confindustria commissioned the OECD and the Dutch university to develop a strategic vision for urban renewal, economic development, and rebranding. After six months of investigation, a number of international urban studies experts and regional development specialists presented their preliminary analysis in a draft policy report, "Abruzzo Toward 2030: On the Wings of L'Aquila," which received much local attention.[19] In March 2012, now almost three years since the earthquake, the experts summarized initial findings at a public meeting. The event was held in the smaller auditorium of L'Aquila's municipal theater, which had not sustained major damage in the earthquake. The meeting, organized by a leading international body in the field of redevelopment, drew a crowd: a few hundred Aquilani filled the comfortable red seats. The experts sat at a long, illuminated table on an elevated stage. Since most of them did not speak Italian, their statements were translated simultaneously. The setup showed that this was a high-profile gathering of international experts who had come to L'Aquila to help. In his opening remarks, Frank Vanclay, a professor of cultural geography from the University of Groningen, offered words of praise to the city:

> I have been to many countries in the world. I can tell you that L'Aquila and the Abruzzi have potential.[20] And the earthquake has added outside interest, in a perverse way. Earthquakes are an integral part of the city's fabric, and the earthquake experience forms part of local identity. L'Aquila has to embrace the earthquake and a process of living with the earthquake. I sympathize with your loss, because I come from an area of the world that is significantly affected by disasters, too, Australia. But L'Aquila's problem is not just the loss of life and buildings: it's a lack of action.[21]

The speakers' nameplates provided details of their titles and signaled institutional prestige; their suits and language registers distinguished the scientists, economists, and advisers. Presentations used such buzzwords as "strategy-based development" or "environmental assets." Vanclay urged L'Aquila to implement the "smart city" strategy for urban renewal. "Transformation" and "strategy" were his key terms when he identified four pathways to urban renewal and economic recovery: eco-cultural tourism; international competition for innovative architecture projects; becoming the EU's capital of culture in 2019; and turning L'Aquila into a twenty-first century smart city. He received applause for his suggestion to start a competition for students of architecture to design new buildings for the city.

Another expert, Matthias Ruth, sought to comfort and inspire the audience by suggesting that Aquilani focus on the opportunities that have opened up rather than only the difficulties. He proposed urban redevelopment and rebranding to construct a twenty-first century city and to forge a new identity by turning L'Aquila into an example for other regions in the world, moving away from an overcome past toward a more innovative and smarter urban form. Listening to the simultaneous translation, Aquilani started murmuring to each other. Some shook their heads; a few nodded.

After a handful of presentations from the experts—which could be summarized as a recommendation to embrace new perspectives and development strategies and a warning to survivors not to become trapped in the past—audience members were invited to comment. Looking around, I saw familiar faces. Many of those present regularly organized or at least attended discussion evenings to debate alternative futures for the city, where they would confidently share their opinions and viewpoints. In the grand auditorium of L'Aquila's old theater, facing international experts, even those who were used to public speaking hesitated to comment on what they had heard. After a pause, someone finally raised his hand—an elderly Aquilano. A steward passed him a microphone as others turned around in their seats to see him. He stood up and said, "I'm just an Aquilano, and so perhaps I don't know much about this, but I think the first priority should be the restoration of our houses. You didn't say anything about the repair of buildings in the historic center in your presentations. It was all about long-term strategies, far into the future, but we need something done now. Tourism, digital economic development, smart city—that is not important for us. We need to get people back into their homes."[22]

Before he could finish, audience members supported his statement. He received long and loud applause, with shouts of "Bravo!" and "Bravissimo!" The ice had been broken, and more hands shot up. An English-speaking woman explained, in Italian, that she had been living in L'Aquila for many years. She then switched to English to say, "The situation in L'Aquila can only be described as a humanitarian crisis. I have been living in five different places since 2009— that is the real issue. Ecotourism will not do the trick. Here, we are without rights and without representation. That must be tackled. We don't need to talk about the earthquake's 'potential' or 'opportunities,' but about what needs to be done *now*, about the issues we all face every day."

Others then echoed her concerns. A young social worker asked why nothing had been said regarding the weakest members of society. She stressed the need to restore social life, not just architecture. Others highlighted the importance of fighting organized crime and urged measures to reverse the flight of young people to cities such as Rome or Pescara. Many comments denounced the incapacity of the local administration and the mayor in particular. Others expressed a feeling of abandonment at the hands of the national authorities, addressing a government minister, Fabrizio Barca, responsible for post-disaster reconstruction, who sat in the audience. A young woman was more conciliatory: "Your projects are interesting, but they are not our priority. The historic center must be reconstructed; the rest is only relevant if it supports heritage restoration."

A well-known Aquilana, who had been an active member of a popular grassroots association, Assemblea Cittadina, that met on a fortnightly basis to discuss urban renewal projects, commented: "Is all this really new? During the past three years, have we Aquilani done nothing? No. We weren't waiting for this plan. We have written proposals with our own ideas for heritage restoration. What you're proposing isn't about L'Aquila. You're using us as guinea pigs for a generic social experiment. These proposals are an imposition from the outside that don't engage at all with our particular situation here. We won't accept them."[23]

A local man, who introduced himself as an architect by profession, then challenged the term *smart city*, which was always used in the original English: "L'Aquila is already smart and intelligent—using a foreign word won't change that. This is just an empty slogan, and it doesn't address any of our concerns." The atmosphere got tenser. Most comments from the floor dismissed the experts' proposals as lofty and decried the fact that local projects put forward by associations over the past years had not been considered or engaged with by the experts. Then, however, a young man leapt to their defense, saying, "When an important international organization comes to L'Aquila to help us, it's embarrassing that we only talk about our houses and about what's gone wrong with local politics. I would like to thank the OECD and the University of Groningen for showing this interest in our situation here. And I reprimand us Aquilani for our embarrassing performance (*brutta figura*) and small-mindedness this evening. We must really change our mentality!"

Many audience members disagreed and told him to sit down, accusing him of being part of the establishment. Others mumbled and shook their heads, while a minority applauded. Someone then rose from his seat to respond directly: "I am sure we did not show a poor performance today. Our concerns are sincere. We don't have many opportunities to share our opinions on these issues. No one ever listens to us. These comments show what we really need here for recovery."

The discussion lasted over three hours. Outside the theater, against the backdrop of old buildings held together by steel braces, Aquilani continued to argue about plans to rebrand L'Aquila as a global model for post-disaster renewal. In closed-off corners of the small square, in front of stabilized eighteenth-century houses that had not been inhabited for three years, heaps of debris from tiles and broken windows were overgrown by moss. It was apparent that the urban redevelopment strategies put forth by nonlocal experts did not align with the more basic aspirations expressed by many Aquilani during the assembly: stop the talking, the commissions, and the paperwork, and instead listen to survivors, look at their plans, repair, and rebuild. Francesca, a key figure from a leading civil society grassroots group, concluded her criticism during the session, noting, "We are always guinea pigs: first for Berlusconi and the Civil Protection Agency, and now for these international organizations. They want to study how we behave in a disaster situation, or, as they called it, after 'shock.'"[24] This fear of being studied or exploited by outsiders was something I heard expressed often; not speaking Italian did not help the experts, since many Aquilani wondered how they could understand their concrete local situation without knowledge of the language. The result was skepticism toward projects that did not take into account the work of local initiatives and include homegrown visions for renewal. The lack of references to local activities hurt pride and suggested that concerns could be ignored in expert panels deliberating the urban future.

Furthermore, the abstract smart city concepts—employing innovative digital information and communication technologies to facilitate everyday city life—did not respond to concrete recovery needs. As a result, the Aquilani who showed an interest in the event and Smart City project were divided over the proposals; some had little trust in external expertise that appeared remote from the work done by local assemblies and associations, while others continued to hope that outsiders might launch new recovery initiatives and break the deadlock that prevented urban recovery. As I learned through subsequent discussions, negative responses to the OECD plans centered on four key aspects: disappointment that the experts failed to engage with expectations regarding repair; disempowerment, since community-based visions or ideas were absent from the proposals; suspicion toward outsiders, who were accused of exploiting the local situation for their own careers; and general skepticism that this initiative was yet another talking shop that would not result in action.

After the event, I spoke to some of the OECD experts, who expressed frustration that Aquilani had not appreciated their advice: "It's not like I necessarily wanted to be here," one of them said, "but the Confindustria asked us to provide input to inspire change and move on from the standstill." Another participant lamented the hostile atmosphere: "They only talk about their old houses—they've got no visions or ideas beyond that. It's quite parochial."[25] Frank Vanclay told me that their project would continue with public consultation exercises involving Aquilani and was optimistic that local concerns regarding a lack of visibility would be addressed in open discussion formats over the coming months.

Following the event and coverage in local papers, the term "smart city" seeped into everyday conversations. Few Aquilani, however, were familiar with the concept's focus on using information and communication technology to connect citizens and services more effectively. Instead, my friends and other locals filled the conceptual void with their own expectations and aspirations. Those favoring authentic restoration—com'era e dov'era (as it was and where it was), a slogan that was popular among conservationists who refused any addition of modern architecture—either rejected the smart city concept or interpreted it narrowly to mean improved communication infrastructure and renewable energy use.[26] Others argued that a smart city required a profound transformation of the urban infrastructure—new buildings with modern materials, not limestone, to withstand tremors. Some dismissed the whole proposal and OECD public consultation process as an imposition that lacked ambition with regard to restoration and repair in the old city and was therefore irrelevant. There was no consensus on what smart city concepts could mean or add to discussions on the future of L'Aquila and its buildings. Critical reactions also illustrated that the OECD time frame did not correspond to what many considered urgent local priorities.

Smart city initiatives that aimed at transforming L'Aquila by 2030 failed to address the questions that were crucial for many people in the city: When will the heritage in the old center be restored? What kinds of jobs will people have in the meanwhile? Which incentives can be given to young people to stay in L'Aquila now? How can the city fight against the presence of organized crime in the construction industry? How can one live in an urban environment without squares and public places? What will be done for the elderly and the disabled who remain tucked away in remote resettlement sites?

Figure 4.4. OECD and University of Groningen experts discussing smart city proposals

The OECD experts especially disheartened displaced Aquilani. They used the open meeting to criticize proposals that did not address their limbo state in isolated resettlement sites. Those who supported the initiative were cautious with vocal approval. The topic was too divisive. With a time frame of almost twenty years, L'Aquila 2030 was not how especially those living in Progetto Case or MAP resettlement sites conceptualized their future. Over the following months, the OECD and University of Groningen researchers asked students to gather data with survey questionnaires and held a number of events, including a World Café—the English term was used—during the course of which eighty local stakeholders, identified by the OECD, worked in small groups to propose ideas for L'Aquila's future. Participants highlighted the importance of the revival of the old center and its economic and social activities, as well as its architectural beauty, while others put forward visions for a polycentric city with a greater distribution of economic activities, private and public offices, and social infrastructure to urban areas outside the centro storico. Having attended dozens of association meetings over the previous months, where local people discussed how they could escape from the misery of isolation and urban decay, I knew that Aquilani had identified their own recovery strategies—even though serious disagreements about future visions continued.

A few months after the first OECD presentation, an image circulated on social media. It showed an abandoned car covered in debris. Its roof had caved in under the weight of tiles and rubble; small shrubs were growing on top. More than three years after the earthquake, the car had not been removed from a narrow alleyway in L'Aquila's old center. The car was a Smart. On social media, the caption "L'Aquila: Smart City?" ridiculed ideas dismissed as out of touch with the needs of a city whose ruined center remained abandoned.

Unlike the 2030 smart city vision, another significant building project did materialize in 2012. L'Aquila's new concert hall divided the population of survivors and illustrated divergent views on the meaning of heritage, identity, and belonging. Those who supported the construction of the modernist auditorium hoped that L'Aquila could rise from ruins and gloom in the same way as the Spanish city of Bilbao had successfully reinvented itself after deindustrialization and decline: with help from a celebrity architect.

A NEW AUDITORIUM

In the 1990s, the Basque city of Bilbao, in northern Spain, was struggling with decline, economic depression, and unemployment in the wake of the region's deindustrialization. In response, the authorities commissioned US architect Frank O. Gehry to design a spectacular building for the new local branch of New York's Guggenheim Museum. There was hope that his building could halt the downward spiral and turn Bilbao into an attractive destination for visitors, companies, and capital.[27] The unusual architecture of the new Guggenheim Museum indeed transformed Bilbao into an exciting destination for weekend trips and left many other European cities looking with envy to the Basque Country.[28] The "Bilbao effect" fascinated politicians and planners hoping to rebrand their own cities through the work of a world-renowned architect.[29] Following Bilbao, the construction of singular iconic buildings sat alongside large-scale public urban redevelopment schemes, since officials—at a time of dwindling resources and small-state ideology—expected such projects to have a major impact and attract investors to fund urban revival privately.[30] When transformative urban redevelopment becomes difficult to sustain financially, big buildings are cheaper substitutes and might spur further investments.

Renzo Piano is arguably Italy's most famous architect; he designed, among other projects, London's Shard skyscraper and the New York Times Building in New York City. Piano won the prestigious Pritzker Architecture Prize in 1998, and Italians call him an *archistar*.[31] In response to the serious damage that had rendered most of L'Aquila's concert halls and theaters inaccessible, the late Claudio Abbado, then Italy's best-known conductor, proposed the construction of a temporary auditorium.[32] Abbado asked Piano to design the building and convinced the wealthy northern Italian Trento province to fund the project, which cost almost seven million euros. Piano designed an ensemble of three interconnected cubes. The concert hall would be located in the largest, central building, with 238 seats. The other two structures contained a green room and a foyer. The city administration, championed by the mayor, Massimo Cialente, was enthusiastic when the project was presented. In public discussions, Cialente expressed faith in the prestige of an eminent architect to render L'Aquila more attractive to investors and tourists alike. Proponents made reference to the Bilbao effect. Construction began in spring 2012 in an urban park surrounding the Spanish Fortress, outside the medieval walls. The park features trails between spruce and fir trees, with iron benches lining wider paths. A pedestrianized cobbled avenue connects the Piazza Battaglione degli Alpini—an unsightly square dominated by a twentieth-century fountain and modernist buildings—with a path surrounding the fortress. The new auditorium was placed halfway between the piazza and the fortress.

The concert hall's inauguration had been scheduled for the summer but was eventually delayed until October 2012. I visited the building site frequently. Piano set up a workshop for twenty-two engineering and architecture students from the University of L'Aquila. Based in a red container on the edge of the construction site that occupied a central section of the park, the workshop students shadowed professional engineers and architects, wrote progress reports, and explained the project to visitors. I attended weekly open days, intrigued by reactions to a controversial project. The twenty-two students had gone through a selection process administered by Piano's office. The workshop was a great opportunity for their professional development. One of them, a twenty-four-year-old Aquilana, recalled her excitement when she had first heard about the project: "I couldn't believe that Renzo Piano was coming to L'Aquila. I had always loved his work, and I wanted to be involved. When I got the offer letter after their entrance examinations, I had tears in my eyes. It was what kept me going. Every day, after lectures, I drove to the construction site and spoke to the engineers about what they had done that day. It was like my baby. It gave me a purpose. The other students here became close friends of mine. We are a close-knit group now."[33]

Overseeing progress on an exciting construction site provided a daily routine and meaningful practical work for the students who supported Piano's vision of diversifying architecture and design in the city and saw the earthquake as an opportunity for urban innovation. They envisioned a city in which restored patrimony and modern architectural forms would complement each other. The students from the workshop represented the opposite pole to the conservationists who demanded detailed and authentic reconstruction, as it was and where it was. On a warm summer afternoon in August 2012, Franco, a PhD student in engineering and the student group leader, explained the project to a dozen Aquilani at one of the weekly open days on the construction site. Wearing a vest and red hard hat, he pointed to the large crane behind him and said:

> Before the earthquake, the park around the Spanish Fortress was in a bad state. Benches were broken; paths were overgrown. People never really used it as a park to spend time or meet friends here. They only passed through it to get to the city center. The concert hall will develop this area into an urban space in its own right, which did not exist here before. This is great. It will be a central space for people to socialize, especially since so many sites in the centro storico are still closed off. We are also remaking the social and cultural fabric with this project.

The two dozen visitors nodded at Franco's suggestion that the project would be an important accelerator for the cultural revival of post-disaster L'Aquila. As he talked, he walked around a large table in the center of the workshop's wooden container and pointed at different architectural sketches displayed on the walls. On one side of the container, a large glass window revealed a view of the three cubes under construction. Wooden beams in a range of colors had already been attached to the buildings. Pointing at illustrations, Franco explained:

> The form of the three cubes is intentionally plain. Renzo Piano didn't want to distract from the Spanish Fortress. The cubes don't have any elaborate decorations, and they are made from wood. We use a range of different natural colors for the facades—green, yellow, orange, and light red—to match the tree leaves changing colors throughout the seasons. The concert hall won't dominate this space; the buildings are low and tucked away behind the trees. The building material is inconspicuous. This isn't meant to be a permanent building either. As soon as the auditorium in the Fortress has been repaired, the three cubes will be dismantled and relocated to a different area of L'Aquila, perhaps near one of the Progetto Case resettlement sites to redevelop the periphery and provide cultural and social spaces outside the centro storico.[34]

He added, with a dose of irony, "But then, as we all know, in Italy nothing lasts longer than the provisional." The others chuckled. Franco continued, "The main cube leans forward; it stands on its edge. This is a reference to the earthquake that rocked our city. At the same time, the concert hall illustrates L'Aquila's revival: it is a model for reconstruction, for the birth of a new city."[35]

For Franco and the other students, the Auditorium del Parco was exciting because it showcased how traditional architecture and innovative design could be combined to shape recovery and transform L'Aquila into a more forward-looking urban environment. It was an experiment with new materials and styles, complementing historic limestone architecture through contrast while respecting the park environment. Furthermore, the plan to relocate the new auditorium following the repair of the old concert hall was conceptualized by the students, as well as by the leading architects and planners, as a contribution to the revitalization of L'Aquila's periphery. Piano's project challenged urban traditions—stone architecture, baroque and Renaissance forms, and the preeminence of the centro storico. For the students, it heralded an alternative urban future, and furthermore, they could participate in its construction and realization as aspiring architects and engineers. Speaking to Franco after his presentation and tour of the building site, an elderly Aquilano expressed his approval:

> Since when I was small, people have avoided this area. It was known for drug users and prostitutes. You couldn't go with kids because there were needles everywhere. People left rubbish bags and didn't clean up dog dirt. The authorities never made an effort to keep it tidy. It would be nice to create a real urban park in L'Aquila now. We don't have them in southern Italy. I was in Turin recently, and they have a beautiful park there, where young people have picnics and spend free time together. We have a big university here, with lots of students. I hope we can create that kind of urban park in the future.[36]

One of the workshop students had overheard the remark and asked the Aquilano whether he would mind being recorded for a promotional video clip on the project website. He declined: "I'm sorry," he apologized, "but people here know me. I used to work as a policeman and I cannot be seen to support this publicly."[37] I was surprised by the refusal, but the students accepted his explanation in a matter-of-fact way. "We hear this every week," Franco told me later. "The project is so controversial. People just don't want trouble with their friends or families. There are too many divisions and conflicts already, but people fight over this."[38] The Auditorium del Parco, designed by an eminent architect and funded by a wealthy Italian province, divided local opinion. In social media, public discussions, and private conversations, supporters and opponents clashed over visions for the city's future and priorities for regeneration. No shared vision for the remaking of L'Aquila as an urban space with

Figure 4.5. Construction site for the new auditorium

distinctive features, buildings, monuments, and public places for shared community life existed. Much like the smart city proposals, the new auditorium was
rejected by its critics as an imposition from the outside that disregarded—and
for some eroded—the material foundations of the city's identity.

OPPOSING INNOVATION

The reasons for which Aquilani criticized the project were many and included
political affiliation, since the new concert hall became contested in campaigns
for the 2012 municipal elections. While the incumbent mayor, Cialente, from
the center-left Partito Democratico, supported Piano's project, his political
rivals denounced the three cubes as a vanity project that ignored local concerns. Abbado's initiative, Piano's design, building materials, and the project
as such were dismissed as being removed from repair priorities.

In March 2012, Ettore Di Cesare, the head of a popular grassroots movement, Appello per L'Aquila (see chapter 5), and also a contender for the office of
mayor, attacked the auditorium in an interview with a local television station.
He described the project as a lost opportunity for civic involvement, suggesting that the mayor ought to have involved local people and their views in the

design process early on. As a result, Di Cesare claimed, the project appeared as yet another imposition. Di Cesare also questioned the mayor's ability to sympathize with displaced Aquilani, since Cialente had already moved back into his private pre-disaster home following repairs. Not everyone embraced the Bilbao narrative and rebranding visions espoused by the local administration; many Aquilani considered the auditorium extravagant. In his defense, Cialente argued that the Trento provincial administration would not have provided seven million euros for heritage restoration. Declining the project would have been a lost opportunity. He urged Aquilani to appreciate how culture could support recovery.

Besides the way in which the project had been decided—unilaterally by the city administration without public consultation—some of my interlocutors deplored that the press conference during the course of which the concert hall plans were presented had taken place in Trento, not L'Aquila. As a result, critics saw the project as an unwanted gift handed to a poor disaster site in Italy's south by its more prosperous northern cousins. For many, the project served to reinforce stereotypes of benevolent northerners and passive aid recipients from the south, an image the survivors had been struggling to cast off. The companies providing the building materials as well as construction workers also came from Trento. L'Aquila-based architects or businesses were not involved in the construction; even many of the workshop students were nonlocal.

My friendship circle was fragmented, but there were no clear patterns of division. Young, middle-class, and better-educated people tended to be more open to new architectural forms and experiments, including Piano's auditorium, yet there were also young and educated Aquilani with staunchly conservationist views on architecture. Those who still lived in resettlement sites were more skeptical of architectural innovation than others who had already returned home. The politicization of the relief effort and construction projects added layers of complexity to an understanding of why certain people rejected innovative schemes for urban renewal and others embraced them, leaving aside aesthetic preferences. Judging from public discussions and newspaper reports, the majority of Aquilani who expressed their opinions disliked the auditorium; supporters were usually quieter about their views. Those who found it objectionable often framed their criticism by referencing history and identity. A social media exchange between two of my close contacts illuminates how debates about the auditorium became contentious even among those who would otherwise be aligned in political and other views.

Davide, a young freelance journalist who had recently left university, supported Piano's project. Davide was an Aquilano in a long-term relationship with someone from the coastal area; they were renting a small flat together. When I first met him, he was working on a freelance basis for a local television station. Davide found the work dull, since it consisted of covering mostly trivial stories from across L'Aquila's neighborhoods, but it paid the bills. He was driven, ambitious, and left-leaning and had supported alternative and anti-Berlusconi movements after the earthquake. For him, the concert hall was exciting and signaled a new direction for the city. Amedeo, a social scientist at the University of L'Aquila, opposed the project. Born and raised in a small town near L'Aquila, he was around ten years older than Davide and had a young family. With his relatively secure job at the university, Amedeo had not been affected as much financially by the earthquake, even though he now lived in a Progetto Case resettlement site. Amedeo had been a vocal Berlusconi critic in the aftermath of the earthquake and had published many texts on the earthquake and its effects on Aquilani. The following discussion took place on Amedeo's Facebook wall, where he had published a post denouncing the auditorium:

> Amedeo: This isn't an either-or question—either restoring heritage or building the auditorium. It's about priorities. If, after having repaired homes, some celebrity architect had built a superfluous concert hall, OK. But at this stage, given the ongoing decay of my former home, I'll ask the authorities to let me move into the auditorium instead.
>
> Davide: The auditorium will become an important place for the city if the authorities know how to manage it. This was a unique opportunity for the students that support the project in the workshop. This redevelops a part of L'Aquila that nobody cared about before. This is typical for L'Aquila: people who do something and roll up their sleeves get attacked, ridiculed, and snubbed. And this from people who don't even bother to see the project before judging it.
>
> Amedeo: Nobody cared about the area before? What are you talking about? It was a park. It did what a park did. Think about most people here: they are still in the same situation in which they found themselves the morning after the earthquake. Those who ran businesses in the old town have had no support. When you break your leg, the first thing you want to do is to have that fixed. Only when you've recovered from injury, you'll think about buying new kitchen equipment, for example. It's the same here: wrong priorities. And these oversized boxes don't sit well with the fortress; they disfigure the park. They contaminate it. A good architect turns an unattractive space into something beautiful, instead of aggrandizing himself by inserting something into a stunning space parasitically. It's typical L'Aquila provincialism: people hope to flourish in the shadow of a big name. We need to defend our own identity as citizens! Of course,

whoever built the Spanish Fortress five hundred years ago waited for
Renzo Piano to dump painted boxes next to it. Come on!

Davide: What would you have done? I don't believe you would have wanted
the auditorium in one of the Progetto Case resettlement sites. The historic
buildings in the center are a totally different matter. It's not up to Trento
to fix that for us. This isn't provincialism, but a realization. This city needs
outsiders to create something beautiful. People here, and I include myself,
aren't capable of it. They always criticize and bubble and complain, and
today more than ever before.

Amedeo: When people criticize local politicians, they aren't simply typical,
pessimistic Aquilani. You're just defending the city's establishment, as
always. I bet you also got invited to the inauguration, no?

Davide: Establishment? What are you talking about? I'm not part of this
city's bourgeoisie; I never got help from anyone. I didn't get invited to the
inauguration either. I just love this hard-hit city, and I appreciate it when
something is done well.[39]

The exchange illustrated that construction initiatives were no niche issue;
the allocation of funds to heritage repair or innovative design projects mattered.
Concerns about the future of property in the old center fused with opinions on
the intersection of heritage and identity. For Amedeo, the auditorium was the
wrong project at the wrong time. Aquilani impatient to repair former homes
viewed Piano's project as out of kilter with the priorities of a post-disaster city.
Amedeo expressed a desire for stability and permanence, which a temporary
concert hall did not provide. He also criticized the design for ruining a historical space. Amedeo and Davide accused each other—and, by extension, project
supporters and critics—of provincialism, either because they refused innovation and change or because they were parochial and starstruck when Piano
came to L'Aquila. Both expressed negative views of other Aquilani, whom they
accused of being narrow-minded and pessimistic in ways they considered at
least partly responsible for the city's state. This episode shows how the absence
of heritage restoration plans produced conflict. Aquilani were spread across
a disconnected urban territory and disagreed over effective strategies for its
revival. While Amedeo emphasized the preservation of heritage as the guiding
principle for recovery and dismissed distractions, Davide expressed hope that
outsiders could bring innovation and accelerate renewal.

The auditorium's inauguration on October 7, 2012, did not end the controversy. Given the concert hall's limited capacity, the ceremony was attended
mainly by important people connected to the project. These included local
and regional politicians, as well as the then president of the Italian Republic,

Giorgio Napolitano, Piano, and sponsors from Trento. Few local citizens were among the invitees. Because of the president's participation, the army, the Carabinieri, police forces, the Civil Protection Agency, and other state authorities closed off a wide perimeter around the building. Opposite the concert hall, a large screen had been erected to livestream speeches and a concert. A few dozen people braved the autumn weather to follow the inauguration. Other Aquilani staged a protest. Their banners read "President, please help us" and "L'Aquila is still April 6, 2009."

Giorgio Napolitano addressed such concerns during his inauguration speech: "It is time to reconstruct L'Aquila, not so-called *new towns* or resettlement sites far away from the city's real center."[40] Piano concurred in his speech: "The Progetto Case resettlement sites are places without a soul, without a logic, and without emotion. Everywhere in the world, peripheries are becoming a thing of the past. L'Aquila is the only place where a periphery was built from scratch."[41] The following day, the new auditorium was closed again. Because of delays, its anti-seismic shock absorbers could not be tested before the official opening. Since the president's attendance could not be rescheduled, however, the building had been inaugurated before completion. High fences returned to the construction site for a couple of months as work continued. Aquilani stayed out. In the city and beyond, news coverage about the botched and mislabeled inauguration documented local controversies.

MATERIALITY VS. IDEALISM

Those opposed to the auditorium often cited frustration with wrong prioritization. Displaced Aquilani in particular had strong views on the succession of urban repair and redevelopment projects, as the hostile reactions to the auditorium, as well as to smart city proposals, illustrated. Amedeo argued that nothing had changed since April 2009. He and his family were still displaced. Their old apartment continued to decay. He was frustrated with a sense of powerlessness; he could do nothing to accelerate recovery and a return to normality. The temporary character of the concert hall exacerbated a sense of limbo. Resettled Aquilani were anxious that others were not taking their longing to return seriously; instead, they worried that a shift in priorities from ending displacement to fanciful urban rebranding and architectural experiments wasted resources and prolonged their suffering.

In his analysis of the post-socialist transition in the East German city of Hoyerswerda, anthropologist Felix Ringel shows how local people experienced the disappearance of hope regarding the future; since neither socialist nor capitalist promises came true, a sense of hopelessness and despair took hold. A prolonged period of stagnation and dashed expectations precluded visions for a hopeful future, as a number of other analyses of the post-socialist transition period have also shown.[42] In L'Aquila, three years after the earthquake, local experiences were not yet consumed by the chronic and irreversible disappointment with the transition period and political projects described by Ringel and other writers on post-socialism. Aquilani continued to debate recovery visions, and while some people attached their hopes to the transformative power of high-profile architects, others attended weekly association meetings to discuss proposals for decentralization and urban innovation; still others defended the focus on preservation and conservation, as it was and where it was. The future was undecided. Opposition to—but also support for—the auditorium reflected a resistance to an extension of the provisional into the future.

At the time of their social media discussion, Davide had already returned to his pre-disaster flat in a postwar neighborhood, whereas Amedeo was still living in a Progetto Case apartment with his wife and two young children. His neighbors had two large—and as he would say, aggressive—dogs that were rarely kept on a leash. Amedeo was scared that they might attack his children on the staircase or the communal lawn. The dogs gave him nightmares. Amedeo had been assigned the apartment at random. He had no power to relocate, did not know the neighbors, and struggled to reason with them about their dogs. He was an anxious person, and his powerlessness exacerbated his situation. "When I talked to the police, they told me to leave poisoned sausages in the staircase. Apparently, they can't do anything about it. Poisoned sausages. It's like we're living in the Third World, not in Italy!," Amedeo told me with exasperation after another visit to the local authorities.[43] He negotiated with the city administration for months to be moved to a different apartment and was eventually granted permission to relocate to another Progetto Case rehousing block. Dependent on the goodwill of the local authorities, Amedeo was frustrated with the disempowering loss of personal sovereignty caused by post-disaster displacement, which also helps to explain his opposition to a temporary concert hall—a far cry from what he believed the first construction priority ought to be.

It frustrated Amedeo and other displaced Aquilani when outside commentators questioned the insistence on heritage restoration and argued that the focus on stone architecture was parochial and dangerous in an earthquake-prone area. Experts advocated modernization and the use of new building materials. In November 2012, almost two months after the concert hall's inauguration, *New York Times* art critic Michael Kimmelman commented on the urban recovery initiatives in the wake of Hurricane Sandy. The storm had devastated New York City and large parts of the eastern coastline, and Americans discussed whether, how, and where buildings should be reconstructed near the water. Following a recent visit to L'Aquila, Kimmelman compared the two disaster scenarios. He urged Americans to reject the architectural conservatism he had discovered in conversation with Aquilani. Kimmelman called Piano's auditorium a "sign of progress" and criticized Pietro Di Stefano, L'Aquila's municipal officer responsible for post-disaster restoration and reconstruction. He recalled a walk through the city: "At the suggestion of wooden buildings, Mr. Di Stefano stiffened. He started to pet the nearest stone building as if it were the family Labrador. 'Impossible,' he said. 'This is a city of stone,' he insisted. 'These homes were built by families here over hundreds of years, and they have their histories. What would Florence be without Giotto, or Pisa without the tower? The buildings are who we are.'"[44]

Kimmelman portrayed Di Stefano as a backward conservationist obsessed with stone and held back by a lack of architectural imagination. He contrasted a theory of urban life that challenged Di Stefano's focus on materiality: "Is a city the assortment of its buildings or the life that happens in and around them? L'Aquila has fine architecture, including Baroque churches and early-20th-century Rationalist office blocks. These could be retrofitted and reopened, and a couple already have been. But it is really the public spaces—the streets and piazzas—that make the city special. Officials charged with saving the center, fixated on buildings instead of urbanism, seem not to realize this, and let L'Aquila die a little more each day."[45]

The article was translated and circulated widely on social media, where Aquilani discussed its merits. A few days later, Di Stefano penned a defense for the local daily, *Il Centro*:

> Michael Kimmelman is a *New York Times* journalist and art critic, born and raised in the city's cultural heart, Greenwich Village. This historic quarter has, for centuries, and despite various urban redesign initiatives, preserved its disorganized, original road pattern, and even real street names, rather than following the widespread use of anonymous numbers to distinguish one road from another. I believed that for that very reason, Kimmelman, more than his fellow countrymen, would understand why the historic center of L'Aquila— the city founded by Frederic II—has to preserve its history.
>
> The kind of urban renewal (of public spaces) that is needed in L'Aquila will certainly not come about by demolishing architectural, historical, and cultural patrimony. It will not come about by replacing stone with wood, disfiguring the identity and the collective memory of a medieval city,

purportedly to speed up the reconstruction process, which, thus far, has been held up solely by unclear legal norms.[46]

Di Stefano's reply was directed at a local audience rather than Kimmelman, and conservationists applauded him for his response. Kimmelman's idealistic definition of a city—social interaction and everyday life—challenged a common materialistic view. The debate between Kimmelman and Di Stefano was reproduced in everyday conversations, where it aligned with controversies regarding the OECD proposals and the concert hall.

A POLYCENTRIC CITY

Soon after the earthquake, a group of predominantly better educated and socially successful Aquilani, including students at the university, founded an initiative called Policentrica. The group promoted the vision of a polycentric city that would create a more equal urban territory, which would no longer concentrate all functions in the centro storico. Policentrica opposed the traditional urban form many Aquilani desired to remake, and its supporters argued that a city with lots of different clusters of economic, political, cultural, and social activity would also be more resilient to future shocks than an urban entity with one single important center. A few days after Kimmelman's article, the University of L'Aquila hosted a symposium, "The Centro Storico of L'Aquila: Reconstruction or Regeneration?" The event had been organized before the publication of Kimmelman's article, but the debate between the art critic and Di Stefano found an echo in diverse contributions. Walter Cavalieri, a retired history teacher, had been one of the founders of Policentrica. In his presentation at the symposium, Cavalieri outlined Policentrica's vision of decentralizing L'Aquila:

A city is like a body; if it doesn't adapt to a changing environment, it will die. Before the earthquake, L'Aquila wasn't a healthy and livable city. We tend to forget this today. We romanticize the past. Remember: There was too much traffic, and rubbish littered our streets. We could not park anywhere. The city was noisy. We had to drive everywhere. For many people, this was not a good place to live. We should not think about the past as something we must blindly return to. That's a sign of stasis. We should think about the before and after differently, and use the earthquake to turn L'Aquila into a polycentric city. The mayor just wants to move all services, offices, functions and so on back into the centro storico. But that won't create a livable urban space. In Policentrica, we want to diversify the entire urban territory, including the center, and transform L'Aquila. We believe that, by creating a polycentric urban space, the center will become more attractive as well, because it will be less crammed.[47]

His presentation captured a minority position, and there was much criticism from the audience during the subsequent discussion session. Opponents cited history by referencing the ways in which Italian cities had grown organically from the center outward, and many expressed a fear of ongoing displacement. At the same time, young Aquilani in particular shared Policentrica's view that the city needed an innovative overhaul. The plan to move the new auditorium into one of the Progetto Case sites after a few years expressed this aspiration for a more balanced urban topography, where services and cultural activities would be relocated to the places where people lived. A few months earlier, I had visited Walter Cavalieri in his home on the outskirts of L'Aquila to hear more about Policentrica. "Do you know about the history of L'Aquila?," he asked me while we were sitting at a table in his comfortable living room. He drew a sketch of L'Aquila's heart-shaped old town and said:

> Most cities in Europe were founded at a crossroads as marketplaces. They then grew over time. When they expanded, new villages and neighborhoods appeared in the periphery. But L'Aquila didn't grow this way, organically. L'Aquila was founded on purpose (*città di fondazione*), following an initiative of around eighty monasteries and castles in this area. People here still believe in L'Aquila's lucky number—ninety-nine settlements founded L'Aquila—but roughly eighty is historically accurate.
>
> In the Middle Ages, each settlement had specialized in a certain type of production: wine, wool, or food, for example. In this mountain territory, they needed a central trading place, and so the emperor planted what was then called Aquila. Every settlement contributed to the new market village: a square, a fountain, a street, a church. So, in a way, L'Aquila emerged out of its periphery. The new marketplace and the settlement around it mirrored the fabric, the culture, and the economic relations of the new town's hinterland.
>
> With time, the marketplace grew and became more powerful. From around 1500, it dominated the settlements that had once founded it. Power was reversed. People inside the city considered themselves citizens (*cittadini*), and those outside the walls were seen as peasants (*contadini*). This had a profound psychological effect: citizens and peasants looked at each other with suspicion. During Fascism, Greater L'Aquila was established. More villages were municipalized. Subjected to the power of the center, the lives of people in the periphery were progressively neglected. They had to drive to work and socialize in the centro storico. That is why people in the Progetto Case resettlement sites talk about restoring the city center "as it was and where it was": they want to reclaim the same status and privileges they had before.[48]

On his sheet, he had arranged a circle of dots and drawn arrows from each dot to the center, where they converged in the centro storico. Walter then added reverse arrows to illustrate relocation to Progetto Case sites: "This area has traditionally been polycentric. Every village has its own history, dialect, and tradition. With Policentrica, we propose to go back to our roots—we are also aligned with L'Aquila's history, as it was a long time before now." Policentrica conceptualized the Progetto Case sites as an opportunity to reconnect Aquilani with the hinterland they had disregarded. "We need to recalibrate the unhealthy imbalance between the centro storico and the postwar *periferia*," as Walter called it, before elaborating: "Most people didn't live in the city center before the earthquake, but in the modern neighborhoods from the 1960s and 1970s. We should use this situation to render these quarters more livable, rather than focus all our efforts and money on restoring everything as it was before in the old city. This doesn't mean abandoning the centro storico, but to realign different parts of the urban fabric in the process of restoring heritage. We should relocate economic, political, social, and cultural services to other sites outside the old town."

Much like the students at Piano's construction workshop, Aquilani involved in Policentrica wanted to view the earthquake as an occasion to rethink L'Aquila as an urban space. They used the city's historical origins as a blueprint for reconnecting parts of the city's territory differently, namely, not to focus all energy on the old center. L'Aquila's past became the source of conflicting approaches regarding the extent to which community life and local identity depended on materiality and the unique position of the centro storico and how closely the city's future as an urban space should recreate its pre-disaster past.

Policentrica and Piano's auditorium challenged traditionalist views that emphasized the exclusive status of the old center for identity, history, and belonging. Nonlocal pundits with seemingly radical opinions about urban culture and architectural innovation, such as Piano or Kimmelman, advocated embracing opportunities for change through a process of rethinking what a city is. These innovative voices inspired and fell on fertile ground in initiatives such as Policentrica. The same views faced opposition from others, however, such as Amedeo, who remained resettled and concerned that premature urban innovation would prolong the powerlessness and uncertainty he experienced as a consequence of displacement.

CONCLUSION

From the beginning of my stay in Abruzzo, I found Aquilani very expressive about their disappointment with the mismatch between quick resettlement in temporary accommodation and the subsequent lack of initiatives with regard to repairing and reviving the old town center, including visions for the urban future of the wider territory. As a result, there was much interest in city planning, urban design, architectural experiments, and modernization proposals. This interest took the form of town hall meetings, initiatives, organized or spontaneous activities involving grassroots associations, such as Assemblea Cittadina and Policentrica, and discussions hosted by the local authorities or the university. Frequently, conversations about urban space became a manifestation of conflict, rather than of a confidently enacted sense of involvement in shaping L'Aquila's future as a city collectively. No project—the concert hall, smart city proposals, polycentrism, or conservationist as-it-was-and-where-it-was visions—found support across a population with very different experiences of post-disaster life and recovery, clashing political leanings, and resultingly divergent visions for the future and how best to achieve it.

In her discussion of uncertainty and precariousness in Japan following the triple disaster of earthquake, tsunami, and nuclear meltdown at Fukushima in March 2011, anthropologist Anne Allison stresses the importance of imagination in attempts to remake life after catastrophe. For self-reflective processes that can nudge people into hopefulness and action, Allison argues, we need visions of the future to serve as "presentiments of what we might, or would like to, become."[49] New forms of sociality depend on people's ability to imagine promising personal and collective futures.[50] This and previous chapters have explored how different experiences in the wake of the earthquake undermined such a sense of collective fate, fragmented survivors physically as well as socially, and generated struggles over visions regarding the future. There was no shared understanding of how L'Aquila got into the mess it was in, nor an imagination of how the city and its population could escape stagnation. After April 2009, the relief effort and displacement disenfranchised survivors; the wheelbarrow initiative sought to counter victimization but remained short-lived. The 2012 municipal elections intensified experiences of powerlessness regarding the capacity to act as informed citizens and shape the course of public affairs. Finally, as I have shown in this chapter, Aquilani also struggled with the non-repair of cherished parts of their city—and the concomitant uncertainty for businesses and homeowners.

Art critics, local officials, *archistars*, national politicians, urban renewal experts, and urban design scholars further complicated local opinions. Different groups developed different views on the trajectory of urban recovery, disagreeing with one another on priorities, aesthetics, and the extent to which innovation could interact with repair. Nuances were lost on both sides, and many people preferred to keep their views to themselves in order to avoid negative social repercussions.

The experiences of loss and division that I have conveyed so far in this book were nonetheless countered by local initiatives seeking to build bridges, connect survivors, and create mutual understanding. The next three chapters examine such grassroots activities, which were aimed at reversing misrepresentation, disenfranchisement, and envy in the wake of an earthquake that had wrecked community life.

NOTES

1. Nick Dines, *Tuff City: Urban Change and Contested Space in Central Naples* (New York: Berghahn Books, 2012), 29–30. See also Roberto Dainotto, "The Gubbio Papers: Historic Centers in the Age of the Economic Miracle," *Journal of Modern Italian Studies* 8, no. 1 (2003): 67–83.

2. Pier Luigi Cervellati, *La città bella. Il recupero dell'ambiente urbano* (Bologna: Il Mulino, 1991); Jeffry M. Diefendorf, *In the Wake of War: The Reconstruction of German Cities after World War II* (New York: Oxford University Press, 1993); and Christopher Klemek, *The Transatlantic Collapse of Urban Renewal: Postwar Urbanism from New York to Berlin* (Chicago: University of Chicago Press, 2011).

3. Dirk Schubert, ed., *Contemporary Perspectives on Jane Jacobs: Reassessing the Impacts of an Urban Visionary* (London: Routledge, 2016); Jane Jacobs, *The Death and Life of Great American Cities* (New York: Random House, 1961).

4. Dines, *Tuff City*, 31.

5. Domenico Cerasoli, "De L'Aquila non resta che il nome. Racconto di un terremoto," *Meridiana* 65/66 (2010): 35–58.

6. Sydel Silverman, *Three Bells of Civilization: The Life of an Italian Hill Town* (New York: Columbia University Press, 1975); Giovanna Del Negro, *The Passeggiata and Popular Culture in an Italian Town: Folklore and the Performance of Modernity* (Montreal: McGill-Queen's University Press, 2004); and Eamonn Canniffe, *The Politics of the Piazza: The History and Meaning of the Italian Square* (Aldershot/Burlington: Ashgate, 2008).

7. Jeff Pratt, *The Walled City: A Study of Social Change and Conservative Ideologies in Tuscany* (Göttingen: Rader, 1986); and John Agnew, *Place and Politics in Modern Italy* (Chicago: University of Chicago Press, 2002). For an account of attempts to transform local identities (or *campanilismo*—from *campanile*, the local bell tower) into national ones, see Gene Brucker, *Living on the Edge in Leonardo's Florence: Selected Essays* (Berkeley: University of California Press,

2005), chapter 3. For comparative analyses of the roles of urban squares in politics, social life, and culture, see Setha M. Low, "Spatializing Culture: The Social Production and Social Construction of Public Space in Costa Rica," in *Theorizing the City: The New Urban Anthropology Reader*, ed. Low (Piscataway, NJ: Rutgers University Press, 1999).

8. Frisch, *L'Aquila. Non si uccide così anche una città?* (Naples: Clean, 2010a). Frisch even called the project an attempt to "annihilate" the old city of L'Aquila.

9. The Civil Protection Agency constructed most of the MAP settlements economically in a functional style. Other organizations, such as the Italian Red Cross, sought to create more picturesque and sociable MAP villages by using decorative materials and varying street patterns, so as to render the relocation experience less grueling for survivors.

10. Amedeo [pseud.], in discussion with the author, Castel Volturno, Italy, January 26, 2013.

11. *Zieta* is Aquilano dialect for *zia tua* (your aunt).

12. Luca [pseud.], in discussion with the author, L'Aquila, Italy, July 13, 2012.

13. Low, "Spatializing Culture," 115.

14. See, for example, Charles Rutheiser, "Making Place in the Nonplace Urban Realm: Notes on the Revitalization of Downtown Atlanta," in Low, *Theorizing the City*, 317–341; Lisa Yoneyama, *Hiroshima Traces: Time, Space, and the Dialectics of Memory* (Berkeley: University of California Press, 1999); Andrew Herscher, *Violence Taking Place: The Architecture of the Kosovo Conflict* (Stanford: Stanford University Press; 2010); and Oleg Pachenkov, "Every City Has the Flea Market It Deserves: The Phenomenon of Urban Flea Markets in St. Petersburg," in *Urban Spaces after Socialism: Ethnographies of Public Places in Eurasian Cities*, ed. Tspylma Darieva, Wolfgang Kaschuba, and Melanie Krebs (Chicago: University of Chicago Press, 2011).

15. See, for example, Gary McDonogh, "Discourses of the City: Policy and Response in Post-Transitional Barcelona," in Low, *Theorizing the City*; and Donald McNeill, *Urban Change and the European Left: Tales from the New Barcelona* (London: Routledge, 1999).

16. For an analysis of urban branding strategies under globalization, see Anna Klingmann, *Brandscapes: Architecture in the Experience Economy* (Cambridge, MA: MIT Press, 2007).

17. Marc Augé has found that precisely such attempts to remodel Western cities render them increasingly indistinguishable under late capitalism, producing more "non-places." Augé, *Non-Places: Introduction to an Anthropology of Supermodernity*, trans. Johns Howe (London: Verso, 1995). See also Frederic Jameson, *Postmodernism, or, the Cultural Logic of Late Capitalism* (Durham, NC: Duke University Press, 1991).

18. See Igal Charney's analysis of how such urban renewal in London enhanced the city's brand but disregarded the expectations of residents. Charney, "The Politics of Design: Architecture, Tall Buildings and the Skyline of Central London," *Area* 39, no. 2 (2007): 195–205.

19. In Italian, *Abruzzo Verso Il 2030: Sulle Ali dell'Aquila.*

20. The term *Abruzzi* became obsolete with a regional reform in 1963 that split the previous region, called Abruzzi e Molise, into two autonomous regions, Abruzzo and Molise, respectively. Outside of Italy, the use of the old name has continued.

21. Frank Vanclay, at a public meeting to discuss the draft policy report *Abruzzo Verso Il 2030: Sulle Ali dell'Aquila,* L'Aquila, Italy, March 16, 2012.

22. Unknown person, at a public meeting to discuss the draft policy report *Abruzzo Verso Il 2030: Sulle Ali dell'Aquila,* L'Aquila, Italy, March 16, 2012. Subsequent statements from the same event were also made by contributors that are unknown to the author, unless otherwise stated and cited below.

23. Alessia [pseud.], at a public meeting to discuss the draft policy report *Abruzzo Verso Il 2030: Sulle Ali dell'Aquila,* L'Aquila, Italy, March 16, 2012.

24. Francesca [pseud.], at a public meeting to discuss the draft policy report *Abruzzo Verso Il 2030: Sulle Ali dell'Aquila,* L'Aquila, Italy, March 16, 2012.

25. Both spoke on the condition of anonymity, in discussion with the author, following a public meeting to discuss the draft policy report *Abruzzo Verso Il 2030: Sulle Ali dell'Aquila,* L'Aquila, Italy, March 16, 2012.

26. For a discussion of the com'era e dov'era slogan in debates about the future, the past, identity, and reconstruction in L'Aquila, see Antonello Ciccozzi, "«Com'era-dov'era». Tutela del patrimonio culturale e sicurezza sismica degli edifici all'Aquila," *Etnografia e ricerca qualitativa* 2 (2015): 259–276.

27. Elsa Vivant, "Who Brands Whom? The Role of Local Authorities in the Branching of Art Museums," *The Town Planning Review* 82, no. 1 (2011): 99–115.

28. Ultimately highlighting the city's success as a popular and hip location, Bilbao's Guggenheim Museum featured in the opening scene of the 1999 James Bond film, *The World Is Not Enough.* For a discussion of the use of culture in Bilbao's urban rebranding, see Deyan Sudjic, *The Edifice Complex: How the Rich and Powerful Shape the World* (London: Penguin, 2006), chapter 11.

29. Davide Ponzini and Michele Nastasi, *Starchitecture: scene, attori e spettacoli nelle città contemporanee* (Turin: Allemandi; 2011); and Klingmann, *Brandscapes.*

30. Charles Jencks, *The Iconic Building: The Power of Enigma* (London: Frances Lincoln, 2005).

31. In Italy, the belief in the power of architecture is particularly pronounced. At least since the Renaissance, architecture and high art have been understood as important factors for successful community life. See, for example, Manfredo Tafuri, *Ricerca del Rinascimento: principi, città, architetti, Saggi* (Torino: Giulio

Einaudi, 1992); David Watkin, *A History of Western Architecture* (New York: Watson-Guptill Publications, 2005), chapter 6; and Paul N. Balchin, *Urban Development in Renaissance Italy* (Chichester, UK: John Wiley & Sons, 2008).

32. Abbado passed away in 2014.

33. Anna [pseud.], in discussion with the author, L'Aquila, Italy, December 1, 2012.

34. Franco [pseud.], in discussion with the author, L'Aquila, Italy, August 21, 2012.

35. Franco [pseud.], in discussion with the author, L'Aquila, Italy, August 21, 2012.

36. Unknown person, in discussion with Franco [pseud.] and the author, L'Aquila, Italy, August 21, 2012.

37. Unknown person, in discussion with Valerio [pseud.], L'Aquila, Italy, August 21, 2012.

38. Franco [pseud.], in discussion with the author, L'Aquila, Italy, August 21, 2012.

39. Davide [pseud.] and Amedeo [pseud.], in discussion on a social media (Facebook) post criticizing Renzo Piano's auditorium, September 29, 2012.

40. Giorgio Napolitano, during the inauguration of Renzo Piano's auditorium, L'Aquila, Italy, October 7, 2012. *New Towns* was the name given by Berlusconi and other politicians to the Progetto Case resettlement sites. Even in Italian, the original English words were used.

41. Renzo Piano, during the inauguration of L'Aquila's new auditorium, L'Aquila, Italy, October 7, 2012.

42. Felix Ringel, "Towards Anarchist Futures? Creative Presentism, Vanguard Practices and Anthropological Hopes," *Critique of Anthropology* 32, no. 2 (2012): 173–188. For a discussion of nostalgic attachments to the past in post-unification East Germany, see also Dominic Boyer, "Ostalgie and the Politics of the Future in East Germany," *Public Culture* 18, no. 2 (2006): 361–381. For more on the emptiness of visions of the future in contemporary capitalism, see Jane Guyer, "Prophecy and the Near Future: Thoughts on Macroeconomic, Evangelical, and Punctuated Time," *American Ethnologist* 34, no. 3 (2007): 409–421; and Hirokazu Miyazaki, "Economy of Dreams: Hopes in Global Capitalism and Its Critique," *Cultural Anthropology* 21, no. 2 (2006): 147–172.

43. Amedeo [pseud.], in discussion with the author, L'Aquila, Italy, October 1, 2012.

44. Michael Kimmelman, "In Italian Ruins, New York Lessons," *New York Times*, November 30, 2012, accessed July 20, 2017, http://www.nytimes.com/2012/12/01/arts/design/in-laquila-italy-lessons-for-rebuilding-from-storm.html?_r=0.

45. Michael Kimmelman, "In Italian Ruins, New York Lessons," *New York Times*, November 30, 2012, accessed July 20, 2017. http://www.nytimes.com/2012/12/01/arts/design/in-laquila-italy-lessons-for-rebuilding-from-storm.html?_r=0.

46. Pietro Di Stefano, "Di Stefano bacchetta il New York Times. L'assessore comunale va all'attacco: non ci servono lezioni, dico no alle demolizioni ideologiche," *Il Centro*, December 8, 2012, accessed July 20, 2017, http://www

.ilcentro.it/l-aquila/di-stefano-bacchetta-il-new-york-times-1.1147042?utm_medium=migrazione.

47. Walter Cavalieri, during a roundtable discussion on the future of L'Aquila's old center, L'Aquila, Italy, December 6, 2012.

48. This, and subsequent quotes in this section, Walter Cavalieri, in discussion with the author, L'Aquila, Italy, July 10, 2012.

49. Anne Allison, *Precarious Japan* (Durham, NC: Duke University Press, 2013), 80.

50. See Henrietta Moore and Nicholas J. Long, "Introduction: Sociality's New Directions," in *Sociality: New Directions*, ed. Moore and Long (Oxford: Berghahn Books, 2012).

FIVE

ACTIVISM AND GRASSROOTS POLITICS

THE PREVIOUS CHAPTERS EXPLORED THE consequences of a loss of access to urban spaces, relocation, uncertainty about recovery, and frustration with the political process in the wake of the 2009 earthquake. When the "extreme interventionism" of the first post-disaster phase morphed into government neglect that, in turn, led to demands for coordinated support, the legacy of destruction, the effects of an uneven political response, and the idiosyncratic repercussions for Aquilani and their social lives generated an experience of crisis.[1] In the coming chapters, I examine the bottom-up initiatives that were developed in response across political, cultural, and other arenas.

I have shown that many Aquilani considered the state relief program and other parts of the official emergency provisions as problematic; for them, disenfranchisement, media disinformation, the lack of a long-term repair strategy, and remote resettlement exacerbated problems caused by destruction. Many Aquilani deplored the access ban to historic neighborhoods, their relocation to faraway hotels and camps, the hosting of the G8 summit, and the construction of permanent resettlement sites instead of recovery schemes for heritage. Since decisions had been taken without consulting the affected population, bottom-up initiatives soon emerged to challenge government decisions and elevate the voices and views of survivors.

In this chapter, I explore grassroots political activities that confronted stasis and disenfranchisement. For the groups and individuals on whom I focus, their resistance fostered a new kind of civic culture that seeks to create spaces for intervention and to reclaim the authority to influence local affairs. I examine how and why certain people chose either established or innovative avenues of

political involvement, including protests, demonstrations, and electoral politics. This chapter explores the possibilities of political participation in a post-
disaster urban context and the aspirations and experiences of those who
activated themselves as citizens as part of their recovery process.[2]

ENCOUNTERS WITH THE STATE

The earthquake aftermath was characterized by encounters with state power:
forced evacuations and rehousing; the presence of police forces, soldiers, firefighters, and the Civil Protection Agency; access bans and regulated camp
life; new types of bureaucracy and documentation, claims forms, and compensation schemes; barriers and fences; visits by politicians and officials; and other
interventions changing local lives. The "faces of the state" that Aquilani confronted during the emergency operation disappointed, angered, and shocked
many, while comforting and consoling others or even the same people at different times.[3] Those who refused to submit to overbearing state authority
inside Civil Protection Agency structures relocated to autonomous emergency accommodations away from official camps. In parks and other locations
across the territory, bottom-up encampments sprung up and were managed
by Aquilani who had strongly critical views of the prime minister, Silvio Berlusconi, and his administration—views that mostly dated back to before the
earthquake. Emanating from these alternative camps, grassroots initiatives
challenged what they saw as a cynical politics of disenfranchisement through
displacement.[4]

One key group was Tre e Trentadue, abbreviated as 3e32—or 3:32 a.m., the
time of the 2009 earthquake. Its members and supporters denounced official
camps as securitized—even militarized—and infantilizing. After having
organized a spontaneous camp for evacuees on a sports field outside the historic center, the group constructed a settlement of durable wooden houses,
called CaseMatte, inside the grounds of an abandoned psychiatric hospital
near the medieval Collemaggio Basilica.[5] On their website, the 3e32 organizers
summarized their activities thus:

> The large "Yes we camp" slogan on the Roio hill during the G8 summit, the
> wheelbarrow protest, and the important anti-government demonstrations
> in L'Aquila and Rome in 2010 are only some of our activities. We have been
> fighting for reconstruction, information, and participation, which are our
> basic, yet negated, rights. In our self-run evacuees' camp, we created a safe
> space for democracy—in a city in which one half was depopulated and
> the other half militarized. We are now based in CaseMatte, at the former

psychiatric hospital, as an autonomous community. We transformed this former place of pain and terror, which was in a state of abandonment and decay when we arrived, into a beautiful space, open to the city, and where everyone can participate in its further development. This place must remain public, and not fall prey to real-estate speculation.[6]

The group was relatively homogeneous; its core activists were left-wingers and university students, as well as anarchists. Criticism of the Berlusconi administration was central to 3e32's agenda. Members denounced what they called the militarization of L'Aquila as a quasi-coup to undermine democracy and impose new political orders on a defenseless population. From the outset, 3e32 members had opposed government initiatives, connecting protest with demands for participation in decision-making processes. They self-identified as defenders of democracy, which was envisioned as direct, bottom-up, and participatory, and accused the Italian state of antidemocratic behavior. The group was involved in the most important protest initiatives. During the initial months of the relief operation, in the spring and summer of 2009, 3e32 activists organized public meetings to discuss such issues as the presence of army personnel in their city, the infrastructure that had to be installed for the G8 summit, living under surveillance in camps, the psychological effects of resettlement, and alternative arrangements in camper vans. Activists clashed with the authorities when they tried to assemble Aquilani in supervised semi-public spaces during the state of emergency.

When I arrived in the city almost three years after the earthquake, 3e32 was still active. Organizers lamented that participation was no longer as enthusiastic as it had been during previous phases, but the initiative survived. The group continued to organize events with a strong left-leaning focus and was an important entry point for my research. One of 3e32's key figures was Franco, a young Aquilano who worked in the press office of a local sports club. I met him at a 3e32 event in the run-up to the municipal elections. We saw each other frequently at similar occasions, and he eventually invited me to his home on the city's outskirts. It had sustained little damage and was soon cleared for habitation. Franco elaborated on the importance of collective grassroots resistance and solidarity during the state of emergency:

> Life in the government camps was crazy. When someone tells you that you're in shock after an earthquake, then you believe that and act like it. The schedule for each day—activities, mealtimes, and so on—changed frequently. People could no longer plan anything. Many just resigned to the authorities, followed the rules, did as they were told, and stopped complaining or thinking for themselves: they sat there, they ate when it

was time to eat, and slept at night, often full of tranquilizers. That was camp reality. The Civil Protection Agency wanted to control every aspect of social life, and the local authorities acquiesced. The mayor kowtowed to Berlusconi. The earthquake fused local with national politics; the two were no longer distinct. Control was total, and it came from the outside. I was a rebel. I questioned the authorities. They kicked me out, and so I moved from camp to camp.

There were two extremes. You'll hear some people say that the summer after the earthquake was the worst one in their lives. There was tragedy and death. But others will tell you that it was their best summer. Living for the day was liberating, and many experimented with activities or ideas that they had never considered before. 3e32 was important for this. The group brought people together for a common purpose: to oppose the state's relief operation that transformed our city and characterized Aquilani in a way that few of us recognized. We discussed every day what was happening to L'Aquila and how we wanted to live in the future. We experimented with new forms of community life. Such a movement would not have existed without the earthquake and the subsequent occupation of our city.[7]

Franco highlighted two aspects that also featured in the accounts of other 3e32 supporters. First, he considered the local authorities defective and incapable of representing citizens' concerns, since the mayor and other officials appeared to be simply executing government orders. Second, he described experiences with state power as the reason why new forms of communitarian associationism against the state were still being pursued by some Aquilani, including people who would otherwise not have been involved in movements that embrace radical political positions and alternative lifestyles. Initiated by left-wingers, 3e32 attracted supporters and event attendees from across local society, since the group offered a space for open discussion in a city under tight government supervision. In the gap between overbearing interventionism and subsequent disinterest, new visions regarding the relevance of active citizenship and civic engagement appeared.

At the time of my fieldwork, 3e32 continued to host events to reflect on the state intervention's impact on local society. In early 2013, I attended a talk by a psychologist, Emanuele Sirolli, on the social repercussions of the relief operation. The central wooden hut in the CaseMatte site contained a small stage, a bar, chairs, and tables. Rock music concerts were organized regularly in the restricted space. Colorful graffiti covered the walls. Despite the cold winter, a few dozen people attended the presentation. After the earthquake, Sirolli had counseled survivors across different official camps. His recollection and analysis mirrored a common theme of 3e32 meetings: a radical critique of government and power.

> Those camps were total institutions, in Erving Goffman's sense: people couldn't establish alternative social environments when they stayed in government accommodation. Survivors were disciplined by the state. The authorities used the state of shock to impose new constraints on people incapable of responding. For Aquilani, shock and exception became normality. Social elaboration didn't happen: people didn't process their experiences collectively. But such social elaboration is important after a traumatic event, just like a funeral. But we were stripped of the possibility of mourning, removed from our city, and relocated to camps and hotels.
>
> Most people spent day and night in these sites. They accepted whatever happened to them. This was state-organized mobbing. The evacuees I spoke to were depressed. They didn't even want to think. They had given up. And this situation of disenfranchisement continued in the resettlement sites. Aquilani felt superfluous. They had no role and no agency. They complained: "I don't get to do anything. They —the Civil Protection Agency—do everything." Elaboration was delayed further. There were no spaces for people to socialize. The camps or hotels were non-places, inhabited by evacuees who developed post-traumatic stress disorders and had no one, or few people, to help them deal with the situation. But there were important exceptions, such as the autonomous 3e32 camp, for example. I helped set it up. We actively brought people together so they could overcome traumatic experiences collectively. We knew about the importance of sharing suffering with others.[8]

A discussion followed the talk. There was widespread consensus that Guido Bertolaso, the head of the Civil Protection Agency, and Berlusconi had sought to impose total social control on survivors. The discussion was heated; anger and frustration with the former Italian administration were still tangible. Years after the earthquake, 3e32 continued to provide a space for critical opposition. The alternative social project still mattered as an initiative that confronted state mismanagement with grassroots activism. In order to assume a more influential position to shape local community life, 3e32 supporters and activists expanded their mobilization to a different plane: institutionalized politics.

APPELLO PER L'AQUILA

In spring 2012, L'Aquila was gearing up for the first local elections since the earthquake (discussed in chapter 3). A new *lista civica* (civic list), called Appello per L'Aquila (Call for L'Aquila), participated in the elections. In the Italian voting system, *liste civiche* are electoral lists without an affiliation to national parties; they campaign predominantly on local issues. Among the founders of Appello per L'Aquila were 3e32 members and supporters, including Franco. He invited me to meetings and introduced me to fellow campaigners. Franco explained that the efforts they had initially pursued through grassroots opposition could not produce the results he and others had expected:

> After the earthquake, there was a host of new grassroots initiatives and movements, and most of them opposed the government. 3e32 was not the only one. Our activities initially focused on the camps. After years of grassroots campaigning through movements, we decided to participate in the municipal elections as a proper political organization. We did this because it was time to shape recovery more actively. Powers had returned from the national government, and our city council deliberated and decided on restoration projects. Many of them favored the interests of a few wealthy construction entrepreneurs, who had good connections to political parties. The normal back-scratching and corruption were back again. We wanted to stop that. We wanted to create an instrument that allowed citizens to control local politics through city councillors that did not belong to the established parties. In 2011, we founded Appello per L'Aquila. This lista civica quickly became bigger than the grassroots movements that had set it up. Many other Aquilani, who were much more moderate than the 3e32 activists, threw their support behind Appello per L'Aquila. It was an inclusive movement.[9]

One of the Aquilani who developed an interest in political participation was Cara, who taught natural sciences at the University of L'Aquila. I met her at an Appello per L'Aquila rally in spring 2012, at the height of the election campaign. Appello per L'Aquila had rented the ground-floor rooms of a building in the city center as temporary campaign headquarters. Reinforcements propped up historic structures along the cobbled street, Via Giuseppe Garibaldi, and prevented the two- and three-story houses from collapsing. Buildings here had been badly damaged. Facades were crumbling to the cobbled floor. Tiles and plaster were strewn along the street. Mold patches marked abandoned homes. Shutters were down on kiosks and pastry shops, the front doors of which were secured with chains. At night, the area was plunged into darkness; only a few streetlights emitted a feeble orange glow.

Appello per L'Aquila had rendered former business premises partly accessible for its headquarters, obtaining special permits. Being located in the old center was a statement: this is the heart of the city and we demand greater reconstruction efforts. The large front window was covered in campaign posters featuring Appello's bright orange colors and the leading candidate, Ettore Di Cesare, declaring the civic list's key demands: participation, transparency, and accountability.[10] The thirty-page manifesto for the election was the result of grassroots meetings with interested participants and the input from expert working groups developing particular sections, such as plans for an innovative city that uses digital technologies to enhance urban life for all, greater investment in the city's parks, and even the vision of a new kind of politics, *governo diffuso* (diffuse government), to shift power from representatives back to an active and participating citizenry. The manifesto also included an emphasis on labor and social services and a commitment to urban development that combined heritage with innovation.

I attended a strategy meeting of Appello per L'Aquila supporters in May 2012, during the hot phase of the municipal election campaign. Di Cesare, the candidate for the office of mayor, was delayed by traffic, while the others arranged plastic chairs in a small circle for two dozen people. Franco used the opportunity to introduce me to other campaigners. When Di Cesare arrived, he gave an impassioned speech that urged supporters to push for a large turnout.

Before campaigners dispersed to hand out leaflets in peripheral shopping centers and along the semi-accessible streets in the old center, Cara, who was competing for a city council seat, invited me to her home after the elections so that we could discuss her commitment to politics. A few weeks later, I drove to her apartment in one of the Progetto Case rehousing sites. With her two adult children, both students, Cara inhabited a lounge/kitchen, two bedrooms, and a bathroom. The place was small. Her partner, who lived outside the city, visited on the weekends. She had opened all windows and doors because of the summer heat, hoping for a breeze. There was no air-conditioning; the top-floor apartment was incredibly hot. Neighbors were sitting on their small balcony below, chatting animatedly in what Cara assumed must be Romanian. She did not know the family. Children were chasing dogs on the parched yellow lawns around the housing blocks. Cara recalled joining Appello per L'Aquila shortly after its foundation. Before the earthquake, she explained, she had not been involved in politics:

> I was born in another town, not in L'Aquila, and this still means a lot here. This city has a problem with racism, particularly toward Eastern Europeans and now Africans, but whenever I argued with Aquilani, someone would say: "You're not even from here yourself! Mind your own business!" That's also why it would have been hard for me to be involved in local politics before the earthquake, and I couldn't have been bothered to fight my way in

against resistance. I would never have considered it. For me, local politics in L'Aquila was all about the self-interest of a small elite—corruption and nepotism were everywhere—and that's why many people here stuck up two fingers to politics. L'Aquila is a small place in the mountains; people tend to be closed-minded. In some ways, the earthquake has been good—it shook up categories; people from the center were evacuated to the coast and then moved into resettlement sites or postwar neighborhoods. They were forced to see different realities and think about what kind of life they want, instead of just living on, passively.

And with this change, I thought differently about my own options and future. The experience during the emergency operation had shocked me—the ways in which the government disregarded local voices and imposed project after project, change after change. That is why I no longer felt comfortable choosing political representatives and delegating decisions to them. I wanted to have a say myself; the local authorities were so useless and sycophantic towards the Berlusconi administration. They didn't stand up for Aquilani. And when I heard about this new political force, Appello per L'Aquila, I got involved. I discovered the importance of critical participation through the earthquake and the state of emergency.[11]

Cara added that 3e32 activists had been a driving force behind Appello per L'Aquila, but she highlighted that the civic list went beyond the more radical left-wing protest movement and sought to attract wider support. She emphasized that her newly found political awareness and engagement contrasted with a lack of commitment before the disaster, when she had experienced rejection as an outsider. Seeking a possibility for political participation after the experience of state emergency intervention, she was convinced by Appello per L'Aquila, also because of its lead candidate, Di Cesare:

Ettore is young, dynamic, and understands communication technologies and the media. He can reach people. He's serious. We chose him unanimously. Ettore has a background in mathematics, so he knows how to read obscure statistics and data—with which we've been bombarded since April 2009. He's lived abroad, so he's seen different realities of governance and democracy. Ettore set up a website, Openpolis, where he and his colleagues publish official documents, figures, analyses, et cetera, to render information public and allow ordinary citizens to assess what the authorities are doing and see how they are spending taxpayers' money. He has been fighting for accountability, transparency, and honesty for years, and we wanted someone like that to lead a political force in L'Aquila, because all of this was missing when the government controlled the city. Since power was taken away by force, it's been a struggle to get the authority over our own lives back into our hands. So many politicians here are motivated by self-interest, but Ettore cares about democratic participation. He's passionate about involving Aquilani in decision-making processes. There's an ongoing democratic deficit in L'Aquila.[12]

Cara recollected a sense of powerlessness felt by many Aquilani, as well as a distrust in local and national authorities. In response, she pursued greater involvement. A lack of participation, accountability, and transparency served to constitute the objectives of Appello per L'Aquila as a political platform. Di Cesare became the lead candidate because he pledged to counter a government approach that Cara, Franco, and others had experienced as too heavy handed and exclusionary.

In a way, the earthquake was a rupture, but a renewed commitment to political institutions also illustrated continuities. Amid what might superficially appear as a general trend toward disillusionment with politics—and which psychiatrists and survivors also described as apathy and resignation, in the camps in particular—other Aquilani found motivation for activities intended to remake political practice. Throughout the election campaign period, Appello per L'Aquila candidates arranged public events to meet with the electorate and convince Aquilani of their agenda for a more transparent and participatory political process during the recovery period. They consulted the public in roundtable meetings across the dispersed city and sought to include popular proposals in their manifesto. Election campaign events were intended to foreshadow the participatory decision-making processes that would take place once Appello per L'Aquila had assumed office, promising an innovative and inclusive approach to local government. Even though not everyone shared the platform's enthusiasm and demands, there was much apparent support for the promised novelty with regard to democratic decision-making processes and influence on public affairs, including repair and recovery. Candidates detailed their expenses painstakingly on the group's website to show that they managed donations responsibly, and supporters proudly carried their orange badges on T-shirts as they walked around the old city center or handed out flyers outside supermarkets and shopping centers.

Cara's reflections capture a common theme in the accounts Aquilani shared with me when they explained how the earthquake had changed them; they had realized that private life was closely entangled with state institutions and the political games that they had ignored before the disaster. Various Appello per L'Aquila supporters and candidates had been alienated from conventional electoral politics before April 2009 but had come to realize that grassroots initiatives and innovative involvement mattered. Protests were not the only way to attain a more active citizenship; through Appello per L'Aquila, participation and change could also be achieved via the electoral process and established institutions. Besides having the capacity to improve local lives, such initiatives also demonstrated to people that they were not the passive aid-seekers they had been portrayed to be, but active citizens who steered their own recovery through both protest and more regular political involvement.

BEREAVEMENT AND POLITICS

For the relatives of the 309 Aquilani who had died in the earthquake, the entanglement of political failure and family life was especially painful. Trying to find others with the same fate and with whom they could speak about loss, the *parenti delle vittime* (relatives of the victims) founded their own grassroots associations. The grieving families transformed suffering into a form of civic associationism to share the burden of mourning and demand rites of memory and places of commemoration. The largest initiative was the Fondazione 6 aprile per la vita (Foundation 6 April for life). It was founded one year after the earthquake and included a large number of grieving relatives. Group members strove to keep the memory of the 309 casualties alive through commemorative measures, including an online platform to share thoughts and recollections.[13] The foundation organized events of remembrance, the most prominent of which was held every year on April 6. It also lobbied the local authorities to construct a memorial fountain in a postwar neighborhood close to the old city center, where many condominiums had collapsed and killed a significant number of Aquilani. The foundation's representatives were taken seriously by politicians and at least superficially consulted, even though discussions around the memorial fountain went on for years without agreement on a concrete proposal. In a country in which Roman Catholic religiosity remains powerful, the grieving relatives attracted both sympathy and attention, which resulted in having a prominent voice on all sorts of matters and developments in the city.

At the time of my fieldwork, the Fondazione 6 aprile per la vita president was Massimo Cinque, a pediatric surgeon. He was working the night shift in a hospital outside L'Aquila when the earthquake struck. His wife and two young sons perished when their multistory condominium outside the old center collapsed and buried them inside the apartment. Homeless and distraught, Cinque had returned to the village of his childhood on the outskirts of the L'Aquila municipality, where he now lived with a sister and his elderly parents.

He was working long hours to stop himself from thinking about loss and hopelessness. At one commemorative event in the old center, we were introduced by a mutual friend. Cinque invited me to his house to talk about the foundation:

> We have two core objectives: memory and safety. Memory is important for our angels—as I like to call them. They might not be here physically, but they are always with us. We feel their presence. As their families, we live with their memory every day. But we also want to make sure their sacrifice wasn't in vain. They lost their lives because of others; they are guilty, they made mistakes. The houses that collapsed had been constructed badly—that's why they caved in. This catastrophe wasn't inevitable or natural. That's why one goal of our foundation is prevention: we want to lobby for safer buildings locally and nationally. We need better laws and controls. It must not be possible for vultures in the construction industry and organized crime to play with our lives by lying, cheating, and building houses that kill people. We don't want others to suffer in the same way that we are suffering every day. We fight for safety and to make sure that restoration and construction projects adhere to the highest standards. There will be more earthquakes. The question isn't whether they will happen, but when. We must make sure that people no longer die in collapsing buildings.
>
> The second objective is the physical memorial. We now use the anniversary as an annual remembrance occasion for the earthquake and the devastation of our city, but we also demand a physical site. We want a fountain, because water is a symbol of life. It would be right to remember our loved ones that way in a beautiful and prominent spot, where we can honor them and others can learn about the people who were taken away.[14]

The foundation's scope went beyond collective commemoration and mutual support; it had a clear political vision, even though members sometimes struggled to turn the attention they received into political projects. Cinque and others worked hard to guarantee that future L'Aquila would not be the same deadly place—rendered fragile by real-estate speculation, corruption, and political ineptitude—that had killed parents, siblings, and children. They organized public events to discuss the impact of real-estate speculation on Italy's housing stock, had engineers explain how a lack of regular checks in the building industry had led to substandard housing that would collapse in similar seismic events, and invited experts to explain the difference between Italian and Japanese approaches to disaster prevention in the construction sector. They sought to raise awareness with local and national politicians through petitions and manifestos. Despite their straightforward aspiration to lobby for greater safety, members of the foundation lamented authorities' indifference. "They would never say 'no' to you," one woman told me during a foundation meeting to commemorate earthquake victims. "They always nod and say how sorry they are, but the politicians don't do anything afterward. They don't act."[15]

Furthermore, occasional scandals revealed that politicians and officials, as well as construction company owners, had seen the disaster as an opportunity for profit or publicity, which undermined survivors' trust in state institutions. Over one year after the earthquake, for example, the Berlusconi administration had appointed a new prefect—the official who represents the national government and serves as a conduit between local and national authorities—for L'Aquila, Giovanna Maria Iurato. Upon her arrival in the city in 2010, she had laid down a wreath and wept at the ruin of a student dorm, where a dozen young people had lost their lives in 2009. Her emotional reaction was appreciated locally. Two years later, however, it was revealed that Iurato had not actually been upset; she had merely pretended to be moved to tears at the *casa dello studente*, which had become a national symbol of L'Aquila's suffering, to meet local expectations regarding sympathy for their plight. After the event, she had talked about the situation in a private phone conversation with a colleague, making fun of the Aquilani who had believed her. At the time, the police had intercepted Iurato's calls in relation to an investigation concerning her previous stint in Naples. During court proceedings in 2013, the recordings, in which she ridiculed gullible Aquilani who had believed her, were made public. The empathetic prefect was exposed as a horrible cynic.

Giustino Parisse had lost two children and his father in the earthquake. He served on the executive committee of the Fondazione 6 aprile per la vita. A well-known local journalist, he published an article in *Il Centro* condemning Iurato and other politicians:

> I knew the former prefect Giovanna Maria Iurato well. That is why my bitterness is even stronger today. I have had long conversations with her.... She asked after our children, looked at their pictures, and asked us to talk about them. Last May, she was here in Onna for a ceremony to plant 40 trees to commemorate those who will never again see the sun in their small village. She seemed sincere. Seemed. That is why I feel betrayed today— also regarding my emotions. She talked to me about her first public act in L'Aquila, the wreath at the student dorm casa dello studente, and asked me to help her write a book about her experience in L'Aquila. Those tears would have been included in the first chapter. Today, for me, they are tears of anger. It is the anger of someone who had believed in her compassion....
>
> Many people have descended on L'Aquila from Rome to exploit the earthquake and make money and further their careers. Some are still around.

We have had bogus ceremonies, bogus commemorative marches, bogus anniversaries, and bogus meetings. Now we discover that the prefect also wore a mask, and it was the most horrible one: the mask of hypocrisy. And what is the consequence? Today, four years on, there is still no memorial where we can weep for the 309 people who did not survive. . . .

The prefect then wanted to organize a religious ceremony in the Collemaggio Basilica around Christmas 2010 to commemorate the victims. During the occasion, she gifted a small angel to each of the victims' relatives. Until yesterday, I had it next to my calendar, underneath an image of my children. Now it's in the bin. . . .

I know that many people—just like you, prefect—have played tricks on me. Not much can hurt me anymore. Everyone has to answer to their own conscience. But here is some friendly advice, prefect: stay away from L'Aquila and from me.[16]

Revelations of attempts by government officials, politicians, journalists, and businessmen to exploit suffering for personal ends were common. As a result, survivors became suspicious toward the public institutions and officials that were tasked with helping L'Aquila rebuild in the wake of disaster. That is why members of the Fondazione 6 aprile per la vita established a proper political platform that challenged traditional party politics in order to effect change. The experience of loss engendered a specific type of civic associationism and grassroots politics with the objective of guaranteeing safety standards through legislation and effective oversight procedures for the construction industry.

L'AQUILA CHE VOGLIAMO

Besides Appello per L'Aquila, a second newly constituted civic list participated prominently in the 2012 elections: L'Aquila che vogliamo (The L'Aquila that we want). Its founder and lead candidate for the office of mayor was Vincenzo Vittorini, a surgeon whose wife and young daughter had perished in the earthquake. Vittorini had remained under the debris of a multistory condominium for hours, until firefighters rescued him. Unlike his wife, he survived by chance when the violent tremors pushed him out of the bed and onto the floor before the ceiling and roof collapsed. Vittorini's son also survived, as he'd been away on a school trip. Vittorini was another important figure in the Fondazione 6 aprile per la vita; he had been a founding member and the first president. With their former home reduced to rubble, in 2012, Vittorini and his son, Federico, lived in a Progetto Case resettlement apartment close to the city center. The underground of the neighborhood where their condominium had collapsed was subsequently tested and found to be too porous and unstable for high-rise constructions. Houses will not be rebuilt in this area and should never have been erected there in the first place, as Vittorini told me, but property developers had pushed for a relaxation of restrictions in the 1970s in order to construct in this underdeveloped area. There had been no construction in the zone because the rubble from previous earthquakes had been buried there, creating a cavernous underground. Such concerns were pushed aside when financial benefits loomed.

In early 2012, Vittorini was dividing his time between the hospital where he worked, the election campaign for L'Aquila che vogliamo, and appearances in court as a witness for the state prosecution in the Major Risks Commission trial (see chapter 7). A few weeks before the elections, Vittorini parked a camper van at the entrance to the historic city center, where Aquilani left their cars to go for walks along the old city's accessible streets. He distributed leaflets and spoke to passersby. Vittorini belonged to a well-known local family; many Aquilani stopped to chat and wished him luck. One week before the elections, mutual friends introduced me to him. Vittorini was enthusiastic about his chances. "This will be a new city after the elections. We will break the chains and liberate L'Aquila from the self-interested elites," he said. "Don't worry, mister anthropologist, you will have a lot to write about after the vote."[17] We exchanged phone numbers and agreed to speak after the elections.

With Appello per L'Aquila and L'Aquila che vogliamo, two *liste civiche* emerged from the engagement of post-disaster grassroots initiatives in response to disappointing experiences with the authorities. Taken together, L'Aquila che vogliamo and Appello per L'Aquila gained over 10 percent of the vote in the May 2012 municipal elections. Both Di Cesare and Vittorini secured seats as city councillors, while L'Aquila's controversial mayor, Massimo Cialente, was reelected (see chapter 3) and commanded a comfortable majority with his center-left coalition in the city council. A few weeks after the vote, the first council session was held in the main chamber of the Abruzzo Regional Parliament, which was situated on the edge of a park area outside the city center. L'Aquila's historic city hall in Piazza Palazzo had still not been repaired and remained inaccessible. The city council had been temporarily relocated to the wooden regional assembly hall. After a turbulent first session, Vittorini spoke to me in a nearby café. He pondered his entry into politics and recalled frustration with his initial attempts to lobby the authorities to promise higher safety standards in restoration and reconstruction projects through the Fondazione 6 aprile per la vita:

Why do houses collapse during an earthquake? Earthquakes in Japan are much stronger, but nothing collapses. This isn't about a natural disaster; it's about culture. They have a culture of safety in Japan. We need that same culture here. We need to build better houses, enforce high anti-seismic construction standards, and have proper checks and oversight. With our Foundation 6 April for life, we lobbied for safety standards, but we didn't get anywhere. The authorities wouldn't really listen to us. They thought we were a bunch of grief-consumed fools that exaggerated and couldn't be taken seriously in politics. That's why some of us created a political platform to participate in the elections: L'Aquila che vogliamo.

This is a conservative mountain city. Change takes longer here than in other parts of the country, but you have to start somewhere even if the struggle is long. There is so much back-scratching and clientelism in Italy. In L'Aquila, politicians have long handed out cushy administrative jobs in exchange for votes. Italian politics is all about self-interest. Our families died because of this negligent lack of professionalism. That's why we set up L'Aquila che vogliamo. Something needs to change, but those in charge won't do it. We need sincere politicians here, who can present genuine projects and convince people to support change.[18]

Reflecting on his own involvement in politics, Vittorini connected loss with the disappointing disinterest from the people responsible for post-disaster recovery. For Vittorini and others organized in both the Fondazione 6 aprile per la vita and L'Aquila che vogliamo, safety was the overriding political objective. Like Cara from Appello per L'Aquila, Vittorini admitted that he had not shown much interest in politics before the earthquake; now, he wanted to promote a type of civic culture that would put citizens' safety first. He added:

Politics in Italy is too short-term. Our politicians only think about the next day, and not about the long-term future of the country. I wasn't involved in politics before the earthquake, because I thought it was pointless anyway. Yes, it's great to build new pavements, but now we also need to have an idea of where we want our city to be in ten or twenty years' time. The game has changed. We need to have a safe city. The crisis we're having in Italy—and L'Aquila is a mirror of it—has been caused by this short-term thinking. It's like the ant and the cricket. The cricket spends all summer singing and frolicking, while the ant builds a place for winter and stores food. It plans ahead. When winter comes, the cricket has got nowhere to go to and dies. The ant survives. That's a good analogy of our political class.

The houses that collapsed in the earthquake weren't the old ones. We had a high death toll in my neighborhood, with buildings from the 1970s. L'Aquila

used to be classified as being at the highest seismic risk, but this classification
was lowered in those decades. It happened because the construction industry
lobbied for lower standards to build cheaper. We had houses here without any
steel frames and built with the cheap fine-grain sea sand rather than the type
that must be used for construction. This disaster has a history, and we need to
lobby back. Deaths could have been avoided. Political decisions and real-estate
speculation killed our loved ones. I cannot just step back and ignore this.

   We will have more earthquakes. Since their time and place cannot be
predicted, we need a culture of safety. This earthquake has been an extremely
tragic event, yes, and I know this more than most. But now, we have to make
sure that the disaster initiates a positive process to make L'Aquila a better
city. Houses can get damaged in earthquakes. But buildings mustn't collapse.
That kills people.[19]

Whereas Appello per L'Aquila supporters envisioned the focus of a new
type of civic culture as being on transparency, active and participatory citizenship, and accountability on the part of political representatives, L'Aquila
che vogliamo foregrounded safety, moral behavior, and construction industry oversight. Following disappointing experiences, Vittorini talked about
reversing cynicism and disinterestedness:

   We don't have real democracy here. It's a democracy facade with no
   substance. They let you say your bit, but it doesn't affect anything, so we
   have to be involved at the top. L'Aquila needs to change. The earthquake has
   revealed that something is deeply flawed in our disinterested and superficial
   lives here in L'Aquila and Italy, with these I-don't-give-a-damn attitudes
   (menefreghismo).[20] If this city learns a lesson, I'll stay. There was a moment
   of solidarity after the earthquake, when something new seemed to be
   taking off and people seemed to share this desire for change, but that's gone,
   unfortunately. If L'Aquila goes back to the past, I'll leave. The past wasn't
   good. It caused all of this pain.[21]

Vittorini described a common nionchalance as being at least partially
responsible for earthquake fatalities. He envisioned a different kind of civic
culture and political practice out of the realization that cynicism had failed
people in L'Aquila. Originally, bereaved Aquilani had set up the Fondazione 6 aprile per la vita as a social forum to share grief and remembrance. The
grassroots association nonetheless had a political scope: guaranteeing building safety throughout the reconstruction process. L'Aquila che vogliamo was
created in order to pursue the goals that the foundation had struggled to reach.
Vittorini's experience on the city council, however, left him disappointed. A
few months after our first conversation, we spoke again. He revealed frustration

Figure 5.1. Appello per L'Aquila campaign poster and supporters

with being in opposition to a powerful majority. The two civic lists lacked the political influence to promote the change and reformed political culture for which they had campaigned.

STRUGGLING FOR CHANGE

While Vittorini's biography rendered L'Aquila che vogliamo particularly authentic in the eyes of voters supporting him, political opponents could also instrumentalize the family tragedy to question his motives and capability as a political operator. Grassroots initiatives did not easily translate into organized politics, as Vittorini had to realize. Ten months after having been reelected, L'Aquila's mayor, Cialente, announced that he would take up additional part-time employment. Before his career in politics, the mayor had worked as a medical professional. Arguing that his pension would otherwise not suffice, he intended to return to work in the city's hospital, writing assessments on public health risks. Vittorini attacked the mayor publicly for this decision in an official press statement released by L'Aquila che vogliamo:

> "Do we need exceptional people in this city? I don't care—I work part-time and beef up my pension." This is the bottom line in our part-time mayor's reasoning, which affects all of us Aquilani. During times of crisis and cuts,

there are people like Cialente, the worst specimen of the old political guard. Oblivious to changing times, he abandons ship to look after his own. This underlines that we have always been justified, as L'Aquila che vogliamo, to express our lack of confidence in him. Before he was elected as mayor, he had already served two terms as a parliamentarian in Rome, earning 12,000 euros per month (which, in seven years, makes a beautiful sum of one million euros, AFTER TAX). Is this not enough for an acceptable pension? No, he still wants to earn more than 3,000 euros with part-time work—and who knows for how long!

This act reveals the profound inadequacy of a mayor who, after seven years in office, has not managed to guarantee his citizens' safety. But we want to help this mayor. We will help him resign so he has lots of time to earn the pension he deserves through genuine work. We will fight, because a politician who puts his own interest before those of the citizens must not and cannot stay in office. This city deserves someone responsible and serious. L'Aquila needs a full-time mayor and a full-time administration.[22]

Cialente responded immediately. He published an official press statement, which many Aquilani subsequently criticized as insensitive and inappropriate:

Doctor Vittorini, a political parvenu and city councillor, attacks me in a vulgar and personal way that regards my private life with sickening reflections. First of all, until a few months ago, he only minded his own business. Thus, he cannot understand that in seven years as L'Aquila's parliamentary representative, I gave over half of my pay, proudly and with conviction, to my party, the Democratici di Sinistra, which was thus able to do politics for Italians across the country. Since 1990, my first election to the local council, I have made my income public. The city has known my private life. It is reviewable like an open book. I thus need to say something on this umpteenth hysterical attack by councillor Vittorini.

Speaking as a medical professional myself, I believe that doctor Vittorini, certainly as a particular kind of response to something, isn't very much himself. He isn't well. We all support him with regard to his private issues, putting up with his messy behavior in commissions and the council, where he acts as if he were at a tenants' meeting rather than part of a civic assembly. But then, while sympathetic to his situation, it seems that, in certain moments, he is taking advantage of our patience. Given the delicate nature of his medical profession, I wish that people close to him engage with the problem and help him overcome this difficult phase.[23]

In L'Aquila, where the tragic history of the Vittorini family was well known, people read between the lines that the mayor accused Vittorini of being mentally unstable and erratic because of his family suffering. The activists from CaseMatte/3e32 openly criticized Cialente, who had always been a contentious figure for the group because of his alleged passivity and acquiescence during the post-disaster emergency intervention:

> We feel the need to intervene regarding the mayor's comments, and declare our solidarity with Vittorini and other bereaved Aquilani. We don't want to comment on the original subject of the discussion. What concerns us is that we had assumed the existence of some kind of respectful behavior in our community, come what may, regarding the personal tragedies suffered by many families in the earthquake. Of all people, the mayor broke this respectful sympathy, using terrible arguments in a polemical debate and thereby insulting the entire city. For months, Cialente has been behaving like a "small tyrant," showering critics and opponents with insults and affronts. But this time he has gone too far. It seemed as if Berlusconi had returned, who, as Prime Minister, accused Aquilani who opposed him of having "fragile minds." Back then, someone responded with a poster: "The only fragile mind is yours!"[24]

On Vittorini's Facebook page, a host of supportive messages appeared.[25] Tiziana wrote: "I can only say that I am completely with Vincenzo Vittorini. I'm speechless." And Erica commented: "I express my estimation and my solidarity. When the first citizen [the mayor] lowers himself to such shameful language, especially regarding someone who lost his loved ones, when he no longer has any respect for suffering and insults pain, then he no longer deserves to be our 'mayor.'"

Antonio agreed: "I voted Cialente, but I condemn his statement about doctor Vincenzo Vittorini firmly. Such insults are already very bad when directed at a city councillor elected by the people, but they become heresy when the mayor conjures up the enormous personal tragedy of doctor Vittorini."

Someone signed off her comment as "a L'Aquila citizen": "Following the dishonorable words about Vincenzo Vittorini, I ask the mayor, Massimo Cialente, to resign before the next earthquake anniversary. This person cannot commemorate the victims of the earthquake in front of their bereaved relatives whom he considers disturbed." Despite the wealth of supportive messages, the incident hurt Vittorini, as he disclosed to me a few days later. He abstained from commenting further on the issue publicly, as did Cialente. Aquilani exchanged their opinions on the matter for a few days on social media and in offline conversations. The majority of voices I heard condemned the attack, even though some people suggested that Vittorini had become irritable—some

Figure 5.2. L'Aquila che vogliamo election campaign event with Vincenzo Vittorini

said obsessive—in his quest to find a purpose and change the political realities. There was widespread consensus that personal suffering must not be dragged into political debate.

Cialente's attack illuminated a difficulty faced by Aquilani involved in new political movements: the established political parties could dismiss them as inexperienced newcomers, unfit for the task at hand. The mayor referenced his long career in politics, which contrasted with Vittorini's more recent entry. While his biography distinguished Vittorini as a credible and authentic representative for some voters, it also led to questions about how serious and long-term his involvement in politics would be. Even though Appello per L'Aquila and L'Aquila che vogliamo had an impact on L'Aquila's political landscape, they remained a minority force. In opposition, Di Cesare and Vittorini could not advance election campaign promises for a safer L'Aquila whose recovery processes would be characterized by transparency and participation. Nevertheless, both civic lists could use their visibility to check on the authorities. Appello per L'Aquila organized livestreaming of city council sessions and published official documents online, providing local citizens with information to assess the work of the city's public administration. Di Cesare also established a number of working groups in which Aquilani could participate and draft petitions for the city council.

The trajectories of grassroots involvement and new political organizations in post-disaster L'Aquila were closely connected with local concerns; both *liste civiche* included "L'Aquila" in their names, underlining a commitment to the city, its specific needs, and its recovery. Supporters for the two platforms invoked experiences connected with the disaster as the origins of renewed types of community associationism, political awareness, and commitment to the public good. The two groups revealed one of the ways in which some Aquilani sought to reconnect with public life in the aftermath of traumatic experiences: by experimenting with new forms of civic culture and political practice as citizens.

CITIZENSHIP IN POST-DISASTER L'AQUILA

This chapter has examined how the aftermath of the earthquake led survivors to reflect on the impact of politics on their lives, and I have traced two particular sets of experiences that induced renewed civic engagement. The group 3e32 reacted to disenfranchisement during the state of emergency by creating autonomous spaces and initiatives to oppose the government. 3e32 offered mutual support during the chaotic emergency phase and challenged the state monopoly on assistance. I found that over three years later, events organized by 3e32 still brought together Aquilani opposed to the government who were striving to analyze the ongoing repercussions of the emergency regime. Seeking to shape the city's future not just through opposition, 3e32 activists were crucial in founding Appello per L'Aquila. Appello per L'Aquila supporters keenly felt the absence of political participation, transparency, and accountability and made it their objective to address these issues through civic initiatives and policy platforms.

The relatives of the 309 Aquilani who had perished in the earthquake founded their own commemorative associations. Vittorini reinvented himself as a community politician striving to secure the built environment. Community activities on the part of grieving relatives did not remain confined to remembrance but spilled over into political engagement. New kinds of citizenship were motivated by pragmatism; if grieving or disenfranchised survivors did not themselves assume public office, other politicians or officials could not be trusted to represent their interests.

Despite success in the 2012 local elections, however, Appello per L'Aquila and L'Aquila che vogliamo members were disappointed with their experience of local politics, as the spat between Cialente and Vittorini illustrated. The impact of the new opposition groups remained limited, even though they introduced more transparency and oversight into the local political process and public administration. Building on this chapter's focus on political campaigns and electoral politics, the next one explores the role of the cultural sector in reconstituting community life and a sense of shared purpose among survivors of the L'Aquila earthquake.

NOTES

1. For a discussion about the concept of "extreme interventionism," see Didier Fassin and Mariella Pandolfi, "Introduction: Military and Humanitarian Government in the Age of Intervention," in *Contemporary States of Emergency: The Politics of Military and Humanitarian Interventions*, ed. Fassin and Pandolfi (Brooklyn: Zone Books, 2010), 22.

2. See, for example, Lina M. Calandra, "Territorio e democrazia: considerazioni dal post-sisma aquilano," in *Sismografie. Ritornare a L'Aquila mille giorni dopo il sisma*, ed. Fabio Carnelli, Orlando Paris, and Francesco Tommasi (Rome: Edizione Effigi, 2012a); Antonello Ciccozzi, "Aiuti e miracoli ai margini del terremoto de L'Aquila," *Meridiana* 65/66 (2011): 227–255; and Fabrizia Petrei, "Democrazia e comunicazione pubblica nel post-sisma: verso quale partecipazione all'Aquila?," in *Sismografie*, ed. Carnelli, Paris, and Tommasi (Rome: Edizione Effigi, 2012).

3. For an analysis of the ways in which citizens confront state power, see Yael Navaro-Yashin, *Faces of the State: Secularism and Public Life in Turkey* (Princeton, NJ: Princeton University Press, 2002).

4. Alfredo Mela, "Emergenza e ricostruzione dopo il terremoto: la resilienza comunitaria e gli interventi di sostegno," *Meridiana* 65/66 (2010): 85–99; Pina Leone, "La mobilitazione cittadina del 2010," in *Territorio e democrazia—Un laboratorio di geografia sociale nel doposisma aquilano*, ed. Calandra (L'Aquila: L'Una, 2012); Alpaslan Özerdem and Gianni Rufini, "L'Aquila's Reconstruction Challenges: Has Italy Learned from Its Previous Earthquake Disasters?," *Disasters* 37, no. 1 (2013); Giuseppe Forino, "Disaster Recovery: Narrating the Resilience Process in the Reconstruction of L'Aquila (Italy)," *Geografisk Tidsskrift-Danish Journal of Geography* 115, no. 1 (2015): 1–13; and Angelo Jonas Imperiale and Frank Vanclay, "Experiencing Local Community Resilience in Action: Learning from Post-Disaster Communities," *Journal of Rural Studies* 47 (2016): 204–219.

5. *Case matte* means *crazy houses*, in reference to the psychiatric hospital.

6. 3e32 CaseMatte, "Chi Siamo," accessed March 12, 2021, http://www.3e32 .org/?page_id=119.

7. Franco [pseud.], in discussion with the author, L'Aquila, Italy, July 10, 2012.

8. Emanuele Sirolli, at a public event discussing the psychological effects of camp life after the earthquake, L'Aquila, Italy, February 20, 2013. Sirolli referred

to Erving Goffman's theory of institutions. See Goffman, *Asylums: Essays on the Social Situation of Mental Patients and Other Inmates* (New Brunswick, NJ: Aldine Transaction, [1961] 2007).

9. Franco [pseud.], in discussion with the author, L'Aquila, Italy, July 10, 2012.

10. Appello per L'Aquila actually had two candidates' lists participating in the elections, In Comune and Cambia Musica, who shared the same program.

11. Cara [pseud.], in discussion with the author, L'Aquila, Italy, June 24, 2012.

12. Cara [pseud.], in discussion with the author, L'Aquila, Italy, June 24, 2012.

13. Fondazione 6 aprile per la vita, accessed March 12, 2021, http://www.6aprileperlavita.it.

14. Massimo Cinque, in discussion with the author, L'Aquila, Italy, March 11, 2013.

15. Angela [pseud.], at a commemoration event for the victims of the earthquake, L'Aquila, Italy, April 6, 2012.

16. Giustino Parisse, "Il terremoto e l'ipocrisia del Prefetto," *Il Centro*, January 20, 2013, accessed July 22, 2017, http://www.ilcentro.it/abruzzo/il-terremoto-e-l-ipocrisia-del-prefetto-1.1163499.

17. Vincenzo Vittorini, in discussion with the author, L'Aquila, Italy, May 4, 2012.

18. Vincenzo Vittorini, in discussion with the author, L'Aquila, Italy, July 18, 2012.

19. Vincenzo Vittorini, in discussion with the author, L'Aquila, Italy, July 18, 2012.

20. *Menefreghismo* is a popular Italian term derived from *me ne frego* ("I don't give a damn"). It denotes indifference and a disregard toward incidents of moral wrongdoing or failure unless they affect one's personal life.

21. Vincenzo Vittorini, in discussion with the author, L'Aquila, Italy, July 18, 2012.

22. Vincenzo Vittorini, "Comune L'Aquila: Servono gli straordinari, e cialente si mette part-time per la pensione," 6aprile.it, March 1, 2013, accessed July 22, 2017, http://www.6aprile.it/featured/2013/03/01/comune-laquila-servono-gli-straordinari-e-cialente-si-mette-part-time-per-la-pensione.html.

23. Massimo Cialente, "Cialente su Vittorini: 'Credo non stia bene, andrebbe aiutato,'" 6aprile.it, March 2, 2013, accessed July 22, 2017, http://www.6aprile.it/featured/2013/03/02/cialente-su-vittorini-credo-non-stia-bene-andrebbe-aiutato.html.

24. 3e32, "Cialente, l'unica mente fragile sei tu. Solidarietà a Vittorini e ai parenti delle vittime," abruzzo24ore.tv, March 4, 2013, accessed May 12, 2013. https://www.abruzzo24ore.tv/news/Cialente-l-unica-mente-fragile-sei-tu-Solidarieta-a-Vittorini-e-ai-parenti-delle-vittime/113779.htm.

25. All of the following comments appeared on Vincenzo Vittorini's personal Facebook page, copied by the author on March 6, 2013.

SIX

—w—

CULTURE AND SOCIAL RECOVERY

HAVING EXPLORED EMERGENT FORMS OF political engagement as one manifestation of post-disaster citizenship in the previous chapter, I now turn to the importance of cultural work in providing spaces for assembly and community. Soon after arriving in L'Aquila, I noticed a vibrant art and culture scene. Posters, social media, local TV channels, and newspapers advertised plays, public readings, exhibitions, book launches, and other initiatives taking place in makeshift venues across the city. Seeking to explore diverse facets of local life, I followed journalists from a local television station—A-TV—chasing stories around the city.[1] Every morning, I drove to the improvised studio on a business and industrial estate on the outskirts of L'Aquila. Following the routine of a morning espresso in a wooden hut that served as a coffee bar, we read through newspapers and social media to identify interesting stories. Most of the staff were precariously employed. They usually worked without regular payment or on short-term contracts covering a few months. Idealism and a desire to avoid gaps on their CV explained the young reporters' dedication.

The 2012 election campaigns, as well repercussions of the earthquake (crumbling Progetto Case sites, financial difficulties, or the latest decisions from Rome), provided a constant flow of newsworthy material. I joined journalists' trips to different parts of the extensive urban territory, where we met a string of artists, writers, and performers. A-TV journalists covered literary and music festivals, plays, film showings, and other public events. This chapter explores the aspirations of Aquilani engaged in cultural activities, illuminating an innovative kind of civic culture through which artists and writers sought to counter the painful effects of displacement, misrepresentation in the media, and mis-understanding and division among Aquilani.

The initiatives on which I focus shared three key objectives: first, to reverse the disappearance of shared urban spaces by providing opportunities for encounter and exchange; second, to permit local people to regain an active voice and render public their recollections and reflections, reversing a period of passivity; and third, to use cultural occasions to bridge divides and foster empathy among estranged survivors.

The lack of shared urban spaces, particularly in the old center, was one of the most detrimental consequences of the earthquake. American urbanist Jane Jacobs has written about the importance of daily social interactions in urban life and how they weave a fabric of trust and reliability into the neighborhoods of towns and cities.[2] In resettlement sites and without access to the center, such spontaneous routine interactions and concomitant trust had become rare.[3] In the Mediterranean context, everyday social interactions and the resulting "cultural intimacy" that give rise to trustworthiness and produce durable social ties are commonly focused on communal public sites in old centers, since pri-vate living conditions used to be restricted and shared with large families, and hence provided limited space for social group gatherings.[4] Regarding the rel-evance of public urban sites to Italian community life, however, there exists a complicating dimension: the official political sphere has been traditionally weak and struggled to integrate society.[5] "Occupied by sectorial or political interests," the public sphere in Italy has been divided—and some would say polarized—even before this became a more widely used descriptor for Western society in the 2010s.[6] This division has seen the emergence of both far-right populism and support for communism, as well as anti-politics sentiment and clientelism as a means of protecting personal interests.[7] The political public sphere has struggled to bring communities together and create a sense of shared purpose.

Given the absence of political institutions with an integrative function, the piazza has been an important space for the development and practice of civic political culture.[8] In the wake of the earthquake, civic spaces were damaged or destroyed and were out of bounds to the dispersed citizenry. Cultural work connected the material and social aspects of recovery, and this chapter illumi-nates the link between the loss of urban spaces and growing estrangement on the one hand and creative work and cultural engagement on the other. These creative initiatives illustrate the emergence of new types of civic culture and political behavior aimed at reversing estrangement and hopelessness after disaster and displacement.

THIS IS YOUR EARTHQUAKE

The earthquake fractured the surviving population in complicated ways, as I realized when reading the foreword to a collection of photographs called *L'Aquila anno zer0*, edited by Marco D'Antonio, that detailed the destruction of homes and monuments, and that was published one year after the disaster. In his foreword to the volume, a local writer, Marco Sebastiani, tried to capture the fragmented experience left by the earthquake:

> In those first hours of sunlight, it stared you in the face. Little was spoken. From your house, the epicenter of your earthquake, you walked further. Aftershocks continued. If you could do more than weep, you sought to understand how much of your life had remained in place. You stumbled briefly around the historic center before they would close it forever, trying to comprehend. Just after the dust blanket had settled and before the aid givers arrived: precisely the moment in which change felt imminent. For the last time, you went to see houses, churches, and the alleys that used to belong to you and to many others. Perhaps you had never been in this chapel, because "it had always been there," it would not have gone anywhere, you could have seen it any day. What a lie.
>
> In the months that follow, your house is a blue tent. The alternative would be a room in some faraway hotel, too far to understand what happens in your city and too far to understand what others are doing to what used to be yours. Control is slipping away. Only a few react: working, organizing themselves, asking to participate, and carving out a role in the recovery. For a short moment, we were all the same. Today, the differences are beginning to weigh down on us. Your friend irritates you when he returns from his coastal hotel resort, wearing his nice, clean shirts but completely ignorant of what others are deciding for his life. But it unnerves him that he does not have a clue about the things that you know, unkempt and worn out as you might be, but on top of events and developments.
>
> Political and other leaders come to L'Aquila these days. The whole world looks at your city, now that it is wounded, not when it was still beautiful. The world comes to the Aquilani, but Aquilani ignore it. They are kept at a distance. Their world is the Red Zone in the historic center, which they cannot access anymore, and now an evacuee compound, in which they are not allowed to do anything. But the real reason why Aquilani ignore the world around them is that they have got more important things to think about, to defend what has remained, and to survive just one more day. There were moments in which you managed not to think about yourself, when you staggered along bent walls, your nose up in the air, staring at cracks. Or when you hoped you could look at yourself in a mirror wearing a bright uniform. It

would have changed everything: you would have been a volunteer. Removed from the catastrophe, you would have come to L'Aquila to help, knowing that all was in order back home, hundreds of kilometers away. But no, you only see yourself wearing your own clothes, in your own skin. This is your earthquake.[9]

Published on the first anniversary of the disaster, Sebastiani's work zooms in on the earthquake's harrowing consequences: isolation, self-centeredness, and resentment. He coins the phrase "your earthquake" to conceptualize destruction and terror as an individual and thus individualizing experience.[10] Those in tent camps envied other evacuees for their comfortable hotel rooms, while Aquilani in holiday resorts resented camp residents for being able to follow the events transforming their city. For Sebastiani, the disaster left every Aquilano and Aquilana with their own experiences, difficult to relate to those of others and hindering solidarity.

At the same time, and in response to division, creative Aquilani devised activities to reverse fragmentation and replace misconception. The intention was not to build some romantically tight-knit community—local people knew that this had not existed before the earthquake—but to lay the groundwork for new types of connectedness and confront the estrangement and poisoning of social relations.

THE PIAZZA

A couple of months into my fieldwork, friends invited me to watch a variety show staged by artists in a makeshift container theater. It formed part of a post-disaster ensemble of temporary cultural venues that framed a purpose-built gravel square, Piazza D'Arti (The Square of the Arts). Near L'Aquila's hospital, on the edge of a postwar neighborhood, grassroots initiatives and artists had turned this previously derelict space into a popular cultural setting. Apart from the theater, wooden and prefabricated metal structures around the square contained a library, a smaller theater, a café, and a support project for people with disabilities. Compared with the scenic squares of the old town, the site was ugly; it seemed unfinished and arranged hastily; a lack of aesthetics underlined the project's emergency character. Piazza D'Arti was cut off from nearby residential neighborhoods; situated in an urban wasteland, the square was squeezed between a major artery, which connected suburbs with the historic center, and the undeveloped retention area of the Aterno River. Visitors reached the Piazza by private transport only, via a newly built one-way street. A couple of damaged schools and kindergartens had been relocated to the area and reopened in prefabricated containers. Illegal dumping was common.

On our way to the variety show, we passed hundreds of cars parked along the street. The tiny gravel parking lot quickly filled up for popular events. The contrast between this make-do arrangement of industrial containers in an urban wasteland with what Aquilani described as the scenic old-town spaces of pre-disaster sociality was strong. The interior walls of the largest structure, which contained the main theater, were covered in black curtains to cover up the metallic exterior. Entering through a fragile plastic door, one had to push through thick curtain cloth. The stage was at ground level, and dozens of seats and benches for the audience had been screwed onto an elevated platform. A scaffolding tower had been erected in one corner of the stage, with lamps attached for illumination. Otherwise, the stage was empty. At the height of political campaigning for the municipal elections in May 2012, the variety show featured political satire and performances by a tango group, dancers, comedians, and poets. The participating acts came from L'Aquila. Two of the mayoral candidates—the incumbent mayor, Massimo Cialente, and his key contender, Giorgio De Matteis—were interviewed during the show. The conversation shifted from serious to entertaining. Since entry had been free, the show host passed around a hat and asked the audience for a small donation. A puppet theater poking fun at the candidates competing in the elections concluded the amusing evening.

Following the show, my friends introduced me to Giulio Votta, a well-known local actor. He had been born in Lombardy, in northern Italy, in the 1970s but then moved to Abruzzo at the age of thirteen, where his father had found work in a factory. After school, Giulio had studied theater and spent a couple of years with a production company touring northern Europe. Ultimately, he had returned to L'Aquila. Months after the variety show, I saw him again in an unexpected setting. Dressed up as a clown, he was entertaining young children in a shopping center. He was nearing the end of his shift and visibly tired. I asked him if he would like to go for a coffee, to which he agreed. Giulio did not enjoy working in the shopping center, but he had bills to pay. His partner had recently lost her employment, and his unsteady income had to support both of them. He told me about a friend of his who had been laid off; at the age of thirty-eight, he had been forced to move back into his parents' house. Giulio dreaded a similar fate. I asked him about the Piazza D'Arti project. He explained that he considered *la cultura* (culture) a crucial part of post-disaster recovery:

> The Piazza D'Arti project was a response to the earthquake. There was an urgent need for public spaces for the displaced population. After the disaster, people were catapulted into this incredible situation: they were dispersed across hundreds of tent camps and hotels, far away from each other. We

Figure 6.1. Piazza D'Arti

needed a space for people to get together, where they could share memories and experiences. We needed a project to reconstruct the disintegrating social fabric [*tessuto sociale*]. The associations and groups that founded the Piazza D'Arti tried to bring together Aquilani through a project that was run by local activists, volunteers, artists, and others involved in cultural work.

We wanted to recreate what everyone had lost in the earthquake— whatever people's personal circumstances with their homes or families—and what continues to be missing today: *la piazza*. It is the place of local civic life, where people meet daily for a chat or to discuss politics, to have a coffee and update each other on gossip and so on. In the piazza, people debate ideas and create new initiatives; it is the city space in which people spend hours with others. There is a market, someone plays the guitar, people chat, and there are newsstands. Everything happens in this place; everyone comes together. In Italy, the piazza is the heart and soul of every village, town, and city. It is the most important place for encounters among citizens.[11]

Giulio was keen to make me understand that Aquilani missed spaces in which they could act as members of a civic urban community, debating and discussing memories, politics, and everyday life. The Piazza D'Arti initiative addressed what Sebastiani, in his foreword to the collection of photographs published one year after the earthquake, had described as one reason for fragmentation: the absence of spontaneous encounters. The results were distrust, sometimes envy. Echoing this concern, Giulio emphasized the need to reconstitute the social fabric as part of recovery.

THEATER

Plays, poetry readings, and other activities that grappled with the earthquake's impact allowed survivors to share their experiences with fellow survivors and other Italians. Tiziana Irti had once studied biology, but after university, she returned to L'Aquila to follow her passion: acting. At the time of my fieldwork, her husband, Giancarlo, had retired from his teaching position at L'Aquila's Academy of Fine Arts. Their two adult children had left to study at northern Italian universities. Tiziana and Giancarlo were very active on the local cultural scene. At the variety show in Piazza D'Arti, Tiziana read poetry. Mutual friends introduced us afterward. A few weeks later, I visited Tiziana and Giancarlo in their home village, thirty minutes southeast of L'Aquila's center. Together, we drove to a nearby town, San Demetrio, which had sustained considerable damage in the earthquake. The facade of its main church had collapsed, and the previously picturesque center resembled L'Aquila's old city; monuments and private houses had been extensively stabilized with scaffolding, debris littered closed-off streets, and green mold crept up on house facades. San Demetrio had to be evacuated after the earthquake. Its inhabitants had first been moved to emergency tent camps and then relocated to a new MAP settlement of temporary wooden huts. Tiziana drove me to a sports field at the edge of San Demetrio. The plateau overlooked the small town. The mountainous landscape formed a long green valley, and L'Aquila's higher-lying neighborhoods could be glimpsed in the distance.

The red, dry soil revealed that no one had played football here in some time. Below the sports ground, there was a small parking lot, little more than an assemblage of potholes; a bar and café from the inaccessible town center had reopened in a log cabin. A handful of elderly men were sitting outside on white plastic chairs and playing cards. Adjacent to the sports field, a large blue container stuck out of the bleak surroundings. Tiziana explained:

> After the earthquake, the Civil Protection Agency set up a tent camp for evacuees on this sports field. This area was really badly affected by the disaster. While not many people had died in San Demetrio, virtually all residents had to leave their homes. The blue container is the theater Giancarlo and I set up next to the tent camp. We used to offer theater workshops for the displaced. Through plays and similar activities, we wanted to offer the camp

residents distraction from their difficult everyday lives. The tent camp is gone now. People have moved into the new wooden resettlement units, where they wait for the repair of their homes.

In order to set up the container theater and fund our work, we collected donations, but most of the money came from our own savings. The theater has ninety-nine seats—L'Aquila's magic number. We inaugurated the venue during the G8 summit in 2009. We named it Teatro Nobelperlapace (The Nobel Peace Prize Theater), since Betty Williams, the Irish Nobel Prize laureate, participated in the inauguration. A few famous American actors, Bill Murray and George Clooney, were also here. They came to the G8 summit and wanted to help. We got a lot of attention. Berlusconi didn't want us to pursue the project because we distracted from his government spectacle, but we didn't let the lack of support discourage us.[12]

Since the earthquake had not damaged their own home in a nearby village, Tiziana and Giancarlo were able to use their professional expertise to support others who were forced to abandon their buildings and struggled with camp life. She elaborated:

Everyone always cares about young children when disaster strikes—but what about older siblings, parents, and the elderly? What do they do? After a while, apart from being terrorized by what they had lived through, many here were just bored. The government didn't let evacuees do anything. Many of them felt guilty for being forced to sit around and just wait for the next meal. Our evacuated friends complained about lethargy. That's why we wanted to bring theater and acting into the camps—to offer people something to do.

We initially set up a temporary theater adjacent to our home village, but the Civil Protection Agency didn't like it. They had no control over what we were doing. They saw us as a risk. They forced us to stop. Luckily, the mayor of San Demetrio then invited us to work with the people in the camp there. He gave us the site for the Teatro Nobelperlapace.[13]

Both Giancarlo and Tiziana highlighted the importance of cultural initiatives to processing the disaster and its aftermath. At the same time, they both considered their engagement an act of resistance to government approaches to disaster relief. Apart from the state agencies, Tiziana also remained critical of the media and their coverage:

Not long after the earthquake, a journalist who worked for an important national Italian broadcaster visited our theater project. He walked around and asked people questions. He spoke to this young girl, she was sixteen years old at the time, who had remained trapped for hours under the rubble of her semi-collapsed home. He asked his cameraman to film her and shoved a microphone in her face: "What did you feel? Did you think of death when you were trapped?" He was just looking for tears and emotions for his story. It was violence. It was sensationalism. As soon as Giancarlo realized what was going on, he grabbed the guy by the collar and threw him out. It was awful. Reporters, journalists, and others came to L'Aquila for dark stories of death and despair. That's voyeurism. They were hunting for pain.[14]

This sense of being misrepresented by reporters pursuing horror stories motivated Giancarlo and Tiziana to produce a more authentic account of life after April 2009. Their narrative was constructed out of survivors' recollections and formed the basis of a popular play, *One Thousand Days*.

ONE THOUSAND DAYS

In the summer of 2012, over three years after the earthquake, a literary festival, Stella D'Italia (Star of Italy), took place in L'Aquila. From across the country, poets and writers marched into the Abruzzo capital on countryside paths crossing the Apennine Mountains. In the city, a weeklong cultural festival celebrated the presence of an illustrious group of creative and critical minds. Across accessible spaces in the historic center, poetry readings and political discussions were organized. At a temporary market with wooden stalls, artisans sold local produce to thousands of visitors. The festival organizers, an Italian activist group called Repubblica Nomade (The Nomad Republic), aspired to launch a cultural reconstruction following what their own publicity called a long period of social and intellectual decline—a thinly veiled reference to the dominance over public life by Silvio Berlusconi, who had been forced from office in late 2011.[15] In the first week of July 2012, Stella D'Italia participants transformed the languishing ruins of L'Aquila's old center. Lively debates, music, and poetry recitals took place at every corner.

I listened to an engaging lyricist perform outside the San Bernardino basilica and spotted Tommaso, with whom I had recently traveled to the earthquake sites in Emilia-Romagna (see chapter 3). He was enthusiastic: "It almost feels like a normal city again. Bars are full of people discussing politics. Others are strolling along the main streets. It is warm, everyone is outside. This is what L'Aquila was like before."[16] One of the most anticipated events during the cultural festival was the performance of a play called *Mille giorni* (One Thousand Days), cowritten and performed by the actor Tiziana Irti.[17] A large crowd attended the *spettacolo* (show) in the Piazza D'Arti theater. In the play, Tiziana encapsulated the experiences and events that had shaped the first three years, or one thousand days, of L'Aquila life since the earthquake in April 2009.[18]

The stage was sparsely decorated with a chair, a cupboard, and a lamp. In *Mille giorni*, Tiziana assumes the role of Antonio, a fictional Aquilano. Antonio's wife has left him. He has just lost his job. It's Saturday night, April 5, 2009. Midnight passes. Antonio is at home, alone. After a while, he steps onto a stool and puts a noose around his neck. He tries to tie the rope to a ceiling lamp. Before he can jump off, he is violently thrown to the floor, covered in dust. It is 3:32 a.m. The earthquake that kills 309 people saves Antonio. This disaster has many stories. The following scenes trace Antonio as he meanders around L'Aquila's streets, thrown to the ground by aftershocks. He encounters distressed Aquilani. He sees dead bodies. He helps firefighters rescue survivors. Tiziana's main character is Antonio, but she also switches into the roles of a narrator and other survivors. Changing her clothes and tone of voice, she performs a range of bizarre encounters and conversations. At the end of the first scene, Tiziana, now as the play's narrator, explains: "The Civil Protection Agency arrives. They install themselves in our towns and villages. Our mayors are reduced to performing wedding ceremonies. People push trolleys to the coaches that take them to the coast, guided by men and women in uniforms. They build the first tent camp. The city is evacuated."

The journey takes Antonio to emergency camps, where confused evacuees share wild conspiracy theories with him. One of them claims that "getting rid of our shit" with portable toilets alone costs the taxpayer thirty-four million euros each year. The narrator continues: "Antonio, like other Aquilani, tours L'Aquila's shopping centers, hoping to find his city. The optician from the high street has reopened in one shopping mall. The place where Antonio used to buy his jackets is in another one. The bar, where he had his coffee, moves next to a supermarket. L'Aquila has been fragmented into lots of shopping centers. Continuous background music. The white of the neon lights in your eyes. Sundays are for consumption in the long corridors, wandering around like stunned ants that have lost their anthill."

Antonio's thousand days are a tale of urban transformation entangled with social dislocation. The historic center disappears; shopping malls and camps are insufficient substitutes. Antonio speaks with evacuees about the difficulties of an existence confined to hotel rooms. They disclose distressing experiences, such as sharing a bedroom with their elderly parents for months, sleepless nights, and the surrender of privacy. Antonio moves into a Progetto Case resettlement apartment. He grapples with the bureaucracy of claims forms and contracts. Tiziana assumes the role of a mother struggling with the constraints of a tiny resettlement apartment. She has been forced to move into the flat with her husband, although the two were separated before the earthquake, and their child. At one point, she exclaims, "Franco! Turn off the television. Go study in our bedroom. Alberto! What is this? The soup is overcooked! Jesus! Why have they forced me to live with you? We separated two years ago and yet you're still here, ruining my life. Now, what are we going to eat? Pizza again? Like yesterday, and the day before yesterday, and before."

Tiziana highlights a range of demoralizing everyday situations in resettlement sites, including spatial constraints and disruptive family reunions. She revisits crucial stages of post-disaster life, including the wheelbarrow initiative. Through Antonio, she denounces how national broadcasters fail to cover what many Aquilani consider a key moment of civic activism: "RAI UNO, Italy's most important television channel, moved our wheelbarrow story to the midnight edition. But we will not stop! We are many, and infuriated with these 'journalists'! Shame on you! Sell-outs! Spineless! How much do they pay you to come here and talk about nothing? You have killed us twice! You say that all is well here. Disgrace!"

At the end of the thousand days recounted in the play, Antonio walks back into the empty city center. Some avenues have been cleared, but most streets remain inaccessible, closed off, and dark. He finds an open pub on the edge of the old city and drinks himself into a stupor. Antonio surrenders his hope that L'Aquila will be restored. He has given up. Closing her eyes, Tiziana says:

> This is the story of Antonio. Unemployed. Divorced. Dead—if the
> earthquake had not saved him. Now, he has forgotten, like many others, but I
> haven't forgotten. In my mind, I walk to the Piazza Duomo. The market with
> the fruit and vegetables stalls. There are chickens and pecorino cheese. Shoes,
> underwear, vests, socks, tights. "Ciao Alessia! Shall we have a coffee? What?
> At the Rocco stall? No, I'll go there later. Too many people now." Nurses,
> students, elderly ladies with their walking frames. I stroll underneath the
> nearby cloisters. At the next corner, I take a look at Grimaldi's music shop. I
> bought my first LP here, *Imagine*, by John Lennon.
>
> Further along, I spot a photograph of the L'Aquila rugby team, proudly
> dressed in our colors: black, for the pain of the 1703 earthquake, and green,
> for hope. I am in Piazza Palazzo. On a bench, a student studies for her biology
> exam. Piazza Dei Gesuiti. Colacchi's shop window is full of books. The
> newsagent. The florist. Walking towards Piazza San Pietro, I pass the *trattoria*
> Da Lincosta. After the play in L'Aquila's theater, the actors will dine together
> here. It's the evening. Music, laughter, voices. Thursday. Student night.

When the play ended, Tiziana stood in the center of the stage, her eyes still shut. The lights went off, and the stage plunged into darkness. Many in the audience had tears in their eyes. Aquilani and visitors alike rose from their seats. "Bravissima!," many cheered. Audience members discussed the play for hours afterward. On a warm summer evening, Aquilani reflected on their biographies and shared them with friends. "I know someone who had to move into a Progetto Case flat with her husband after the earthquake, even though they were no longer together, because he had an affair with his secretary," someone told a friend. "I guess I should be glad to live with my parents in their home village again," her interlocutor responded, "but I still really miss my independence."[19] A young man told his seat neighbor, "After work, I still often drive back to the site of my old house, which has since been demolished, and only then I realize that I missed the exit for my Progetto Case resettlement site. It's just so natural for me, and it shocks me a little more each time I spot the hole where my house used to be."[20] Outside visitors asked Aquilani whether their experiences matched Antonio's life. Lively conversations continued for hours. *Mille giorni* stimulated exchange among Aquilani and presented visitors with more authentic interpretations of the everyday challenges in a city struggling to recover from disaster and division.

A few weeks later, I visited Tiziana again in the container theater at San Demetrio. Giancarlo was holding a theater workshop for a dozen locals, while Tiziana was rehearsing for another role. We sat in a small greenroom crammed with documents, costumes, and press articles about Teatro Nobelperlapace. Music from the stage was interrupted by Giancarlo's instructions. Tiziana explained the background to *Mille giorni*:

> At the beginning of *Mille giorni* was the desire to tell a story. Time had to pass in order to gain distance to the earthquake. It wouldn't have been a lucid account otherwise. Three years was the right time. A few months after the earthquake, I began reciting people's testimonies, which I had found on the internet or in conversations with friends. We organized a tour, and I performed testimonies in northern Italy in late 2009. It was direct and powerful, since the experiences we staged were about the earthquake: trauma, fear, death, destruction, evacuation. After that tour, the project fell dormant. Then, with the things that happened in 2010 and 2011—the wheelbarrows, scandals, displacement, and decay in the center—the necessity to talk about events from our perspective returned. The earthquake had been covered widely in the media, but many of us in the city felt that there weren't many authentic accounts. Reporters said what they wanted to say or what others wanted them to say. It was propaganda, not information. In

L'Aquila, there was great desire to share our views—to tell this story through the eyes of the people who were living it.

In the play, we highlight the earthquake's human dimensions, which were ignored during the emergency operation. People were reduced to numbers. There was a need to give space to people's voices and reach the audience emotionally. Theater is very powerful for this. A friend of mine, who had experience in narrative theater, joined our project. We interviewed over thirty Aquilani, aged twenty to seventy, about their memories and circumstances. We spoke with people who had had losses in the family and others who did not even have property damage. Some had been evacuated to the coast; others had stayed in tent camps. Some lived in the Progetto Case resettlement sites, while others had returned to their repaired homes. We had a range of different narratives and we wanted to bring out this multitude of experiences. People had an enormous desire to talk and share, from the head of the firefighters to a local teenager. But they did not just want to talk as a therapeutic thing; they wanted to communicate experiences to help others understand.[21]

Tiziana established three key aspirations for *Mille giorni*: countering misrepresentations, giving space to people's voices, and furthering mutual understanding. She expressed her wish to highlight the human dimensions of suffering, which Tiziana contrasted with the bureaucratic indifference of the relief effort that had reduced real stories to numbers.[22] She talked about the *bisogno* (need) or *necessità* (necessity) to provide authentic accounts of the past and the present, since many Aquilani continued to live in a limbo state of displacement. Tiziana found a great desire to share stories across L'Aquila. The objective of such storytelling was to convey the idea of a shared fate in order to counter envy. Real stories were combined to form a single, fictional character, Antonio. Tiziana explained that this permitted a more lighthearted introduction, which is why the play could begin with his unsuccessful suicide attempt. The earthquake saved at least one life. Tiziana smiled and evaded the question when I quizzed her about whether she had taken the idea from a real story. She told me instead, "We didn't have preconceptions when we collected accounts. Obviously, being both the actress and a personal witness who experienced the earthquake first-hand, my point of view does feature. But there are many aspects I had never thought about. That is why I didn't just want to talk about my own experiences. The play is a monologue, but it reveals a range of stories. It is as if lots of people were merged into one."[23]

In the fictional character of Antonio, the experiences of diverse Aquilani became a single story. Antonio personified everybody's and nobody's earthquake, permitting Aquilani to identify with him and understand the lives of others at the same time.[24] One year after the earthquake, Sebastiani described social fragmentation as being the result of disparate disaster experiences. In the story of Antonio, Tiziana merged idiosyncratic experiences into one narrative. Her performance highlighted the shared dimensions of local biographies, reestablishing connections and enabling communication.[25] For nonlocal Italians, the play also addressed a lack of information and complemented media stories with local voices.

Cultural initiatives were driven by such aspirations to remake an independent public sphere in which ideas could be shared and sympathetic exchanges enabled. *Mille giorni* highlighted that, despite the differences between life in tent camps or hotels, all survivors longed to tell their stories and struggled to maintain friendships and hope. Tiziana stressed that this was her understanding of what culture could achieve during crisis: "People think that a cultured person is someone with lots of books. I don't consider that culture [*cultura*]. For me, people are 'cultured' [*colto*] when they are integrated into the social world around them. Culture means being connected with your environment, developing a deep understanding of what happens around you. If an event, such as the earthquake and its aftermath, can make you lose this connection, or at least fracture it, then cultural initiatives can help you reestablish a close link."[26]

Tiziana also described how culture became an important part in her struggle to overcome the earthquake's destabilizing impact on her personal life:

The last years were strange, but they would have been strange anyway. My children left home and my parents died. My childhood home disappeared in the earthquake. Giancarlo retired. It's a time of passage and change. Under normal circumstances, one deals with it. But a violent event like the earthquake precipitates transformation. It becomes more difficult to move on, to metabolize everything. A lot of this would have happened anyway, but more gradually. When it all comes together, it's harder to bear. I can't dissociate the personal changes from the earthquake and what came in its wake. It happened in the same moment. I connect the event and other changes. My mother had to leave her house, evacuated, and could not move back before she passed away. My son had to grow up so fast. He was only seventeen, always joyful and smiling. This thing made him years older.

The play helped me. Performing the disaster through the eyes of different people allowed me to gain distance to the painful changes in my own life. You cannot overcome it completely, but you can look at your own challenges with less fear. During a performance, you need to control your emotions to establish the rapport with the audience you want. I need to organize and to manage my feelings. It is an exercise that has helped me offstage as well. The play is part of my own recovery.[27]

Some months later, I followed Giancarlo and Tiziana to Pescara, on the Adriatic Coast, where they showed *Mille giorni* in a small theater. This was Tiziana's tenth performance as Antonio. Nonetheless, she described performing in Pescara as a challenge, since thousands of Aquilani had relocated to the coastal city after the earthquake. "I could never live in Pescara," Giancarlo noted. "The city is so commercial and full of beach tourists. Cultural life is marginal here, but many parents didn't want their children to grow up in L'Aquila, given the unpredictable situation, which is why they moved."[28] Tiziana expected many relocated Aquilani to come to the show.

Giancarlo's brother, who used to live in L'Aquila, arrived early at the Pescara theater. During the earthquake, he had remained trapped when the ceiling collapsed onto him. Four years later, he still reported pain in his back and one leg. He told me that he found Pescara ugly and impersonal, but the thought of returning to L'Aquila was too painful. A queue formed outside the theater, which contained fewer than one hundred seats. Many had to be turned away. The atmosphere was intimate; Giancarlo greeted the guests personally. Most of them were old L'Aquila friends. The people in the audience were visibly moved by *Mille giorni*'s depiction of struggles that many recognized as their own. After the performance, Tiziana and Giancarlo spoke to guests, reflecting on the past and recent developments in L'Aquila and Pescara. Again, discussions continued for hours.

I found *Mille giorni* a particularly important initiative; it illustrated that a key component of how local people conceptualized recovery involved reconnecting individuals across their social environment. The play addressed two different audiences: non-Aquilani, who needed to know what survivors had really been through, and fellow Aquilani, who had to understand better and reconnect with fellow citizens. Cultural recovery, for Tiziana, focused on reintegrating survivors into their social environment. *Mille giorni* produced an account of the past through which a shared fate transpired, since Aquilani could discuss their struggles and experiences.

I WAS NOT THERE

At the beginning of my fieldwork, I struggled to meet people. The city center population had been relocated, and the historic core remained abandoned. I had asked the authorities if I could move into one of the Progetto Case relocation apartments, but since I was not a *terremotato* ["earthquaked"], I could not be accommodated, despite a large number of vacant flats.[29] Instead, I found a single room in a postwar multistory condominium that had sustained little damage and could be repaired without much delay after the earthquake. I shared a flat with a handful of university students. During the first couple of weeks, I used my car to drive to as many public events as possible, which I found announced online and in the papers. This was how I met journalists from the regional television station A-TV, who were happy for me to shadow them for a couple of months.

One of their reporters, Francesco Paolucci, became a close friend. He was an Aquilano in his early thirties who had studied journalism outside his hometown for a few years. After the disaster, he had been involved in a number of creative initiatives, such as a series of tongue-in-cheek YouTube videos called *dice che* . . . [someone has said that] . . . in which Francesco and a friend mocked post-disaster conspiracy myths. Francesco was not challenged by the job at A-TV, which entailed filming and editing short clips for news items. His dream was to produce a documentary or feature film with a long narrative. During the election campaign period, which spanned the first five months of my fieldwork, politicians hired Francesco as a freelance filmmaker to shoot election clips for local television. One day in April 2012, Francesco and I were sitting in Piazza Palazzo—the square initially cleared by the wheelbarrow initiative—and waiting for Cialente, L'Aquila's mayor.

He had a special permit to enter the heavily damaged historic city hall, which had been off-limits since the earthquake, to film a clip for his reelection campaign. An officer of the municipal police followed the three of us around the semi-ruined building. Francesco filmed Cialente, who was equipped with a yellow hard hat, walking along dust-covered corridors with kettles, files, documents, and office chairs strewn across the floor. The windows were broken. In the council chamber, Cialente pointed to large cracks zigzagging high walls. He was cautious, and the police officer reminded us constantly to mind the metal chains tying the unstable structure together, brutally cutting through walls and furniture. Leaning on the elegant wooden benches reserved for council members and now covered in dust, Cialente stared into the camera as he promised to restore this important space of civic identity and political autonomy after his reelection.

The state of the city hall left an impression on Francesco, who had not previously realized the extent of the destruction. Climbing over piles of debris in the stabilized corridors of what used to constitute a symbol of local pride, he fell uncharacteristically silent. Afterward, we had lunch in a small bar at the edge of the historic center that was frequented by workers from a handful of construction sites in the vicinity. I sought to lift Francesco's spirits. Finally, when I asked him about plans for his future, he beamed. Francesco revealed his idea for a film project, which he was developing with a friend, called *Io non c'ero* (I Was Not There). It was about two Aquilani friends whose paths parted in the earthquake aftermath. Francesco put his pecorino sandwich down and explained enthusiastically:

> In the earthquake night, only one of the two old friends is actually in L'Aquila; the other one doesn't experience the catastrophe, because he's away on a business trip. He returns to L'Aquila afterward but cannot reconnect with the devastated city. Eventually, he decides to leave for good. The two friends argue about the decision. The one who witnessed the earthquake urges his friend not to give up after everything that has happened: the fear during tremors, panic, screams, firefighters, tent camps, celebrities, spectacle, funerals. Everything. But the other one just replies: "I wasn't there!" And then he storms out, and the two don't see each other again. He didn't experience the earthquake and the painful events that his friend recalls, and so he doesn't have the same kind of attachment. He doesn't share the same sense of duty or commitment to fight for recovery.
>
> Thirty years later, the son of the man who left L'Aquila returns here for work. He falls in love with a young woman—the daughter of his father's former friend. When the two get married a few years later in a restored church in the historic center, the old friends meet again for the first time since they parted in an argument decades earlier. The reunion resolves their split and unites two Aquilani after decades of frustration and unsympathetic misunderstanding.[30]

Francesco talked about misunderstandings in his own friendship circle that prompted him to create this film. He used a similar language to Tiziana—speaking of a "need" to tell personal stories—when he reflected on his motivation for the project:

> I feel that there is a need to give stories of what *we* have been through. They deserve being told, also outside L'Aquila. The earthquake made history. Not just for us, but for the whole country. What has happened here is a condensed version of what is happening across Italy; this is about information, communication, corruption, and justice. The earthquake has exposed how the Italian state confronts its citizens, its architectural heritage, and society. It has shown the extent of cynicism and exploitation that corrupt Italy's leadership. This happens across the country, but it has become painfully obvious here. And we should react as citizens in our local realities. But we

wouldn't want this film to be merely political. It is also about people who face difficult decisions in their lives. The stories are personal, but they happen in a broader context. The film raises the question of leaving or staying and fighting. It is a question many people are facing today, because of the economic and political situation in Italy as a whole. We want to give people hope. The decisions we take today will have consequences in the future, even if change takes many years. But reconciliation and reconstruction are possible. That's the positive message we want to tell![31]

Francesco echoed Tiziana's expectations for *Mille giorni* that cultural initiatives could help overcome misconceptions. It was a project aimed at instilling courage for action. At the end of *Io non c'ero*, L'Aquila would be reconstructed, with personal friendships remade.

One year after our first discussion about the film, Francesco and fellow producers showed a short trailer for *Io non c'ero* in a restored historic building in the centro storico. The Palazzetto dei Nobili was one of the first listed buildings to be restored in the old city; it is situated on a picturesque square behind L'Aquila's city hall. Following its restoration, the Palazzetto's bright orange color contrasted with the decay framing it: the pockmarked facade on the back of the city hall and other buildings propped up and clad in gray scaffolding. Soldiers at a nearby army checkpoint stared out of their camouflaged vehicles, scrutinizing passersby. Located at the heart of the uninhabited center, this area of L'Aquila was particularly difficult to access. Visitors had to leave their cars outside the old city and continue on foot. Nonetheless, many Aquilani participated in the launch and fundraising event for the production of *Io non c'ero* and were moved by the professional trailer, which sketched how the film would engage with pressing issues of misunderstanding, departure, disappointment, difficult choices, and reconciliation. Afterward, Francesco explained his aim to realize the film through crowdfunding, which would turn the project into a collective initiative supported by Aquilani.[32]

Mille giorni ended with a nostalgic walk through pre-disaster L'Aquila, recounted by Tiziana. By contrast, Francesco's conclusion for *Io non c'ero* would illustrate how Aquilani had achieved reconciliation. Both projects gave emphasis to personal experiences after the earthquake, when friendships disintegrated and Aquilani had to confront the alienating effects of resettlement.

LILIES OF MEMORY

Tiziana and Francesco drew on their expertise in acting and filmmaking for new initiatives, but I also came across creative activities pursued by Aquilani without such previous experience. One of them was a book project, *I gigli della memoria* (The Lilies of Memory). After the 1703 earthquake, the few medieval houses that had remained intact were adorned with iron flowers. They became known as the lilies of memory, symbols of resilience in the face of adversity. Aquilani would often point to the metal lilies during walks around the old center. When Patrizia Tocci, a schoolteacher, invited a number of earthquake survivors to publish their stories in an edited book, she found inspiration in this history of survival and named her project *I gigli della memoria*. One of the contributors to the book was a friend of mine, who introduced me to Patrizia. In the summer of 2012, Patrizia agreed to meet and speak about her project. She had already published a range of short pamphlets about L'Aquila and her memories of the city. We went for a stroll in the park around the Spanish Fortress, passing the construction site for Renzo Piano's auditorium. Patrizia recalled pre-disaster L'Aquila nostalgically:

> It was such a beautiful city. At this time, in the early evening, people would be walking along the main street, *il corso*, stopping here for a glass of wine and there for an *aperitivo*. The whole city came to the center. There was no need to fix dates with friends. You saw everyone anyway. Our civic life really happened only in the centro storico: cinemas, theaters, restaurants, bars— everything was there. L'Aquila's citizens needed the centro storico for all sorts of activities. The libraries were full of students. It was a young and lively city. It was completely different from what it is today. The earthquake changed me, too. I stay at home now. I don't go out. I can't stand noise or crowds anymore. They scare me. Before the earthquake, every group had their spot in the city: The school students went to one bar, teachers to another one. Left-wing university students had their place, and the more conservative-minded people another venue. Children did not meet their parents on a night out. It was important for different people to have their own spaces, to develop their own social circles and values and separate friendship groups. It is different today: Social life now means heavy drinking. Everyone goes to the same few bars. There are no distinctive places for social groups anymore. It is cluttered. And so many people don't come out anymore at all.
>
> Everything seems so provisional today. I had to change my address so many times since the earthquake, moving from one form of temporary accommodation to another. I wonder how many letters I have lost. Back in my old house, I had a room full of books. I remembered exactly which one stood where. Today, I often buy copies of books I already own. I've lost track. There were shared initiatives, such as the wheelbarrow protest, but the solidarity spirit disappeared soon. People began to associate the wheelbarrows with left-wing politics, and so many did not attend further rallies. You feel

powerless. I have protested against Renzo Piano's auditorium, but it doesn't change anything. We don't need this now; it's a waste of resources. We want the centro storico back. But no one listens to us citizens. There is no public participation in L'Aquila.

Before the earthquake, no one outside Abruzzo knew this city. People thought it was some small place somewhere in the south. Today, when we demand the restoration of the centro storico, outsiders think we talk about a handful of streets. But the historic center was more. Everything used to happen here. The historic center *is* the city. Unless people understand this and see why we need to restore everything, I have little hope.[33]

Patrizia developed her book project to address the rupture created by the earthquake: "I wanted to create a testimony of post-disaster life that includes a wide range of experiences. The fifty-five authors, who each contribute one chapter, write about what happened during the first twelve hours of their 'second lives,' which began at 3:32 a.m. on April 6, 2009. All of us are involuntary witnesses to a burdensome history of destruction and survival, as are the lilies on the medieval houses in the historic center—hence the title."[34]

In early 2013, I followed twenty *I gigli della memoria* authors to a book presentation in Rome. The event was held in the city hall, on the Capitoline Hill, in a small but elegant chamber. The presentation began with a minute of silence for the 309 casualties. Patrizia explained that the initiative's objective was to create what she called a memory bank for future generations. She admitted that it had not been easy for her and others to write about painful experiences and then went on to underline the importance of creating personal accounts: "We need to give a voice to this dispersed community, to a community that has lost its places of encounter. Every single one of our fifty-five stories is a lily, and they all have a different form, but they can only be taken together. We are one big family. Like real lilies, we were born in the dark and live in the light. Memory is our identity. I would like to thank everyone for contributing to the book. This is a collective work."[35]

After Patrizia's introduction, contributors read excerpts from their chapters and discussed recollections with the audience. The stories encompassed diverse experiences and documented how differently the population of L'Aquila had lived through the first twelve hours after the city's destruction. The accounts were intimate, often tragic, in captivating prose. One of the authors had lost her daughter, son-in-law, and grandson in the earthquake. Her second grandson, who was due to be born on April 6, 2009, never left his mother's womb. She read a passage from her chapter about waiting outside the collapsed building that had buried half her family: "I don't listen to my husband when he runs toward me and yells: 'We have lost them all!' I don't believe it. I hope instead. They still find people alive after days. That is how I feel about it. I spend hours waiting. I watch volunteers carry debris away. I wonder how much building material has crushed them. I call out for my loved ones. I only give up hope when the ambulance drives off. It won't be needed here—but perhaps elsewhere."[36]

Sympathetic and encouraging applause followed the readings. Every author described the group as a big family and thanked Patrizia for the initiative and for bringing different people together. The contributors organized presentations across Italy, using coaches to take the group on book tours. They set up social media channels and communicated regularly. Despite the variety in their recollections, the fifty-five lilies had found a way of connecting with each other. One of them explained in her presentation: "I had never dreamt of writing a book or of anything like this, but after the earthquake, I felt that others needed to know. I wanted other Aquilani to understand me, and *I gigli della memoria* helped me understand the suffering others endured as well."[37] Patrizia emphasized that the book contains diverse stories but constitutes a shared project: the struggles that began when Aquilani were thrown into what Patrizia calls their second lives.

Patrizia linked the absence of physical spaces for social groups to the book project. In L'Aquila's old center, she recalled, there had been separate spaces for different social groups. The large diversity in political leanings or generational identities nonetheless used one shared space, the centro storico, which Patrizia hoped would be restored authentically. Their book project resembles the old town that was lost: it contains a range of disparate views and recollections grouped into sections, which nonetheless belong together and constitute a whole.

THE PIAZZA AND CULTURAL RECOVERY

I began this chapter with an account from a collection of photographs published one year after the disaster. The author described how the catastrophe had splintered into a set of personal crises that fragmented survivors. In response, grassroots groups joined forces to create a new square, Piazza D'Arti, as part of the recovery process. Tiziana defined culture as a process of integration between individuals and their social environment; she saw culture as a means of addressing the isolating aftereffects of catastrophe.

With *Io non c'ero*, Francesco focused on hope; his message was that fragmentation and division could be overcome even after decades of bitterness. Reconciliation was possible. Besides its encouraging message, the film project had a practical scope: with crowdfunding, Aquilani could become active supporters of the project.

Figure 6.2. Progetto Case resettlement site

Figure 6.3. Historic buildings in the old center, uninhabited and stabilized

Finally, *I gigli della memoria* encouraged dozens of Aquilani to work together and confront fragmentation. The division of a community of survivors into idiosyncratic crisis experiences was addressed by fusing disparate stories into one shared project, with the additional objective of providing authentic biographical accounts for nonlocal Italians.

The following chapter turns to another important initiative, widely discussed in the city and beyond: a high-profile court case against the members of an expert government body, the Major Risks Commission. While the victims' relatives, who acted as witnesses and plaintiffs, conceptualized their involvement as an act of civic duty and sought to behave as model citizens, the trial attracted global condemnation. Pundits accused Aquilani of punishing innocent scapegoats and misunderstanding science. Bereaved survivors reported disillusionment and frustration when their struggles were misrepresented, and the community of mourners was split over inclusions in the court proceedings. The battle with the legacy of the earthquake took an unexpected turn, complicating recovery and the process of regaining control over local biographies.

NOTES

1. A-TV is not the real name.

2. Jane Jacobs, *The Death and Life of Great American Cities* (New York: Random House, 1961).

3. I have analyzed this in more detail in chapter 4.

4. For an in-depth analysis of the concept of cultural intimacy in the Mediterranean context, see Michael Herzfeld, "The European Crisis and Cultural Intimacy," *Studies in Ethnicity and Nationalism* 13, no. 3 (2013): 491–497; and Herzfeld, *Cultural Intimacy: Social Poetics in the Nation-State* (Abingdon, VA: Routledge, 1997). For a discussion of the importance of public spaces across the Mediterranean as a consequence of small private homes, see also Julian Alfred Pitt-Rivers, *The People of the Sierra* (Chicago: University of Chicago Press, 1971); Sydel Silverman, *Three Bells of Civilization: The Life of an Italian Hill Town* (New York: Columbia University Press, 1975); Jane K. Cowan, *Dance and the Body Politic in Northern Greece* (Princeton, NJ: Princeton University Press, 1990); Herzfeld, *A Place in History: Social and Monumental Time in a Cretan Town* (Princeton, NJ: Princeton University Press, 1991); and Herzfeld, *Evicted from Eternity: The Restructuring of Modern Rome* (Chicago: University of Chicago Press, 2009).

5. Marco Revelli, "A Fragile Political Sphere," *Journal of Modern Italian Studies* 18, no. 3 (2013): 296–308.

6. David Forgacs, "Looking for Italy's Public Sphere," *Journal of Modern Italian Studies* 18, no. 3 (2013): 348–361. See also Paolo Mancini, "The Italian

Public Sphere: A Case of Dramatized Polarization," *Journal of Modern Italian Studies* 18, no. 3 (2013): 335–347.

7. Paul Ginsborg, "Civil Society in Contemporary Italy: Theory, History and Practice," *Journal of Modern Italian Studies* 18, no. 3 (2013): 283–295. See also Alfio Mastropaolo, *La mucca pazza della democrazia. Nuove destre, populismo, antipolitica* (Turin: Boringhieri, 2005); and Sandro Setta, *L'uomo qualunque, 1944–1948* (Bari: Editori Laterza, 2005). In the 2010s, the "digital populism" of the Five Star Movement (MoVimento Cinque Stelle) also capitalized on the weakness of traditional political institutions and a fragmented public sphere. See Giuliano Santoro, *Un grillo qualunque—Il Movimento 5 Stelle e il populismo digitale nella crisi dei partiti italiani* (Rome: Castelvecchi, 2012); and Fabio Bordignon and Luigi Ceccarini, Five Stars and a Cricket: Beppe Grillo Shakes Italian Politics," *South European Society and Politics* 18, no. 4 (2013): 427–449.

8. See, for example, Roberto Bianchi, "Il ritorno della piazza. Per una storia dell'uso politico degli spazi pubblici tra Otto e Novecento," *Zapruder* 1 (2003): 30–48; Eamonn Canniffe, *The Politics of the Piazza: The History and Meaning of the Italian Square* (Aldershot/Burlington: Ashgate, 2008); and Nick Dines, *Tuff City: Urban Change and Contested Space in Central Naples* (New York: Berghahn Books, 2012), 106–112. However, some suggest, urban sprawl and individualization have transformed both the material character of Italy's towns and cities and civic lives, reducing the relevance of the square for political conduct and social belonging. Guido Martinotti, "Empty *Piazze*. The Waning of Urban Civism in Italian Politics," *Journal of Modern Italian Studies* 18, no. 3 (2013): 322–334.

9. Marco Sebastiani, Preface, "L'Aquila anno zer0," in *L'Aquila anno zero*, ed. Marco D'Antonio (Rome: DED'A, 2010).

10. Rebecca Solnit, for example, has documented such emergent forms of solidarity during different kinds of emergency in the United States. Solnit, *A Paradise Built in Hell—The Extraordinary Communities That Arise in Disaster* (New York: Penguin, 2010).

11. Giulio, in discussion with the author, L'Aquila, Italy, January 9, 2013.

12. Tiziana, in discussion with the author, L'Aquila, Italy, December 10, 2012.

13. Tiziana, in discussion with the author, L'Aquila, Italy, December 10, 2012.

14. Tiziana, in discussion with the author, L'Aquila, Italy, December 10, 2012.

15. Antonio Moresco, "Il progetto—Un cammino a piedi per ricucire con i nostri passi l'Italia: 5 maggio–5 luglio 2012," Repubblica Nomade (2012), accessed July 27, 2017, https://camminacammina.wordpress.com/imprese -passate/stella-ditalia/stella-ditalia-il-progetto/.

16. Tommaso [pseud.], in discussion with the author, L'Aquila, Italy, July 7, 2012.

17. Her coauthor was Antonio G. Tucci, who also directed the play.

18. All extracts in this section are from Tiziana, acting in the play *Mille giorni*, L'Aquila, Italy, July 5, 2012.

19. Unknown persons, overheard by the author, L'Aquila, Italy, July 5, 2012.

20. Unknown person, overheard by the author, L'Aquila, Italy, July 5, 2012.

21. Tiziana, in discussion with the author, L'Aquila, Italy, July 30, 2012.

22. Herzfeld has also written about this alienating effect of bureaucratic management and its production of "indifference" in the Mediterranean context in *The Social Production of Indifference: Exploring the Symbolic Roots of Western Bureaucracy* (Chicago: University of Chicago Press, 1992).

23. Tiziana, in discussion with the author, L'Aquila, Italy, July 30, 2012.

24. I would like to thank one anonymous reviewer who reminded me of James D. Faubion, who also representationally merges fragmented experiences of city life into one fictional character, Maro. Faubion, *Modern Greek Lessons: A Primer in Historical Constructivism* (Princeton, NJ: Princeton University Press, 1994).

25. Importantly, Tiziana, a female actress, also chose a male persona, Antonio, as the protagonist, encompassing diverse gendered experiences. Throughout the play, Tiziana assumed different male and female roles, as well as those of young and old people.

26. Tiziana, in discussion with the author, L'Aquila, Italy, July 30, 2012.

27. Tiziana, in discussion with the author, L'Aquila, Italy, July 30, 2012.

28. Giancarlo, in discussion with the author, L'Aquila, Italy, January 12, 2012.

29. In January 2012, when I had just arrived in L'Aquila, local media reported that dozens of Progetto Case apartments remained empty—while hundreds of Aquilani were still living in remote hotel resorts—for bureaucratic reasons or because some Aquilani were unwilling to move into the sites.

30. Francesco, in discussion with the author, L'Aquila, Italy, April 19, 2012.

31. Francesco, in discussion with the author, L'Aquila, Italy, April 19, 2012.

32. By the time I left L'Aquila, Francesco had resigned from A-TV and was pursuing a career as an independent filmmaker, with increasing success. *Io non c'ero*, however, has still not been realized at the time of writing (May 2021). Because of insufficient funds, production was stalled.

33. Patrizia, in discussion with the author, L'Aquila, Italy, July 16, 2012.

34. Patrizia, in discussion with the author, L'Aquila, Italy, July 16, 2012.

35. Patrizia, at a book presentation for *I gigli della memoria*, Rome, Italy, March 26, 2013.

36. Renza, at a book presentation for *I gigli della memoria*, Rome, Italy, March 26, 2013.

37. Sonia, at a book presentation for *I gigli della memoria*, Rome, Italy, March 26, 2013.

SEVEN

—ᴍᴍ—

MOURNING IN COURT

THE PREVIOUS CHAPTER EXAMINED CULTURAL recovery and aspirations to remake the public spheres of a civic community. In this chapter, I analyze a different avenue through which a subset of the surviving population—a group of bereaved Aquilani—attempted to influence the recovery trajectory by shaping the disaster's public legacy and defending their families' biographies through legal process.

After the 2009 earthquake, the police launched numerous criminal investigations because of the high number of casualties, and the state prosecutors initiated lawsuits, most of which concerned the collapse of buildings as a result of criminal negligence on the part of construction firms, engineers, and architects. Casualties could have been avoided, the prosecution argued, if legally required building safety standards had been maintained. Legal proceedings were an important ramification of the earthquake. They shaped how responsibilities and ideas about power were interpreted and had divisive consequences for the surviving population. In this chapter, I analyze the most impactful court case that resulted from the disaster, as well as the experience of bereaved relatives who acted as witnesses and plaintiffs. This chapter examines how the bereaved sought to gain appreciation for their stories of trust and betrayal and to reverse injustice and institutional failure by judicial means.

The specific case I consider involved the seven participants of a meeting of the Major Risks Commission, convened by the head of the Civil Protection Agency, Guido Bertolaso, and which took place in L'Aquila one week before the April 2009 earthquake. The scientists and experts had been expected by the public to assess the risk of a monthlong sequence of seismic tremors.

Seemingly official communication following the meeting reassured many Aquilani that low-intensity shocks were no reason for concern. Seven days later, L'Aquila lay in ruins. Numerous survivors suspected that the expert commission had negligently failed to analyze the possibility of catastrophe and misguided the local population. Following police complaints by bereaved Aquilani, who sought to press charges against the experts for failing to carry out their duty of thorough scientific assessment and informing the public, the prosecution initiated a lawsuit accusing the defendants of criminally negligent manslaughter. The argument for the prosecution was that the superficial assessment and flippant communication had breached the required code of conduct and misled anxious Aquilani, many of whom trusted in the authority of scientists. A proper scientific analysis, the prosecution argued, would have yielded different results, which would not have led Aquilani to abandon habitual precaution, such as evacuating their homes following tremors. The trial revealed that Bertolaso had choreographed the expert meeting in order to soothe the city. He had purposefully instructed the experts to use their authority to calm fears and discredit alarming amateur earthquake predictions. The experts had acquiesced and failed to assess the real danger of a seismic situation—all of this with, the prosecution argued, fatal consequences.

In this chapter, I explore how a group of bereaved Aquilani became committed to the court case in a fight to shape history and correct a defective state. Bereaved survivors described the trial as a source of relief and renewal of political agency. They sought to defend their deceased family members as victims not simply of a natural disaster, but of irresponsible and corrupted public institutions. In the course of the trial, however, these Aquilani experienced disillusionment; legalese and the formal requirements of legal evidence challenged their recollections and transformed their testimonies. What had begun as a process that a group of bereaved survivors believed would be fruitful for recovery became distressing and threatened to taint the reputation of the victims. As the trial unfolded, the metropolitan Italian and global media accused L'Aquila's population of vilifying the Major Risks Commission members as scapegoats. Commentators accused Aquilani of punishing innocent experts to overcome their own guilt. Instead of reporting on responsible citizens who were attempting to bring to justice questionable officials and experts, self-declared pundits reproached the purportedly backward disaster survivors for putting "science on trial."[1] As a result, the trial turned into "one of the most misunderstood" recent cases regarding science communication and risk reduction.[2] Stereotypes of Italians as anti-modern, anti-science, and backward dominated much coverage of the court case.

The L'Aquila trial of the Major Risks Commission took place a few years after the spectacular sentencing of American exchange student Amanda Knox for the 2007 murder of British student Meredith Kercher in the Italian city of Perugia. The case received significant international attention because of the violent killing and revelations of very intimate details regarding young people's liberal sexual behavior. In 2009, alongside codefendant Raffaele Sollecito, Knox was convicted of homicide, but she successfully appealed the outcome and was acquitted in 2011. In addition to outlining the young students' sex lives, international media coverage of the Knox trial had promoted misleading caricatures of the Italian legal system, invoking stereotypes regarding the Italian state, corruption, chauvinism, and generically dysfunctional public institutions.[3] Especially in the United States, the Knox trial shaped how cynically the public perceived Italy's juridical system, and the trial of supposedly innocent scientists for failing to predict an earthquake in L'Aquila aligned with the perception of defective courts and ignorant lawyers. In this opinion climate, and due to sheer temporal coincidence, distortions of their own case frustrated bereaved Aquilani. The professed aim for many of the witnesses was an improvement of public morality and government. Once the trial got underway, however, bereaved Aquilani faced hostile reactions and little sympathy for the fate of their deceased relatives. The attempt to combine ritual remembrance with a fight for compensation and legal as well as social acknowledgment could not bring together a community of mourners.[4]

THE MAJOR RISKS COMMISSION

On the evening of October 22, 2012, three and a half years after the earthquake, the judgment of a municipal court in L'Aquila was reported across Italian and international news broadcasts. The judge found seven expert members of a scientific government commission guilty of criminally negligent manslaughter and grievous bodily harm on multiple counts. Across the media landscape, reactions were hostile. Journalists reported that an Italian court had sent scientists to prison for failing to predict a natural catastrophe. International repercussions were profound. Australia's ABC News, for example, announced, "Italian Scientists Convicted for Failing to Predict Quake."[5] US channel Fox News reported, "Italian Court Convicts 7 Scientists for Failing to Predict Earthquake."[6] In the United Kingdom, *The Independent* ran the headline "Italian Scientists Jailed for Six Years after Failing to Issue Warnings Ahead of Deadly L'Aquila Earthquake."[7] The verdict was broadly condemned as an attack on science and the scientific community, summarized by the *Guardian*: "Jailing of Italian Seismologists Leaves Scientific Community in Shock."[8] The court case was compared with the Inquisition's punishment of Galileo for promoting a heliocentric worldview, meaning a doctrinal medieval condemnation by the Roman Catholic Church was being equated with the modern Italian state's rule of law.[9] An editorial in the leading science journal *Nature*—with the damning subtitle "The Italian System's Contempt for Its Scientists Is Made Plain by the Guilty Verdict in L'Aquila"—opined that "science has little political clout in Italy and the trial proceeded in an absence of informed public debate that would have been unthinkable in most European countries or in the United States. [Marco] Billi [the presiding judge] should promptly explain his decision, and the scientific community should promptly challenge it."[10] The editorial further called the verdict "perverse" and the sentence "ludicrous," even though the author had to admit that the detailed legal explanation had not yet been published.

For Aquilani, such reactions were not unexpected. Pundits from around the world had mocked the court case since its inception in 2010. When the public prosecutor's office in L'Aquila first initiated the lawsuit, Italy's National Institute of Geophysics and Volcanology (INGV) asked the Italian president to interfere, publishing a pledge signed by over "4,000 members of the international scientific community" who called the accusations "unfounded."[11] Alan Leshner, president of the American Association for the Advancement of Science (AAAS), sent Italy's president, Giorgio Napolitano, an open letter:

> The charges against these scientists are both unfair and naïve. The basis for those indictments appears to be that the scientists failed to alert the population of L'Aquila of an impending earthquake. However, there is no way they could have done that credibly. Years of research, much of it conducted by distinguished seismologists in your own country, have demonstrated that there is no accepted scientific method for earthquake prediction that can be reliably used to warn citizens of an impending disaster. To expect more of science at this time is unreasonable. It is manifestly unfair for scientists to be criminally charged for failing to act on information that the international scientific community would consider inadequate as a basis for issuing a warning.[12]

From the beginning, there had been assumptions about the case by metropolitan Italian and international commentators that I found to be at odds with how bereaved Aquilani and other survivors talked about the trial. In the main, critics alleged that scientists had been sentenced to spend several years in prison for having failed to predict an earthquake—a claim that belied local views as well as my analysis. For months, I joined Aquilani in the courtroom's public gallery for hearings throughout 2012; I interviewed the plaintiffs, legal professionals, state prosecutors, and the judge, and I consulted official court documents. The following paragraphs reconstruct the background of the trial, starting even before the 2009 earthquake.

In October 2008, seismographic instruments began to register a sequence of light earthquake tremors in the area around L'Aquila. Over the coming weeks, the shock intensity and frequency grew steadily.[13] People close to the respective epicenters began to perceive tremors in December 2008. While magnitudes continued to increase in early 2009, such seismic phenomena were not unusual for the area. Local newspapers published details regarding the intensity and epicenter location in a matter-of-fact way; Aquilani were used to occasional tremors. In February 2009, however, the municipal authorities evacuated schools after a particularly powerful quake. Cracks appeared on buildings. Throughout February and March 2009, dozens of tremors were strong enough to be felt by locals, rather than just registered by sensitive instruments. A friend recalled this period: "We were like zombies: always tired, but unable to rest. I couldn't sleep or shower. I didn't want to end up trapped under rubble in the bathroom. At work, I couldn't focus or think. We spent nights outdoors, sleeping in our cars. We were terrorized. Walking around L'Aquila, you saw that people were exhausted, nervous, and anxious."[14]

Others, however, remembered fatalistic resignation or casualness. One Aquilano reflected: "I wasn't nervous. There was nothing to do. We'd had such tremor clusters before—for example, in 1985—and nothing happened. When you live in a seismically active area, you have to accept this. But many others were terrorized, absolutely. My sister was mortified, and I could say whatever I wanted, nothing would calm her down. To be honest, looking back, I guess she was right and I was wrong about it."[15]

The early months of 2009 were characterized by confusion about the appropriate response to not uncommon—but disconcerting—seismic activity. On March 30, 2009, seven powerful tremors struck in one day. Many Aquilani fled from houses and offices in panic. The widely publicized statements made by Giampaolo Giuliani, a local man with a reputation as a vocal amateur scientist, added to uncertainty and even panic for some. He claimed to have invented a technique relevant to earthquake prediction: in measuring radon gas emissions, he forecast a destructive seismic event for the town of Sulmona, south of L'Aquila. Giuliani convinced the mayor that an earthquake was imminent. In response, the local authorities sent loudspeaker vans to warn Sulmonesi, many of whom left their houses in fear and slept in their cars for days. When the prediction did not come true, Giuliani was banned with an injunction from issuing future warnings and threatened with a criminal prosecution for raising a false alarm.[16] In Rome, the national authorities were concerned about reports of anxiety and confusion in L'Aquila. In response, Bertolaso ordered a meeting of a scientific body—the Major Risks Commission—for March 31, 2009. A Civil Protection Agency press release, reported in the local media, stated that the experts would convene in L'Aquila to "provide the Abruzzo citizens with all the information available to the scientific community concerning the seismic activity of the past weeks."[17] Since ongoing seismic activity and amateur alarms seemed to contribute to panic, the national authorities summoned renowned scientists to provide a definitive answer.

The Major Risks Commission is an expert advisory body that connects the Civil Protection Agency with the scientific community.[18] It includes a range of experts on catastrophes, including earthquakes, volcanic eruptions, chemical, nuclear, or industrial accidents, and forest fires. The commission's president convenes relevant members whenever a risk situation arises. The experts then examine scientific findings, developments, and risk factors, analyze the given scenario, and provide practical advice concerning risk reduction to the authorities. On March 31, 2009, a selection of Major Risks Commission members and high-profile regional officials gathered in the seat of the Abruzzo regional administration. The key members and later defendants were four scientists: Franco Barberi, volcanologist and vice president of the Major Risks Commission; Enzo Boschi, Italy's most prominent geophysicist and president of the National Institute of Geophysics and Volcanology (INGV); Giulio Selvaggi, seismologist and director of the National Earthquake Center; and Claudio Eva, seismologist at Genoa University. They were joined by two engineers: Gian Michele Calvi, president of the European Center for Training and Research in Earthquake Engineering; and Mauro Dolce, specialist for anti-seismic engineering and director of the Civil Protection Agency's Office for Seismic Risks. The final defendant was Bernardo De Bernardinis, deputy head of Italy's Civil Protection Agency.[19] The session's aim was to examine the risk situation constituted by the tremors affecting L'Aquila and the surrounding area. The panel concluded its deliberation after less than one hour, and a couple of the experts remained in the venue to participate in a press conference chaired by the regional Civil Protection Agency coordinator, Daniela Stati. Since no official press statement was released, Aquilani consulted media reports from this press conference. Local reporters treated the panel's conclusion as a decisive statement that there was no risk or reason to assume that a catastrophic earthquake could take place in the foreseeable future.

The state prosecution would later present news coverage and interviews given by some of the experts to illustrate that the session had attempted, superficially and incorrectly, to comfort local people and reduce panic, rather than to assess the real risk situation and inform the population, the local authorities, and the Civil Protection Agency about potential precautionary measures to reduce the risk of damage and casualties. In their interviews with local news outlets, some of the experts generically discredited earthquake forecasting, apparently in response to Giuliani's apocalyptic amateur predictions. A television interview by Bernardo De Bernardinis, the deputy head of the Civil Protection Agency, contained some of the most vivid phrases that Aquilani remembered years later: "It's just a situation we have to be prepared to live with. There is no danger. That's what I told the mayor of Sulmona, too. On the contrary, the scientific community continues to confirm that we have a positive situation. There is a continuous discharge of energy. That is why we have had a sequence of noticeable seismic events, but nothing too strong."[20]

The reporter asked De Bernardinis—who had grown up in Abruzzo— whether Aquilani could sit back and relax with a glass of wine. He responded: "Absolutely, absolutely. One of those great local Montepulciano ones, I'd say. That's important."[21] Everyone in L'Aquila said that they remembered this above all: the memorable, and soon infamous, phrase about how everyone should sit back and relax with a glass of Montepulciano. Coming from a top-level official, who emphasized his local roots and expressed sympathy for fellow Abruzzesi, this statement had an effect.

In the following days, the tremors continued. Aquilani relied on the expert information reported by key sources: local officials, newspapers, and social media. No drills were held, no evacuation plans published, and no night shelters opened. Since the authorities seemed to place trust in the experts' judgment, many Aquilani accepted that new tremors were no reason to be distressed or spend the night in their cars. On Palm Sunday, April 5, a strong tremor occurred at 10:48 p.m. and another soon after midnight, now April 6, 2009.[22] Many of those who felt the earth shake later claimed that they had evaluated the seismic phenomena, which would have alarmed them previously, differently; experts had described the tremors as normal and even positive. Aquilani consulted the latest measurements provided by Italy's leading geophysics institutes, which seemed to confirm that magnitudes were decreasing. A few hours later, at 3:32 a.m., the city was devastated by one of Italy's deadliest and most destructive postwar disasters.

THE TRIAL

Vincenzo Vittorini—who was instrumental in founding the political movement L'Aquila che vogliamo, which represented the bereaved and their desire for a safer L'Aquila (see chapter 5)—acted as a plaintiff and key witness for the court case. We spoke regularly during breaks in the hearings, standing outside the makeshift courthouse in the Bazzano quarter on the outskirts of the L'Aquila municipality. Since the earthquake had rendered L'Aquila's grand *tribunale* (court) inaccessible, a temporary venue had been made available in the peripheral business and industrial park containing warehouses and other functional buildings. The temporary court complex consisted of a number of structures with offices for the state prosecution, judges, and other legal professionals. The courtroom was small—like a school classroom—and sat at the edge of the site. The adjacent fence was adorned with protest posters calling for punishments or acquittals in different trials. While the hearings were public, only a few uncomfortable plastic seats were available at the back of the courtroom. The presiding judge, Billi, sat on an elevated platform at the other end, under a crucifix and a large marble slab with the inscription *La legge è uguale per tutti* (Everyone is equal before the law). The defendants and their legal representatives occupied desks at the front of the room; behind them sat the plaintiffs and their lawyers. The room was jam-packed when high-profile witnesses were cross-examined, such as the defendants, Cialente (L'Aquila's mayor), or Bertolaso. In the warmer summer months, the air was hot and sticky. The small windows permitted little circulation; there was no air-conditioning. When the sun was shining outside, the white interior walls reflected uncomfortably bright light. Hearings lasted for hours and were exhausting for all participants.

One day in May 2012, Vittorini and I were standing outside the courtroom, watching army soldiers check vehicles that entered the area. In the distance, still snow-capped mountains flanked the L'Aquila valley. Vittorini spoke of his motivation to press charges against the Major Risks Commission's members:

> Many people think I'm doing this for vengeance or money, but that isn't true. I don't care about that. If someone, from Bertolaso to Cialente, said publicly, "I made a mistake. I underestimated the risk. I'll take the responsibility. I didn't understand what was going on," then I would withdraw my complaint. If someone assumed their responsibility, it would show that something is changing in Italy. But this never happens, so what do I do? I could take the law into my own hands, but I don't think it would be a good idea to be a vigilante. So I have to ask the judiciary to investigate. In a civilized country, people assume responsibility for their mistakes and resign. And that is how things change. But Italy isn't a civilized country. And so you have to get the courts to establish who is responsible for what. Hopefully, people will be banned from holding public office again. The administration will change

slowly. Eventually, this country will become more civilized, like Germany or the United Kingdom, but it will take time—and battles like this one.[23]

In interviews with the local and metropolitan media covering the trial, Vittorini repeatedly underlined this aspiration to initiate political change and "civilize" Italian public institutions. His motivation to be involved in the trial echoed his work for L'Aquila che vogliamo. His vision of himself as a plaintiff in the trial was of the good citizen doing his duty to reform defective state practice and enhance public morality. Others involved in the case shared his aims. They agreed with an assessment that public institutions were defective but saw themselves as part of the solution, and rejected the accusations, prominent in the media, that they were motivated by anger or even greed.

For the state prosecution, there had been nothing exceptional about the ways in which the lawsuit was initiated, as one of the prosecutors told me at the outset of the trial: "This started like any other case. After the earthquake, residents pressed charges with the carabinieri and the state prosecution. They described their habitual caution with regard to tremors and earthquakes, which had always led them to leave their houses after a strong seismic event and remain outside fearing aftershocks. This caution was transformed by the advice from the Major Risks Commission's experts. When they were buried under rubble or lost their loved ones, these citizens complained about having been tricked."[24]

The opening court hearing took place in October 2011, two and a half years after the earthquake. The state prosecution had a difficult task: to prove a causal link between the expert commission's assessment and Aquilani deaths. The prosecution included 29 casualties, out of 309 earthquake victims in its case and was confident that it would be able to demonstrate that the experts' assessment had changed individual behavior. The trial did not consider all deaths nor all injured Aquilani, but instead focused on a sample of deceased victims whom friends and relatives testified had altered their response to tremors as a consequence of the Major Risks Commission's session on March 31, 2009.[25] The court case became a fixture of my research. Every other Wednesday morning, a few dozen Aquilani made their way to the temporary courthouse to see how some of Italy's most prestigious lawyers defended the Major Risks Commission's experts. Developments from the court case were reported in local newspapers and discussed widely.

The hearings were peculiar. The case had already received significant international attention, but its reputation as one of the most spectacular trials in recent Italian history contrasted with the banality of the container venue and the informal character of the proceedings. Court sessions were interrupted for long lunch breaks, when the state prosecution, the plaintiffs' lawyers, De Bernardinis—the only defendant who participated regularly—and others walked across the road outside the court compound to buy sandwiches or pasta in a large café. Predominantly frequented by staff from companies in the industrial park, the café had a spacious interior that resembled a motorway service area, with functional plastic chairs and tablecloths made from recycled paper. De Bernardinis talked casually to the plaintiffs over a coffee or sandwich. As we returned to the courtroom for one afternoon session, I asked a father who had lost a child in the earthquake how he felt about De Bernardinis. He insisted that he bore no grudge: "He's a broken man, just look at him. He is the only defendant who attends every hearing. The guilt must be enormous, and I feel sorry for him."[26] There was no talk of revenge. In addition to the relatives and friends of the twenty-nine selected casualties, experts in neuroscience, communication, seismology, and other disciplines gave testimony for the state prosecution or the defense. They sought to establish or discredit connections between the meeting and the casualties. In the final hearing, the seven defendants were given a chance to speak themselves. Over a hundred witnesses and experts were heard in total. The case was concluded quickly, in just over one year.

One of the first people to testify was Maurizio Cora. In the earthquake, his multistory condominium outside the old center had collapsed; his wife and one daughter were killed instantly. Another daughter passed away four days later in the hospital. Cora survived. In his testimony, he recalled why his family had stayed inside despite the tremors:

> Until April 6, our behavior had been instinctive. We had always left our house after tremors. That night, unfortunately, we reasoned differently. This reasoning would not have existed without the evaluations made by the Major Risks Commission. After months of shocks, we had been expecting their advice like manna from heaven. We had been through six months of tremors. You can only know what this means if you've been through it yourself. We lived every day with fear. We were tense. After months of panic, our behavior changed following the experts' session. Unfortunately. We reflected on what had been our previous and instinctive reactions. We placed complete trust in these people. They were the representatives of considerable scientific expertise in Italy.[27]

Other witnesses confirmed that they, or their deceased friends or relatives, had felt relief after the experts had supposedly established that the tremor swarm did not signal danger, but rather indicated a positive energy discharge. Cora explained to the court how the expert judgment had toppled fears:

> In the earthquake night, there was a strong tremor at around 10.30pm. We noticed that its intensity was lower than during previous quakes. The Major

Risks Commission had predicted this. They had spoken about a normal tremor cluster, which we saw confirmed. My wife said: "They are so great, the Major Risks Commission's experts. They were precise. They predicted it correctly." The Commission's analysis profoundly conditioned our behavior. Until that day, our behavior had always been the same, at least since an earthquake that took place in 1985. We always left our house for a long period of time, until no sign of risk remained. This also happened after the powerful tremors on March 30, 2009. We left our house and went into the park near the L'Aquila fortress, where Aquilani gather during seismic events. I remember it well: my daughter Alessandra had a temperature, 39 degrees. She was wrapped in blankets. But still, we stayed in the car, in the open, for a long time.[28]

Cora told the court that his oldest daughter had been in Naples for work. He advised her to stay away from L'Aquila while the tremors continued, despite the upcoming Easter holidays. After reassuring remarks from the Major Risks Commission, he told her she could return to L'Aquila. A week later, the Cora family ceased to exist. Cora told the court: "I shouldn't even be alive. I fell down eighteen meters when my house collapsed. I lost my entire family. I am a living dead."[29] He and other witnesses claimed that the experts had changed what they thought the tremors represented—a reassuring energy discharge rather than a potential danger to life—and thus they behaved in a way that caused death later the same night of April 6, 2009. This was a point underscored by Vincenzo Vittorini, who also testified to the court:

We knew that L'Aquila was a seismic city. Instructed by my father, who had an instinctive fear of earthquakes, we were used to behaving in a specific way. When I was young, we lived in the old center, in a historical building. Whenever there were tremors, we had to run to the supporting beam and hide underneath. As soon as the shaking stopped, we left the house quickly. When a tremor struck during the night, my father looked out of the window to see what our neighbors were doing, whether they turned on their lights or not. When the lights in our neighborhood came on and people left their houses, we also went outside and slept in our car, covered in blankets, with our mother. Our father waited outside, smoking and talking to the other men. This is what our father had taught us, and what we had always done.

When the meeting of the Commission was announced, my wife and I talked about it a lot. We were thinking: "Well, if they hold a session with top-level experts, there is probably something that is not quite right—why else convene a meeting like this in L'Aquila?" And so we waited anxiously for the outcome. On the evening of March 31, we followed the news. I remember an interview with [Franco] Barberi [a volcanologist by training and vice president of the

Major Risks Commission], who said that earthquakes cannot be predicted, and that the situation could be defined as "normal." And I remember the press conference. Besides what was said, I looked at their faces. The scientists weren't terrified. Their calm expressions underlined the comforting statements. I listened to them saying that the more shocks there were, the better. This was one of the phrases I heard and that struck me, and which I recalled, unfortunately, one week later. Everyone, everywhere repeated it: the more discharge, the better. It meant that the earthquake was losing energy. It was a good thing that there were lots of weak quakes instead of a strong one.

On the night of the earthquake, just before 11 p.m., there was a tremor. My wife Claudia and my daughter were frightened. I said: "Be calm." And then I said to Claudia: "How did this quake compare with the one last week?" And she said: "It was less strong, but it scared me nonetheless. What are we going to do? Leave?" I looked out of the window, and there were no people in the streets. And we talked again about how this recent shock compared with the one the week before, and she repeated that it had been weaker. Perfect, I thought, the more discharge, the better. That evening, I took the wrong decision. I went against what had been a habit, something that my father had inculcated in me: always to escape. That evening, we reflected on this behavior. We received a phone call from my brother, who lived in Bologna. He had heard about the first tremor on television. He said: "Leave! Get out of the house!" He repeated this I don't know how many times. I told him: "Calm down, the situation is calm. There have been lots of tremors in this period, and they told us that it was a normal phenomenon: the more discharge the better. They told us that it is all under control." But he shouted: "Leave! Get out!" He is a bit like my father. Earthquakes leave an impression on him. Despite his insistence, we stayed inside, precisely because we trusted what the experts had said. As a surgeon, I take science seriously.[30]

His testimony to the court presented the Vittorinis as a rational family; a few hours before the disaster, they had used scientific explanations to comfort a nervous brother. Vittorini alleged that the scientists had misled him and his family, with fatal consequences.

To corroborate the testimonies of bereaved relatives, the state prosecution invited expert witnesses. Among them was Antonello Ciccozzi, an anthropologist at the University of L'Aquila. He was invited to provide a scientist's opinion regarding the link between expertise and human behavior under extreme circumstances. Ciccozzi wrote an expert evaluation for the prosecutors, was cross-examined, and subsequently published his advice as a book, *Parola di scienza* (which translates as "Word of Science").[31] In his statement to the court, he examined the role of scientific knowledge in Western societies. Ciccozzi argued that scientists command an

Figure 7.1. Temporary container courthouse in the Bazzano industrial park

almost religious authority, by virtue of which they are capable of influencing human reasoning. He invoked Serge Moscovici's theory of social representation to argue that certain forms of knowledge can assume enough persuasiveness and power to transform human interpretations of the world and the ways in which we behave. Science, he suggested, was endowed with high credibility and thus a capacity to condition human representations of the world—as well as to change behavior.

Ciccozzi suggested that well-educated Aquilani, in particular, with their faith in scientific knowledge, had trusted the experts and changed their reaction to tremors: "The social representational notion of the 'energy discharge,' disseminated by the scientific authorities and transformed into common sense, had the highest plausibility among better-educated people, before it all collapsed alongside the buildings. They habitually place trust in scientific opinions communicated in the media."[32] In so doing, he argued, the experts had predicted a non-earthquake and reduced risk perception among Aquilani, reversing local traditions and a culture of caution.

Ciccozzi, the state prosecution, and others grappled with the difficulty of demonstrating that an event—the meeting of the Major Risks Commission—had altered behavior.[33] Even though Ciccozzi admitted in his testimony on April 11, 2012, that no clear cause-effect model of human behavior exists since countless factors are involved in decision-making processes, he nonetheless emphasized the impact of cultural determinism. Others, however, disagreed with Ciccozzi's approach and interpretation.

In a subsequent hearing, an expert in human communication, Mario Morcellini, of Rome's La Sapienza University, rejected Ciccozzi's models of behavioral determinism. As sociologist Federico Brandmayr, who studied the trial closely, observed: "Whereas Ciccozzi emphasized an all-embracing and unsophisticated faith in science, Morcellini stressed the heterogeneous character of modern societies, in which individuals can freely consider different opinions in making their choices."[34] Morcellini refuted Ciccozzi's interpretation—that science had such a high authority that it could condition behavior directionally—and placed the information Aquilani had received about the expert meeting alongside other factors, including media coverage and views reported by friends and families. Causation, Morcellini countered in response to Ciccozzi's testimony, could not be proven.

POLITICAL INTERFERENCE

In addition to illustrating a link between the expert's assessment and individual choices, the state prosecution had to present evidence that the defendants had not conducted their risk analysis properly. Scientists were invited as expert witnesses to scrutinize the statements made by the defendants as reported in two sets of minutes from their meeting and as recalled by session participants. The two meeting transcripts contained inconsistent and generic statements, which the judge later described as "incomplete, imprecise, and contradictory information regarding the nature, the causes, the danger, and the future developments of the seismic activity under consideration."[35] Session participants confirmed that the evaluation had not met the required standards for a thorough and scientific investigation into a concrete risk situation, which had already resulted in evacuations and property damage. In 2009, Cristian Del Pinto was a geophysicist and seismologist who worked for the Civil Protection Agency in the neighboring Molise region. He attended the meeting of the Major Risks Commission in L'Aquila on March 31, 2009, but without contributing to the discussion.[36] In his testimony during the trial, Del Pinto explained to the court that the opinions he heard from the experts had left him bewildered: "It was said that it would be unlikely for events with a magnitude greater than four to occur within a seismic swarm. Someone claimed that the earthquake the previous day [March 30] had already had the maximum intensity. Other events were expected to be of the same magnitude, not stronger. But this was a prediction for the intensity of future tremors, for which no scientific basis existed."[37]

Del Pinto also told the court that the experts had misleadingly defined the swarm as "normal"; "I don't think a swarm is ever normal. It should always be treated as an anomaly." The state prosecutor asked, "This definition of normality, to what would it lead in practical terms?" Del Pinto replied, "The phenomenon could be underestimated."[38] The prosecution thus strove to demonstrate that the experts' assessment of the concrete seismic situation had been generic, not the thorough analysis of all available data that had been required under the circumstances of a concrete risk situation. The state prosecution furthermore presented as evidence an interview given by Enzo Boschi, the former head of the National Institute of Geophysics and Volcanology (INGV) and arguably the most esteemed scientist at the L'Aquila meeting. A few months after the earthquake, Boschi had spoken to a news magazine and confirmed that the March 2009 meeting had not met the standards to which he was accustomed from the Major Risks Commission:

> Ridiculous. In many years, I had never seen such a meeting by the Major Risks Commission. It was over after half an hour, without a written statement. The minutes were only signed on April 6, after the earthquake had struck. I thought we would sit together until the early hours the next morning. In such cases, facing serious events, in one of the highest risk zones in Italy, the Commission can only conclude the meeting after having taken a unanimous decision, put down in a written transcript of the minutes. As far as I could remember, whenever a session had been called in the past because of a specific event, the transcript of the minutes had been signed immediately.[39]

During his hearing in May 2012, Boschi was asked why he had not raised concerns over irregularities in the commission's conduct. Boschi replied, "Look, let me be clear about this. When we have an emergency, the head of the Civil Protection Agency becomes my superior. So, when he calls me and says, 'I want to know this,' I respond. And once the emergency is over, he can get lost."[40]

Boschi referred to the fact that Bertolaso, the head of the Civil Protection Agency, had given the experts instructions before their session. Bertolaso had summoned the experts not to analyze the concrete risk situation, but to calm down concerned Aquilani by discrediting Giuliani's radon-based predictions. A telephone conversation between Bertolaso and his regional Civil Protection Agency coordinator, Stati, which was made public during the trial, showed that

Bertolaso had instructed Stati to organize a media stunt aimed at rubbishing Giuliani with the authority of science. During their phone call, Bertolaso said:

> You have to organize the details for a meeting I have called about this matter with the tremor cluster: to shut up these imbeciles immediately, to stop speculation, anxieties, etc. I am not coming, but Zamberletti [the then president of the commission, who did not participate due to illness], Barberi, Boschi. So basically Italy's greatest experts. I will make them come to L'Aquila as a media stunt [*operazione mediatica*], got it? Then, the greatest earthquake experts will say: this is a normal situation, these are phenomena that happen, it's better to have one hundred tremors with a magnitude four on the Richter scale instead of silence, because these one hundred shocks serve to release energy and so the bad shock, the one that really hurts, will never come. Then, spread the word that the meeting is called not because we are frightened or worried, but because we want to comfort people. And rather than having you and I talk about this, we will let the biggest names in earthquake science speak.[41]

For many Aquilani, the conversation, made public in January 2012, demonstrated that the authorities had not taken seriously local fears; a "media stunt" had been the official response to panic. In the closing statement, the prosecution made reference to this media stunt as evidence that the experts had not behaved as they ought to have done and claimed that their negligent behavior misled and killed Aquilani. Boschi confirmed that instructions to comfort local people had been his overriding concern during the meeting. For Vittorini and others involved, it was the corruption of scientific procedure through political manipulation that had caused suffering. The court case was an immensely complex affair, with numerous statements from witnesses and experts on earth sciences, human communication, and psychology, as well as testimonies from dozens of Aquilani.[42] Nonetheless, in the end, the municipal court reached a clear verdict.

THE JUDGMENT

On October 22, 2012, Judge Billi concluded the case. The seven defendants were each sentenced to six years in prison and barred from holding public office. The plaintiffs were entitled to financial compensation. The charge: criminally negligent manslaughter (*omicidio colposo*). Three months after the verdict, the court published a detailed judgment, the *motivazione*, in which Billi explained the legal reasoning, which followed in large part the state prosecution's indictment. The judge found that the Major Risks Commission had not failed to evaluate the concrete risk situation in L'Aquila on March 30, 2009.

The experts had been instructed by Bertolaso to comfort an anxious population. The members of the commission had followed orders, even though they had noticed irregularities with regard to the commission's usual conduct. In so doing, they had ignored the concrete risk situation affecting the area and its resulting threat to life.

Even if well-intended—and the state prosecution acknowledged this—the media blitz that had the objective of discrediting Giuliani's radon-based predictions had ignored the commission's key responsibilities: the rigorous analysis of risk factors and the provision of clear advice to the Civil Protection Agency. The judge underlined that a press release issued the day before the experts' meeting had announced that the commission would "provide the Abruzzo citizens with all the information available to the scientific community concerning the seismic activity of the past weeks."[43] Aquilani reasonably believed, Judge Billi concluded, that the experts had analyzed their specific situation.

The *motivazione* explained that the experts ought to have examined a concrete risk, which the Civil Protection Agency defines as constituted by three factors: seismic peril, vulnerability of buildings, and human exposure to potential events.[44] The experts' duty would have been to scrutinize these dimensions independently. Their focus on assessing and rejecting claims regarding earthquake forecasting had therefore been negligent. A thorough risk analysis ought to have considered L'Aquila's earthquake history, the judge ruled, as well as the well-known fact that many buildings in the city would not have been able to withstand stronger seismic events—a fateful condition of which at least some of the defendants were acutely aware. The experts had not advised the authorities on how to improve structural stability or devise evacuation plans for vulnerable areas. Such advice, the judge ruled, could have reduced the risk to the population since, at the point of the expert meeting, future tremors had been likely to occur, even though their intensity was unpredictable.

The court located the defendants' guilt in the gap between their broad expertise regarding the various factors constituting a danger for the city of L'Aquila and their generic statements and insufficient communication to the population and the authorities: "What the defendants are accused of is not, with hindsight, the lack of a prediction of an earthquake or the non-evacuation of the city of L'Aquila. The defendants are not punished for their lack of prophecy. Instead, they stand accused of the violation of specific duties concerning the evaluation, forecasting, and prevention of a seismic risk required by the law in force on March 31, 2009, and of the violation of specific duties concerning the provision of clear, correct, and complete information."[45]

The judge confirmed that the earthquake victims had behaved correctly when they followed scientific advice that was later found to have been vague

and misleading. By neglecting their duties regarding forecasting and prevention, the commission's members had failed a citizenry justifiably expecting
a serious analysis. Their negligence revealed an instance of what others have
called the "ineffective national culture of emergency information" in a country
that regularly experiences devastation by natural and other disasters.[46] The
trial of the Major Risks Commission exposed a lack of seriousness and prep-
aration, as well as dangerous collusion between politics and science, which,
the court ruled, had rendered the population more vulnerable. The court case
seemed to achieve the objective desired by Vittorini and others: to define official responsibilities and improve Italian public institutions. It appeared that a
desire to influence social and political realities through legal redress was bearing fruit for the citizens who had served as plaintiffs and witnesses.

Despite the seemingly straightforward verdict, the court case was often a
harrowing experience for the relatives of the earthquake victims: their desires
to commemorate family members and tell their stories clashed with established
patterns of legal practice, such as cross-examination and exposing inconsis-
tency in testimony. Furthermore, the selective inclusion of only some families as plaintiffs by the state prosecution created envy , since the court verdict
entailed significant financial redress for a small fraction of Aquilani. Subsequently, the initial convictions were overturned in the court of appeals, and
the anticipated closure and the improvement of state institutions and public
morality became more complicated.

MEMORY, BIOGRAPHY, AND LEGAL SCRUTINY

Exposing personal pain to public scrutiny in the course of legal proceedings can
have devastating repercussions for the witness. Analyzing women's testimonies
for South Africa's Truth and Reconciliation Commission (TRC), anthropologist Fiona Ross shows that women who testified in hearings regularly found
their memories distorted and exploited. Complexity and nuance were disfig-
ured into sensationalist accounts. Having a voice in legal procedures produces
ambivalent results because "once spoken, claims do not rest but are reworked
and revised in accord with various conventions."[47] Including personal memories in court proceedings exposes intimate recollections to external forces that
can disturb and scar the remembering person.[48] In L'Aquila, too, witnesses and
plaintiffs seeking to turn their suffering into a means for improving state institutions experienced a reworking of recollections. The trial conflated a struggle
for legal recognition as injured parties with commemorative practice. When
legal procedure entered what plaintiffs described as the sacred space of the

family, bereaved relatives were faced with the questioning of, and challenges to, their recollections of the past and their family biographies.[49]

In response to testimonies, the defense invited an expert witness to comment on the capacity of individuals to reconstruct the past after traumatic experiences. Stefano Cappa, a professor of cognitive neuroscience at the University of Pavia, had read witnesses' accounts alongside the press coverage from the commission's meeting. On the morning of Cappa's expert testimony to the court, the atmosphere in the small courtroom was particularly tense. The relatives of the earthquake victims sat on the edges of their chairs. Outlining his scientific expertise on human memory, Cappa calmly explained that the process of remembering was not like a camera: "Memory is a reconstructive process. Our brain reorganizes fragmented information in the cerebral cortex. On the basis of this organization, our brain constructs a story. In all cases, the story then becomes a truth, in which we believe completely."[50]

Cappa further explained the unsaid bias: "This is the tendency to remember selectively all the elements that favor an eventually realized event, simultaneously suppressing aspects that would work in the other direction. This is something we do all the time; we cannot control it, this is simply how our brains work."[51] As Cappa continued, Aquilani plaintiffs in the audience became agitated. Cappa said he considered it unlikely for the statements released by the commission to have altered decades-old instinctive behavior, as plaintiffs had claimed. He argued that people did not behave rationally in exceptional risk situations and that the assumption that scientific expertise could supersede established behavior patterns in a scenario marked by panic was implausible. As Cappa proceeded, Vincenzo Vittorini whispered to me: "I remember what happened, I'm not inventing anything; I *did* feel reassured, otherwise I wouldn't have stayed inside with my wife and daughter, would I?"[52] He also attempted to speak to his lawyer, who gestured to Vittorini to be quiet. Instead, Vittorini started talking to other plaintiffs. As the muttering increased, the judge requested silence. In the session break, Vittorini paced up and down the courtroom before speaking to the assembled reporters: "I know what I remember. I felt reassured. Otherwise I would have left the house, or not? I'm not crazy! I remember what happened that night! You can believe me!"[53]

In his analysis of how legal proceedings affect testifying witnesses, legal scholar Austin Sarat writes that "public scrutiny invades some of the most personal aspects of our lives—the ways we suffer and grieve."[54] In his testimony to the court, delivered a few months before Cappa analyzed survivors' recollections, Vittorini had recalled the decision-making processes that had led him to dismiss his father's childhood advice and his brother's insistence to leave the house. Cappa challenged these recollections, as well as Vittorini's story as an Aquilano who had abandoned a family history of precautionary flight due to expert recommendations. Even though the bereaved relatives might honestly report their recalling of how events had unfolded, Cappa suggested, their memories were not precise. Recounting personal suffering for the purpose of judicial proceedings dislocates memories from the intimacy of the family, friendships, or the local community, in whose presence they would not be subjected to such scrutiny. The trial produced ambivalence; bereaved Aquilani who testified turned into defendants, their memories questioned and their biographies challenged. The gap between popular understandings of the truth and its legal forms disturbed witnesses.[55] Rather than providing a space to commemorate death, the courtroom constrained or at least reordered priorities. The most relevant people in the trial were not the dead nor the bereaved, but the defendants, most of whom did not even attend hearings regularly—unlike the grieving Aquilani.

Surrendering family history to cross-examination created agony. Two months into the court case, Massimo Cinque—the then president of the Fondazione 6 aprile per la vita, which represented relatives of the 309 casualties—expressed his anguish over the court case. Cinque's wife and his two young sons had lost their lives in the earthquake, and he acted as a plaintiff in the case. In an open letter to *Il Centro*, a local paper, which he signed on behalf of the bereaved, he noted the discrepancy between his expectation of a respectful and appropriate treatment of the deceased and the trial's routines:

> We demand respect for our angels and for our city. Being in court during the hearing last Wednesday was another painful experience for me. I will explain. It felt like my three angels (Daniela, Davide, and Matteo), together with the other 306 victims, together with the whole city of L'Aquila, were treated like meat in a slaughterhouse. I had to listen to the words of those who, back then, had been asked to guarantee the safety of the local population. I watched a never-ending blame-shifting, a never-ending tirade of "I don't remember," "I'm not sure," "that was not my responsibility," and on and on like this. Then, of course, the carefree, student dorm atmosphere in the courtroom, with lots of people who had nothing to do with the case—some dodgy characters, neither here nor there—continuously leaving and re-entering the courtroom. It was curious intrusiveness, without any consideration for those who are no longer, and for those who live with never-ending pain. Oh no! This is not how it should be!
>
> Apparently, we are a city—or better, a nation—of mediocre people. Perhaps we deserve being represented by mediocre officials, who keep assuring us that they bear no responsibility, despite the fact that the evidence

is so obvious and glaring that there should not be a need for a court case. I am convinced that everyone knows of his or her responsibility. I wish that the truth will come out and that it will become clear who has acted negligently and failed to do his or her duty with regard to the 309 angels who entered into heaven that night and with regard to an entire city that was betrayed.[56]

One aspect of the trial that Cinque lamented concerned its public character; anyone could enter the courtroom, listen to testimonies, and leave freely. I also found the casual behavior unusual; it was very informal, with members of the public checking their smartphones during testimonies, answering calls at the back of the room, and rushing outside on numerous occasions. The makeshift atmosphere of the temporary courtroom did not provide an appropriate context for intimate commemorative occasions, and Cinque and others were upset by the lack of sobriety and respect. Quips and ironic comments from the state prosecution, the defense, and the judge left them disappointed.[57] As a result, over the course of the trial, fewer and fewer Aquilani with painful memories from the earthquake, including the plaintiffs, attended hearings. For them, the courtroom—with its peculiar routines, arrangements, and practices—became a daunting space and the trial experience added insult to injury and increased frustration with public institutions.

SPLITTING THE COMMUNITY OF MOURNERS

When nonlocal commentators portrayed the court case as the attempt by angry rustics to punish scapegoats, they failed to notice how divisive the trial was for bereaved family members and Aquilani more broadly. While a number of the bereaved professed their goal to exercise a civic duty to address corruption and institutional failure, others had more mundane aspirations. Halfway through the trial, I spoke to an Aquilano who had lost many family members in the earthquake. I call him Domenico. He had not sought to be included in the court case as a plaintiff but told me that other family members had fabricated a story to suggest that the experts had influenced deceased relatives:

> On the night of the earthquake, I spoke with my family on the phone after the two tremors that preceded the fatal one. They didn't mention the Commission and the experts at all. They were just tired and worn out by months of tremors. They could not be bothered to leave their house and sleep elsewhere. That is why they died. The experts made mistakes, but I have no one else to blame but myself for not insisting more, or them, really, because they didn't leave. My in-laws made up this other story [about how the experts

had changed the behavior of the deceased] and told it to the court. They want financial compensation. I haven't spoken to them in a while. I find it horrible that they use our dead family for their own benefit. They are distorting their history for money, but obviously I can't speak up about this. I just don't want to see them again. For me, these people don't exist anymore.[58]

Among a population already divided by recovery experiences, repair speed, and compensation levels—the "war among the poor" of previous chapters—the trial created further fractures. It was important for Domenico to remember and talk about his relatives in a way he found authentic, and so his in-laws' fabrication left him sad and helpless, since he could not challenge them without risking a scandal. In the local papers, Domenico read about testimonies involving his deceased loved ones that he knew were false, producing an incorrect biographical account. Domenico deplored the consequences of the court case: "I know that some people felt calm after the experts' meeting. I know that a lot of Aquilani said they believed the scientists. But I don't know what goes on behind closed doors. My in-laws are lying through their teeth to get their hands on the money. Who knows how many fake stories are told in court? I believe Vittorini. But I am angry that the whole trial is twisting my family history. They are writing an account for the history books that is simply untrue."[59]

On the day of the verdict—October 22, 2012—the small square outside the makeshift *tribunale* was thronging with journalists, reporters, television-crew vans, and curious onlookers. The hectic jostling was in contrast with other hearings over the past year, which had been largely ignored by the nonlocal press. Now, eager for the outcome, dozens of reporters filmed the final statements by the state prosecution, the defense, and the civil parties. The courtroom hosted a media spectacle that would feature in sensationalist news coverage across the world. This was an unprecedented event, many claimed, in the history of Western legal systems and modern science. They would not be disappointed.

Just in time for the European evening news, Judge Billi returned to the packed, silent courtroom. Billi's voice was barely audible at the back of the small container when he delivered the verdict in only a few sentences. The state prosecution had requested four-year prison terms; the judge handed down six years, imposed a ban on holding public office for all seven defendants, and ordered substantial redress. Most people were surprised by the sentence, including bereaved witnesses. Vittorini, Cora, and others had tears in their eyes and embraced one another. Shortly after the verdict, Vittorini commented on the outcome for a television interview. The reporter congratulated him on what he called a victory, but Vittorini rejected the description and instead voiced disappointment:

This trial should have become important for the entire city, but the population kept its distance from the court case. Most Aquilani never came to any hearings. The city did not support us. We had lots of lip service, but no action. L'Aquila remained distant from those fighting for justice and for truth, not for vengeance. That hurts. I hope that everyone will understand eventually that this was done not for revenge or hatred. The court case was necessary to change this country and to avoid seeing others suffer as much as we have suffered. This is what has motivated me, nothing else.[60]

Despite the convictions, witnesses and plaintiffs reported bitterness about the ways in which the trial had become an increasingly lonely battle for remembrance and justice, with most of the local population distant to the proceedings. The trial crystallized one of the most challenging legacies of the disaster and its aftermath: recovery was not collective, but followed different trajectories, with different paces. While some were ready to move on and remake normality at speed, others demanded adequate spaces and rituals for appropriate commemoration.

Immediately after the verdict, the defense announced that it would appeal the judgment, further delaying conclusive legal recognition for the bereaved relatives. In addition, Vittorini and others faced accusations of being privileged mourners. The state prosecution's decision to include some injured parties as plaintiffs and to exclude others who had also asked to be represented by the prosecutors had a divisive effect on the community of mourners. Suffering became the subject of battles over inclusion and legal recognition. One local lawyer, who represented various injured parties, explained this to me:

Unfortunately, less formally educated Aquilani, such as people with only primary school education from the rural villages, were not able to explain what the Major Risks Commission was, or how precisely their friends or relatives had behaved. They simply said: "That's what the experts told us." But in a criminal case culpability has to be proven beyond doubt. These people could not demonstrate that their family members had remained indoors as a consequence of what the experts had told them—that there was nothing to be concerned about. I don't know whether those deceased Aquilani had felt reassured by the experts or not. In any case, it is the style of their relatives' accounts that caused their exclusion from the lawsuit. The law is not fair sometimes, and I know many people who are upset because of this.

Some recollections were not legally convincing because they were not expressed in the kind of language the court would have recognized as evidence. Around thirty families demanded to be included additionally as offended parties, but the state prosecution dismissed them to avoid weakening the indictment. This was painful. Many people came to me and asked if I could help them with my legal expertise, but I could simply explain that the prosecution had to present a persuasive case. The state prosecutor is constrained by legal requirements; he's not a nasty man. But still, many felt that they were left alone with their guilt for stupid legal reasons they couldn't understand. They had to suffer quietly. They did not get the same acknowledgement or space to talk about their pain.[61]

The prosecution also rejected further parties demanding inclusion, aside from those Aquilani who struggled to present a legally convincing narrative. Dozens of earthquake victims were university students who had been born and raised outside L'Aquila. Vittorini or Cora could demonstrate that their families had always behaved in a certain way when faced with seismic tremors, because they had been a constant feature in L'Aquila. For nonlocal residents, this was difficult to demonstrate. The parents of nonlocal students also claimed that their children had mentioned the experts as the reason for their belief that there was no danger. Since these students had only recently moved to L'Aquila, however, their parents were not able to demonstrate that their children had changed a previous routine—namely, to escape and seek shelter. As a result, they were not included as injured parties by the prosecution. A number of parents appealed this decision, and the state prosecutor had to defend their exclusion in a separate hearing. Lawyers representing the bereaved parents accused the prosecution of dividing victims into first-order and second-order deaths, with preferential treatment for local casualties.

After a number of hearings on this matter, L'Aquila's municipal court confirmed the state prosecution's exclusion of nonlocal casualties from the trial, which left bereaved parents unsettled. After the decision to divide the casualties into local and nonlocal cases, the father of a twenty-three-year-old student from a town on the Abruzzo coast, who had studied at the University of L'Aquila and died in the earthquake, told a local newspaper: "We have been abandoned. No help. No psychological support. No tax breaks or financial help. The families of the nonlocal students [who perished in the 2009 earthquake] only got one thing: a coffin. But the ruins are inside our homes. The empty chair at the table still stands there."[62]

French sociologist Pierre Bourdieu called the law "the quintessential form of the symbolic power of naming that creates the things named, and creates social groups in particular. It confers upon the reality which arises from its classificatory operations the maximum permanence that any social reality has the power to confer upon another, the permanence which we attribute to objects."[63] The acknowledgment that the deaths of twenty-nine Aquilani had been caused by the negligent behavior of state institutions and the compensation of the surviving relatives forged a distinctive social group with its specific reality. The judiciary confirmed that some deaths had been caused by state negligence and thus recognized that the deceased and their relatives had behaved correctly and were entitled to both an apology and compensation. This official recognition was withheld from others. The classificatory power of the law that Bourdieu described created a new social group and bestowed on its members a more powerful identity of being innocent and having been wronged by the state. By assuming responsibility for the demise of twenty-nine people, the state left most survivors alone with their sorrow and guilt for the death of other loved ones.

DIFFICULT LEGACIES

During the final months of my fieldwork, Vittorini faced a frustrating setback for his endeavor to reform defective state practices. In January 2013, a series of seismic tremors occurred in the Italian region of Tuscany. In response, the National Institute of Geophysics and Volcanology (INGV) issued a warning to the Civil Protection Agency that a new fault line could open during the following twenty-four hours. The national government passed on this information to local mayors, who advised citizens to leave their houses and stay outside until the danger had subsided. Thousands of people hastily abandoned their homes and slept in their cars or in evacuation areas set up by the authorities.

Eventually, no strong tremors occurred. After twenty-four hours, the authorities retracted their warnings and people returned home. Commenting on the evacuations, the new head of the Civil Protection Agency, Franco Gabrielli, called the situation "the poisonous fruit of the L'Aquila judgment."[64] He acknowledged that the mayors had acted with the best of intentions when they advised their citizens to leave their homes but also emphasized that earthquake tremors were common across Italy. He warned of disruptive consequences if voluntary evacuations became a new standard reaction to seismic events, which in the majority of cases did not cause damage. Gabrielli described the L'Aquila court case as a watershed moment that increased panic, since the authorities now feared criminal prosecution as a result of inaction. In L'Aquila, many interpreted the authorities' reactions positively. The mayor, Cialente, criticized Gabrielli for his statements about the court case's legacy. He told reporters that he would have acted the same way. A few days later, I met Vittorini. He was furious about Gabrielli's remarks: "Instead of talking about a 'poisonous fruit,' Gabrielli should call it 'an act of civilization that has its origins in L'Aquila. We have learnt from what went wrong in L'Aquila.' It is so important that mistakes will not be repeated, and the head of the Civil Protection Agency speaks about a poisonous fruit. I cannot believe this is happening. What did we fight for?"[65]

Gabrielli's comments illustrated that key officials continued to misunderstand the ramifications of the court case. The October 2012 convictions did not bring closure for the bereaved. Two years after the first verdict, the Abruzzo Court of Appeals overturned the initial sentences. Six defendants were acquitted. Only De Bernardinis received a reduced two-year prison sentence because of his remarks about the supposedly positive energy discharge. In their detailed judgment, published in February 2015, the Court of Appeals judges held De Bernardinis responsible for the misleading pronouncements. The judges underlined that a proper session of the Major Risks Commission would have required the participation of at least ten members. Thus, the session in L'Aquila had not been a meeting by the Major Risks Commission, but simply a gathering of experts without any responsibility for risk prevention. Unlike the experts, De Bernardinis, then the deputy director of the Civil Protection Agency, was punished for his negligent conduct as a state official. This decision was upheld by Italy's highest court, the Court of Cassation, which pronounced definitively on the matter in autumn 2015.

Whereas the first court case had permitted bereaved Aquilani to tell their stories, the second and third instances evaluated the quality of the original judgment and evidence. When the three judges in the Court of Appeals read out the verdict, the bereaved relatives sitting in the courtroom were outraged and shouted, "Shame on you!" In the days following the acquittal, as metropolitan and international commentators voiced relief, some bereaved Aquilani organized protests in the historic city center. They called their events "Justice for L'Aquila" or "Truth and Justice: Communal Sit-In," but only a few hundred people attended. There was decreasing interest in the case and its ramifications. The explanations offered by Ciccozzi, the local anthropologist who had suggested that the superior authority of the scientists had induced behavior change, were also torn apart. Both courts rejected his reasoning and asserted that Ciccozzi, as an anthropologist and earthquake survivor, had already expressed his views on the scientists' culpability in a newspaper article in 2010, therefore casting doubt on the objectivity regarding his subsequent analysis.

Ciccozzi published a defense of his methodology of knowledge production in an Italian anthropology journal in which he criticized the courts for their narrow-minded obsession with the "hard sciences" and their particular approach to presenting empirical evidence. He was frustrated and complained about a "systematic process against me personally that in many ways resembled a degradation ritual, that is, a practice that essentially involves redefining the social identity of an individual by lowering his or her social status."[66] This struggle for honest coverage and recognition for local experiences has been a constant feature of post-disaster life in L'Aquila.

For an important group of bereaved Aquilani, the court case constituted a key aspect of how survivors envisioned recovery: an act by responsible citizens. Some of them made explicit reference to their goal of transforming the country's public administration. David Alexander, an authority on the trial, has called it "a brave and concerted attempt to restore seriousness to the judicial system, bring morality back into public life and redefine the role of science in the management of hazards in Italy."[67] Most outsiders, however, saw and misrepresented these "brave" Aquilani as irrational and vindictive witch hunters.

The court case disappointed expectations because of its irreconcilable objectives. For bereaved relatives, the trial was an opportunity to honor deceased family members. What the bereaved might have regarded as "their" trial was reordered on other levels as some of Italy's most seasoned legal professionals picked apart testimonies and memories. The condemning international reactions removed the court case further from the original desire to tell local stories of loss and suffering. As a consequence, the court case shifted between incommensurate levels: the intimacy of family life and grief, national law and the requirements of legal evidence, and metropolitan Italian and international interventions and their defense of science. In most coverage, there was no recognition for the efforts and motivations professed by the plaintiffs. Instead, the case's inclusions and exclusions, made necessary by the requirements of legal evidence, created new categories of mourners. Only those with the capacity to present elegant and persuasive narratives could expect recognition. Envisioned as a process of writing earthquake history, defending the memory of the dead, and improving public morality and institutions as a way of finding meaning in suffering, the court case produced a more complicated legacy, mixing partial recognition with ongoing misrepresentation and exclusion.

NOTES

1. See Stuart Clark, "From Galileo to the L'Aquila Earthquake: Italian Science on Trial," *The Guardian*, October 24, 2012, accessed August 1, 2017, https://www.theguardian.com/science/across-the-universe/2012/oct/24/galileo -laquila-earthquake-italian-science-trial; and Warner Marzocchi, "Putting Science on Trial," *Physics World* (December 2012): 18–19.

2. David E. Alexander, "Communicating Earthquake Risks to the Public: The Trial of the "L'Aquila Seven," *Natural Hazards* 72 (2014): 1159–1173.

3. See Sarah Annunziato, "Knox Case Has Put the Italian Legal System on Trial in the US," The Conversation, January 30, 2014, accessed November 10, 2020, https://theconversation.com/knox-case-has-put-the-italian-legal-system-on-trial-in-the-us-22606.

4. On ritualized mourning and community-making see, for example, Sarah Farmer, *Martyred Village: Commemorating the 1944 Massacre in Oradour-sur-Glane* (Berkeley: University of California Press, 1999); Katherine Verdery, *The Political Lives of Dead Bodies: Reburial and Postsocialist Change, The Harriman Lectures* (New York: Columbia University Press, 1999); Veena Das, *Life and Worlds: Violence and the Descent into the Ordinary* (Berkeley: University of California Press, 2006); Heonik Kwon, *After the Massacre: Commemoration and Consolation in Ha My and My Lai* (Berkeley: University of California Press, 2006); and Kwon, *Ghosts of War in Vietnam* (Cambridge: Cambridge University Press, 2008).

5. Mary Gearin, "Italian Scientists Convicted for Failing to Predict Quake," ABC News, October 22, 2012, accessed August 1, 2017, http://www.abc.net .au/news/2012-10-23/italian-scientists-convicted-over-earthquake-warning /4328046.

6. Fox News, "Italian Court Convicts 7 Scientists for Failing to Predict Earthquake," October 22, 2012, accessed August 1, 2017, http://www.foxnews .com/science/2012/10/22/italian-court-convicts-7-scientists-for-failing-to -predict-earthquake/.

7. Michael Day, "Italian Scientists Jailed for Six Years after Failing to Issue Warnings Ahead of Deadly L'Aquila Earthquake," *The Independent*, October 22, 2012, accessed August 1, 2017, http://www.independent.co.uk/news/world /europe/italian-scientists-jailed-for-six-years-after-failing-to-issue-warnings -ahead-of-deadly-laquila-earthquake-8221905.html.

8. Lizzy Davies, "Jailing of Italian Seismologists Leaves Scientific Community in Shock," *The Guardian*, October 23, 2012, accessed August 1, 2017, https://www.theguardian.com/world/2012/oct/23/jailing-italian-seismologists -scientific-community.

9. Clark, "From Galileo to the L'Aquila Earthquake."

10. *Nature*, "Shock and Law," October 23, 2012, accessed August 1, 2017, http:// www.nature.com/news/shock-and-law-1.11643.

11. Edwin Cartlidge, "Aftershocks in the Courtroom," *Science* 338, no. 6104 (2012): 184–188.

12. Alan I. Leshner, "Open Letter," AAAS, June 29, 2010, accessed March 20, 2021, https://www. https://www.aaas.org/sites/default/files/s3fs-public/10_06 _29earthquakelettertopresidentnapolitano.pdf[o].

13. Jordi Prats, "The L'Aquila Earthquake: Science or Risk on Trial?," *Significance* 9, no. 6 (2012): 13–16.

14. Carlo [pseud.], in discussion with the author, L'Aquila, Italy, December 2, 2012.

15. Giovani [pseud.], in discussion with the author, L'Aquila, Italy, July 11, 2012.

16. After the earthquake on April 6, 2009, the investigations were dropped. In the post-disaster confusion, many papers depicted Giuliani as a maverick genius who had correctly predicted the L'Aquila earthquake, even though his forecast had concerned another place and a different time. Giuliani used the publicity to promote his new amateur earthquake science foundation (http:// www.fondazionegiuliani.it). See John Dollar, "The Man Who Predicted an Earthquake," *The Guardian*, April 5, 2010, accessed August 1, 2017, https://www .theguardian.com/world/2010/apr/05/laquila-earthquake-prediction-giampaolo -giuliani; and Nick Squires and Gordon Rayner, "Italian Earthquake: Expert's Warnings Were Dismissed as Scaremongering," *The Daily Telegraph*, April 6, 2009, accessed August 1, 2017, http://www.telegraph.co.uk/news/worldnews /europe/italy/5114139/Italian-earthquake-experts-warnings-were-dismissed-as -scaremongering.html.

17. Tribunale di L'Aquila, Motivazione, Sezione Penale: n.253/10 R.G.N.R, n. 1497/10 R.G.G.I.P, n. 448/11 R.D.Dib., n. 380/12 R, Sent, L'Aquila: Tribunale di L'Aquila (2013), 3.

18. The official name is National Commission for the Forecast and Prevention of Major Risks (Commissione Nazionale per la Previsione e la Prevenzione dei Grandi Rischi). When the experts convened on March 31, 2009, the commission's role was defined as follows: "The National Commission for the Forecast and Prevention of Major Risks serves as an organ of the National Civil Protection Agency. It is both an advisory body and an active organ [*organo consultivo e propositivo*] concerning all civil protection activities with regard to the forecasting and the prevention of various risk possibilities [*ipotesi di rischio*]. The Commission provides necessary guidelines for the definition of exigencies concerning civil protection study and research, proceeds to examine the data provided by authorized institutions and organizations regarding caution [*vigilanza*] toward events defined by the present law, to assess related risks and resulting interventions, and to examine all other questions concerning activities referred to by this law." (Tribunale di L'Aquila, Motivazione, 70-71). This definition was changed in 2011, in light of the L'Aquila court case (Dipartimento della Protezione Civile 2011).

19. Of those seven, only four were nominal full members of the Major Risks Commission: Barberi, Boschi, Calvi, and Eva. During the court case, the state prosecution argued that the other three had been acting members by virtue of their presence and their expertise. In the initial trial, the judge accepted this argument, and all seven defendants received the same sentence as a result. This was later overturned during the appeals process.

20. Tribunale di L'Aquila, Motivazione, 96.

21. Tribunale di L'Aquila, Motivazione, 96. This interview was given before the session had started, which suggests that the outcome and recommendations had been predetermined politically by Bertolaso, the head of the Civil Protection Agency, as the court case confirmed.

22. The 10:48 p.m. tremor on April 5, 2009, had a magnitude of 4.0 (Richter scale). The 12:39 a.m. tremor measured 3.5. The strongest previous quake in the swarm had occurred on March 30, measuring 4.1 on the Richter scale. Intensity appeared to be decreasing.

23. Vincenzo Vittorini, in discussion with the author, L'Aquila, Italy, May 30, 2012.

24. Fabio Picuti, in discussion with the author, L'Aquila, Italy, December 5, 2012.

25. In addition to the twenty-nine casualties, the state prosecution also included five Aquilani as injured parties, as they suffered from post-traumatic stress disorder.

26. Umberto [pseud.], in discussion with the author, L'Aquila, Italy, May 16, 2012.

27. Maurizio Cora, during a public hearing for the case Repubblica Italiana In Nome Del Popolo Italiano contro BARBERI Franco, DE BERNARDINIS Bernardo, BOSCHI Enzo, SELVAGGI Giulio, CALVI Gian Michele, EVA Claudio, DOLCE Mauro, N. 253/2010 R.G.N.R. N., Tribunale di L'Aquila, L'Aquila, Italy, November 30, 2011. (Subsequently 'Italy vs. Barberi et al.').

28. Maurizio Cora, during a public hearing for the case Italy vs. Barberi et al., L'Aquila, Italy, November 30, 2011.

29. Maurizio Cora, during a public hearing for the case Italy vs. Barberi et al., L'Aquila, Italy, November 30, 2011.

30. Vincenzo Vittorini, during a public hearing for the case Italy vs. Barberi et al., L'Aquila, Italy, November 30, 2011.

31. Antonello Ciccozzi, *Parola di Scienza: Il terremoto dell'Aquila e la Commissione Grandi Rischi. Un'analisi antropologica* (Rome: DeriveApprodi, 2013).

32. Ibid., 118.

33. The importance of scientific knowledge in Western societies, whose citizens rely increasingly on experts and their interpretations of the world, has been studied across academic disciplines. See Karin Knorr Cetina, *The Manufacture of Knowledge: An Essay on the Constructivist and Contextual Nature of Science* (Oxford: Pergamon, 1981); Knorr Cetina, *Epistemic Cultures: How the Sciences Make Knowledge* (Cambridge, MA: Harvard University Press, 1999); Steven G. Brint, *In an Age of Experts: The Changing Role of Professionals in Politics and Public Life* (Princeton, NJ: Princeton University Press, 1994); and Harry

Collins and Robert Evans, *Rethinking Expertise* (Chicago: University of Chicago Press, 2007).

34. Federico Brandmayr, "How Social Scientists Make Causal Claims in Court: Evidence from the L'Aquila Trial," *Science, Technology & Human Values* 42, no. 3 (2017): 346–380.

35. Tribunale di L'Aquila, Motivazione, 2.

36. The Molise region shares a border with Abruzzo and was affected by the earthquake swarm tremors. Its regional Civil Protection Agency branch sent Del Pinto to report on the scientists' findings.

37. Cristian Del Pinto, during a public hearing for the case Italy vs. Barberi et al., L'Aquila, Italy, December 7, 2011.

38. Exchange between the state prosecution and Cristian Del Pinto, during a public hearing for the case Italy vs. Barberi et al., L'Aquila, Italy, December 7, 2011.

39. Manuela Bonaccorsi, "Verbali Volant," *Left*, December 11, 2009.

40. Enzo Boschi, during a public hearing for the case Italy vs. Barberi et al., L'Aquila, Italy, May 30, 2012.

41. In March 2009, Bertolaso's phone conversations were recorded on behalf of the Florence state prosecutor's office, which was investigating possible corruption in construction projects for Italy's G8 summit, managed by the Civil Protection Agency. In 2010, Bertolaso resigned under pressure. The recording became relevant during the court proceedings in L'Aquila. The recording is available at: Giuseppe Caporale, "Bertolaso e il terremoto: 'Sia un'operazione mediatica'," *La Repubblica*, January 17, 2012, accessed May 15, 2021. https://video.repubblica.it/le-inchieste/bertolaso-e-il-terremoto-sia-un-operazione-mediatica/85961/84350.

42. As Michael Yeo has argued, responses to the case can be channeled into four main interpretations. The first one was the anti-science interpretation suggesting that Italians and the judicial system used scientists as a scapegoat to overcome guilt. The second line of interpretation focused on insufficient science communication, with experts choosing registers that laypeople cannot understand. The third interpretation regards the confusion of roles, with the experts not being clear about their responsibility as scientists and government advisors. The fourth one highlights the "conflation of science and politics," with experts bowing to political pressure. See Michael Yeo, "Fault Lines at the Interface of Science and Policy: Interpretative Responses to the Trial of Scientists in L'Aquila," *Earth-Science Reviews* 139 (2014): 406–419.

43. Tribunale di L'Aquila, Motivazione, 93.

44. Tribunale di L'Aquila, Motivazione, 262–264.

45. Tribunale di L'Aquila, Motivazione, 304.

46. Mara Benadusi, "The Earth Will Tremble? Expert Knowledge Confronted after the 2009 L'Aquila Earthquake," *Archivio Antropologico Mediterraneo Online* 18, no. 2 (2016): 17–31.

47. Fiona C. Ross, *Bearing Witness: Women and the Truth and Reconciliation Commission in South Africa* (London: Pluto Books, 2003), 10.

48. See, for example, John M. Conley and William M. O'Barr, *Just Words: Law, Language, and Power* (Chicago: University of Chicago Press, 1998); Richard A. Wilson, *The Politics of Truth and Reconciliation in South Africa: Legitimizing the Post-Apartheid State* (Cambridge: Cambridge University Press, 2001); Brandon Hamber and Wilson, "Symbolic Closure through Memory, Reparation and Revenge in Post-Conflict Societies," *Journal of Human Rights* 1, no. 1 (2002): 35–53; and Priscilla Hayner, *Unspeakable Truths: Transitional Justice and the Challenge of Truth Commissions* (New York: Routledge, 2002).

49. See also Mindie Lazarus-Black, "Law and the Pragmatics of Inclusion: Governing Domestic Violence in Trinidad and Tobago," *American Ethnologist* 28, no. 2 (2001): 388–416.

50. Stefano Cappa, during a public hearing for the case Italy vs. Barberi et al., L'Aquila, Italy, May 16, 2012.

51. Stefano Cappa, during a public hearing for the case Italy vs. Barberi et al., L'Aquila, Italy, May 16, 2012.

52. Vincenzo Vittorini, in discussion with the author, L'Aquila, Italy, May 16, 2012.

53. Vincenzo Vittorini, talking to journalists in court, L'Aquila, Italy, May 16, 2012.

54. Austin Sarat, "Vengeance, Victims, and the Identities of Law," in *Law and Anthropology*, ed. Martha Mundy (Burlington, VT: Ashgate, 2002), 348.

55. On the tension between legal and popular ideas of "truth," see Denis Patterson, *Law and Truth* (Oxford: Oxford University Press, 1999).

56. The letter appeared in L'Aquila's *Il Centro* newspaper on December 10, 2011.

57. On the disappointing form of legal discourse for injured parties, see also Conley and O'Barr, *Rules versus Relationships: The Ethnography of Legal Discourse* (Chicago: University of Chicago Press, 1990); and Pierre Bourdieu, "The Force of Law: Toward a Sociology of the Juridical Field," in *Law and Anthropology*, Mundy (Burlington, VT: Ashgate, 2002).

58. Domenico [pseud.], in discussion with the author, L'Aquila, Italy, February 10, 2013.

59. Domenico [pseud.], in discussion with the author, L'Aquila, Italy, February 10, 2013.

60. Vincenzo Vittorini, talking to a journalist, overheard by the author, L'Aquila, Italy, October 22, 2012.

61. Francesca [pseud.], in discussion with the author, L'Aquila, Italy, November 10, 2012.

62. Matteo Ricevuto, "L'Aquila 5 anni dopo/I morti di serie A e quelli di serie B," Globalist, March 15, 2014, accessed March 20, 2021. https://www.globalist.it /world/2016/05/08/l-aquila-5-anni-dopo-i-morti-di-serie-a-e-quelli-di-serie-b -55700.html[o].

63. Bourdieu, "The Force of Law," 142.

64. Il Centro, "Paura in Garfagnana, Gabrielli: frutto avvelenato dell'Aquila,' February 1, 2013, accessed May 15, 2021. https://www.ilcentro.it/l-aquila/paura -in-garfagnana-gabrielli-frutto-avvelenato-dell-aquila-1.1167731.

65. Vincenzo Vittorini, in discussion with the author, L'Aquila, Italy, February 14, 2013.

66. Ciccozzi, "Forms of Truth in the Trial Against the Commission for Major Risks: Anthropological Notes," *Archivio Antropologico Mediterraneo on line* 18, no. 2 (2017): 65–81 (footnote 33).

67. Alexander, "Communicating Earthquake Risks to the Public," 1171.

EIGHT

—ɯ—

CONCLUSION

A Future for L'Aquila

THIS BOOK HAS EXPLORED POLITICS, democratic life, and civic engagement under exceptional circumstances. In post-disaster L'Aquila, politics became closely entwined with other aspects of local existence: cultural work and storytelling, commemoration and public memory, architecture and urban design, the legal system, and grassroots associationism. These are all facets of the pathway toward *recupero* (recovery). The spectrum of diverse engagements and aspirations illustrates the grit and determination to regain self-control across a citizenry experiencing displacement, disenfranchisement, and division.

At the origin of the analysis lies one of Italy's most devastating postwar natural disasters, the 2009 L'Aquila earthquake. Media coverage of the event captivated television audiences across and beyond Italy, giving the city's destruction more airtime than previous comparable earthquakes. The country's then prime minister, Silvio Berlusconi, came to the city dozens of times after the destruction, bringing attention and television crews to the Abruzzo region. World leaders visited the area during the July 2009 G8 summit, and the pope and Hollywood celebrities comforted survivors. The earthquake became a celebrity catastrophe that garnered global attention through Italian show politics and the willingness of many in the press and the media to become complicit in the misrepresentation—some would say exploitation—of suffering and victimhood. The effects of often heavy-handed government interventionism and an unprecedented media frenzy against the backdrop of the city's ruins were complex; they included, initially, significant expectations regarding recovery and a return to some form of normal life, as well as

226

subsequent disappointment and disorientation when promises were broken and recovery plans abandoned.

As a consequence of uneven political attention, three to four years after the earthquake, survivors struggled with the social impact of increasingly divergent recovery experiences. This local situation was further exacerbated by the financial crisis of the late 2000s and the eurozone crisis of the early 2010s, which also saw frequent government changes in Italy. Misunderstanding and envy led to division—a "war among the poor"—and frustration with the ongoing ruination of the old center. Fragmentation and estrangement chipped away at the vision of a shared purpose, and agreement on the kind of routines and lives people wanted after the earthquake was difficult to achieve. I have sought to document the less well-known implications of a natural disaster and the peculiar state response that followed it, which many of my contacts described as a second earthquake. Top-down management and the pursuit of prestige projects, rather than conclusive restoration and repair strategies involving grassroots participation and public consultation, complicated recovery processes.

In the aftermath of the catastrophe, the state initially was an overbearing—possibly authoritarian—player before turning into a passive bystander. Groups of Aquilani responded in different ways both to the interventionism that characterized the immediate aftermath and to subsequent disinterest. Their approaches to civic culture are revealing. They illustrate how statecraft in the latter phases of berlusconismo—characterized by a hard hand, media spectacle, and a lack of support for projects put forward by citizens' initiatives—shaped conflicts over resources and recovery priorities. In response, the visions of active citizenship that I found shared a number of objectives: to regain control over local lives after an invasive state intervention and media misrepresentation; to shape reconstruction, in the old city in particular, and build stronger connections among different quarters of the urban territory; to find avenues for participation and grassroots engagement for diverse local interest groups; to reverse isolation and fragmentation resulting from uneven pathways marking possible returns to "normality"; to increase understanding for disparate recovery visions and experiences through opportunities for exchange and empathetic storytelling that could create a shared experience; to correct state mismanagement and increase public morality; and to instill hope for a better future and for reconciliation.

Andrea Muehlebach has written about the state's retreat from care and protection in neoliberal Italy.[1] She shows how new moral economies succeed in naturalizing the rollback of welfare and security, leaving social responsibilities in the increasingly busy hands of citizens and civil society. In the wake of the government intervention and subsequent state retreat that many Aquilani experienced, numerous voices nonetheless emphasized that responsibility for reconstruction and recovery lay with the authorities—while simultaneously demanding opportunities for local input. Vincenzo Vittorini's L'Aquila che vogliamo platform, as well as the initiative Fondazione 6 aprile per la vita, insisted that the reconstruction of urban heritage must follow high anti-seismic engineering standards and be supervised by the state. Appello per L'Aquila and other grassroots activists stressed that public institutions committed to democratic life ought to practice transparency and accountability. Not least in the wake of the death of Rocco Pollice, survivors demanded that the state care more for people's mental health, broadening the vision of recovery beyond a narrow material focus on resettling and repair. There was widespread consensus that heritage reconstruction in the centro storico ought to be considered a moral, political, and financial duty for the Italian state—again flanked by local involvement and public consultation. Furthermore, the trial of the Major Risks Commission revealed an expectation that experts working in tandem with state agencies ought to provide genuine scientific knowledge and advice during crises; in the case of dangerous political interference, courts must right wrongs and encourage the exercise of civic duty on the part of citizens who seek to improve public institutions.

All of these activities were facets of the new types of civic culture and political behavior with which different Aquilani experimented, as citizens without a city. The literature on political identity in Italy has often emphasized the concept of *campanilismo* to explain attitudes regarding civic culture.[2] The term describes a predominantly local identity and a location of civic interest that references a village's or quarter's bell tower, *campanile*. It has been suggested that such parochialism hinders the development of a national identity or national civic culture.[3] The new civic cultures that emerged in post-disaster L'Aquila were predominantly local in scope. More importantly, they showed how care about one's city, and indeed its historical bell towers, could become entangled with wider political objectives; the local activities I have described also communicated claims regarding the state to guarantee participation, transparency, and better recovery efforts, including the admission and correction of errors and the improvement of public morality. L'Aquila's active citizens showed concern for their urban neighborhoods but also reflected on the ways in which the citizenry and their state institutions—on local, regional, and national levels—should interact. In this vein, my friends suggested that the transformations they were experiencing in L'Aquila encapsulated what others were seeing across Italy more broadly: manipulative or absent state institutions, growing envy and social estrangement, and the emergence of new forms of grassroots attempts to reverse pessimism and decline and to improve the relations between Italian citizens and their public institutions with a view to rendering the latter more responsive to the citizenry.

In a way, this is also a story of at least two cities. In L'Aquila, there was resignation, envy, and frustration, on which I focus predominantly in the first half of the book, but also a host of innovative activities and powerful ambitions to confront fragmentation and misunderstanding, some of which I outlined in the second half. Ideas regarding citizenship—of the relevant civic culture and political behavior—played important roles in both experiences of the earthquake aftermath and visions for the future. I have sought to sketch divisive and difficult debates on the one hand and attempts to provide spaces for reconciliation and understanding on the other. As I have shown, attempts to reconstitute a sense of solidarity were not always successful; the forces of division in the aftermath of a badly managed disaster, which led to crosscutting hierarchies, misunderstanding, and rivalries, were difficult to overcome.

This is, therefore, not a happy story of closure and social peace, but rather an open-ended account of the numerous, and often concealed, tensions that can exacerbate a situation of crisis as the result of both failed governance and an unwillingness to empathize with the pain, experiences, or views of others. I do not seek to condemn egoism or envy but instead aim to highlight some of the difficulties in remaking an urban community in a highly politicized post-disaster context. L'Aquila's citizens, barred from their city, struggled to identify as a citizenry with shared goals. Laudable and innovative attempts by grassroots activists to overcome division and envy provided spaces of hope and reasons for optimism, but they could not easily reverse the wider, pernicious trends of bitter estrangement.

TEN YEARS LATER

I write these lines in the spring of 2021. When I last returned to L'Aquila, in late 2019, approaching the city on the highway from Rome, I saw a forest of cranes topping the terracotta roofs of the centro storico. Along the main street of the old center, the *corso*, construction sites and a large number of recently restored buildings signaled change. A number of fine buildings had been restored, particularly in the areas flanking the central axis of the old city. Lively colors on brand-new facades, cables waiting to be connected, and stickers on freshly installed windowpanes announced the completion of building projects. A dozen restaurants, bars, and shops had reopened, including a famous ice-cream parlor on the market square, Piazza Duomo. Its tables, placed outside in the shade of the still-inaccessible cathedral, were occupied. On Piazza Regina Margherita, Luca's pub was now closed, and restoration had started; he had reopened his business in a significantly larger venue, a beautifully repaired building on a nearby street. At least economically, Luca was doing better. Nevertheless, he told me that fewer than one hundred businesses had reopened in the old city; before the earthquake, there had been over one thousand.

Outside the city center, the renovation of postwar areas was proceeding faster. Modern postwar condominiums looked fresh and comfortable and in many places were connected with new roads and roundabouts. As a result of such progress, a number of apartments in the Progetto Case resettlement sites were now empty. Aquilani wondered about their future usefulness, since it had become apparent that they would not be transformed into Europe's largest university campus, despite such promises made by the now former mayor Massimo Cialente. Instead, my friends already saw them as the next set of ruins decaying in the periphery. The project, once hailed as an unprecedented and generous rehousing initiative, had outlived its purpose ten years after completion. The repair of old city streets and postwar neighborhoods revealed how short-sighted the massive construction undertaking, which included the addition of apartments for sixteen thousand people to a shrinking city, had been. As in many other parts of Italy, post-disaster property speculation, enabled by emergency legislation, left behind more uninhabited urban wastelands.

The apparent material recovery hid a more complex picture of an uneven return to pre-disaster normality. There were still many streets and squares in L'Aquila's historic neighborhoods that had not changed since I left the city in 2013. Mold and political disinterest continued to wreck abandoned buildings. There were heaps of debris overgrown with shrubs in hidden corners, and gaping holes in semi-collapsed roofs still allowed rain to damage structures further. Most of the newly restored buildings in the old center remained empty; few people lived behind the spotless facades. Trucks and lorries meandering through narrow lanes threw dust into the air all day. Construction workers were shouting in Italian dialects and foreign tongues. Noise from drilling and hammering was ubiquitous. "Would you want to live in such a half-city?" a friend asked me rhetorically.[4] Many Aquilani seemed to answer in the negative.

People were waiting for works to be completed; schools and public buildings remained in a state of disrepair. Some of my interlocutors were certain that the stasis had lasted so long that even promising piecemeal signs of change could not alter their cynical outlook. Although there were now traces of "normal" activity in a few parts of the old center, thousands of local residents had left the city for good—particularly young people and their families—and had spent years building new lives elsewhere. They would not return soon. Many of these Aquilani nevertheless used government funding to reconstruct damaged properties, which remain vacant, waiting for tenants in a city with, ironically enough, now too many buildings available for a dwindling number of inhabitants. In other parts of the most damaged areas, people continue to live in supposedly temporary housing modules, erected over ten years ago, free of charge. Residents complain about mice, mold, and other signs of decay in the prefabricated wooden housing units, but they cannot afford to rent elsewhere while their homes are awaiting reconstruction.

Since renovation still proceeds in slow and inconsistent fashion, with a focus on construction around the central axis in old town L'Aquila and with future funding uncertain, the city will remain a noisy construction site for many years. Brand-new apartments will continue to contrast with abandonment. The temporal and provisional linger on and affect those trying to carve out a new life in the city. Perhaps entrenched cynicism has become one of the most powerful effects of disaster mismanagement and the social divisions resulting from a botched and uneven recovery process. By 2020, the state had already spent eighteen billion euros on the emergency intervention and subsequent recovery projects, with 30 percent of the private building stock still awaiting reconstruction or repair in the city of L'Aquila and 50 percent across settlements outside the municipality.[5] Then, the COVID-19 pandemic halted the recovery process again. For months, building sites were closed, creating more uncertainty regarding the future of the reconstruction process.

In June 2017, the city had changed the local administration. The mayor in charge since 2007, Cialente, could not run for a third term. The candidate intended as his heir, Americo Di Benedetto, leading a center-left coalition as an independent, lost to Pierluigi Biondi, a center-right politician. Turnout was high. Biondi's coalition included far-right groups, such as the anti-immigration platform Noi con Salvini. The tight outcome—53.5 percent for Biondi versus 46.5 percent for Di Benedetto—revealed ambivalence about the correct response to stasis. In the days after the vote, left-of-center Aquilani were exasperated that a candidate supported by the far right had secured so many votes. A video clip shared on social media showed Biondi supporters at a victory rally using the Roman salute, the signature gesture of neofascists. Appello per L'Aquila and L'Aquila che vogliamo, the two civic platforms that were headed by Ettore Di Cesare and Vittorini, respectively, had now joined forces to present one candidate for the office of mayor, Carla Cimoroni. She only gained 6.3 percent of the vote and became a city councillor on the opposition benches. Vittorini and Di Cesare were not reelected to the city council. Their platforms had lost steam.

L'Aquila's future remains uncertain over a decade since the earthquake struck the city. My friends lament that changing local representatives is unlikely to alter their situation. The interplay involving municipal, regional, and national authorities is complex, and they agree that national oversight and resources are needed in order to move the city forward more quickly. While the government remains committed to repairing the city and most of its hinterland, the long delays might mean that many who have left will not return. Experiments with new kinds of civic culture and political behavior constituted important pockets of resilience and attempts at reconciliation, but the unevenness of recovery, for which the state and its particular emergency response and initial lack of long-term strategies are responsible, appears to have had a long-lasting impact on L'Aquila's citizens, who are, in many respects, still without their city.

At the same time, as a local historian told me, this is not without historical precedent: "After the earthquake in 1703, Aquila was first depopulated before new people moved in and rebuilt the town. Perhaps such change is the only constant in our history, as frustrating as it is for those living through the period of renewal."[6] L'Aquila's municipal colors are still black and green; because where there is destruction, as well as active and committed citizens, there is also hope.

NOTES

1. Andrea Muehlebach, *The Moral Neoliberal: Welfare and Citizenship in Italy* (Chicago: University of Chicago Press, 2012).

2. See Herman Tak, "Changing Campanilismo: Localism and the Use of Nicknames in a Tuscan Mountain Village," *Ethnologia Europaea* XVIII (1988): 149–160; Tak, "Longing for Local Identity: Intervillage Relations in an Italian Mountain Area," *Anthropological Quarterly* 63, no. 2 (1990): 90–100; and Tak, *Feste in Italia meridionale. Rituali e trasformazioni in una storia locale* (Potenza: Edizioni Ermes, 2000).

3. See, for example, Gene Brucker, *Living on the Edge in Leonardo's Florence: Selected Essays* (Berkeley: University of California Press, 2005); and Eamonn Canniffe, *The Politics of the Piazza: The History and Meaning of the Italian Square* (Aldershot, UK: Ashgate, 2008).

4. Riccardo [pseud.], in discussion with the author, L'Aquila, Italy, September 14, 2019.

5. Stefania Alessandrini, "L'Aquila 2009–2020: a che punto siamo con la ricostruzione," Ingenio, June 4, 2020, accessed November 18, 2020, https://www.ingenio-web.it/26478-laquila-2009-2020-a-che-punto-siamo-con-la-ricostruzione.

6. Ettore [pseud.], in discussion with the author, L'Aquila, Italy, July 10, 2012.

BIBLIOGRAPHY

Abruzzo24Ore. 2009. "Niente allarmismo, i terremoti non sono previdibili,"
April 1. Accessed August 1, 2017. http://www.abruzzo24ore.tv/news/Niente
-allarmismo-i-terremoti-non-sono-prevedibili/10340.htm.

AbruzzoWeb. 2012. "Terremoto: Sgarbi, 'In Emilia ricostruzione rapida, all'Aquila
si piange adosso,'" May 5. Accessed August 12, 2017. http://www.abruzzoweb
.it/contenuti/terremoto-sgarbi-in-emilia-ricostruzione-rapida-allaquila-si
-piangono-addosso/477684-302/.

Adams, Vincanne. 2013. *Markets of Sorrow, Labors of Faith—New Orleans in the
Wake of Katrina*. Durham, NC: Duke University Press.

Agamben, Giorgio. 2005. *State of Exception*. Translated by Kevin Attell. Chicago:
University of Chicago Press.

Agnew, John. 2002. *Place and Politics in Modern Italy*. Chicago: University of
Chicago Press.

Alessandrini, Stefania. 2020. "L'Aquila 2009–2020: a che punto siamo con
la ricostruzione." Ingenio, June 4. Accessed November 18, 2020. https://
www.ingenio-web.it/26478-laquila-2009-2020-a-che-punto-siamo-con-la
-ricostruzione.

Alexander, David E. 2002. "The Evolution of Civil Protection in Modern Italy."
In *Disastro! Disasters in Italy since 1860: Culture, Politics, Society*, edited by John
Dickie, John Foot, and Frank Snowden, 165–185. New York: Palgrave.

———. 2010. "The L'Aquila Earthquake of 6 April 2009 and Italian Government
Policy on Disaster Response." *Journal of Natural Policy Research* 2, no. 4:
325–342.

———. 2013. "An Evaluation of Medium-Term Recovery Processes after the
6 April 2009 Earthquake in L'Aquila, Central Italy." *Environmental Hazards* 12,
no. 1: 60–73.

————. 2014. "Communicating Earthquake Risks to the Public: The Trial of the "L'Aquila Seven." *Natural Hazards* 72: 1159–1173.

Allison, Anne. 2013. *Precarious Japan*. Durham, NC: Duke University Press.

Amabile, Flavia. 2014. "La vita dei bimbi dell'Aquila mai stati in una scuola vera." *La Stampa*, March 26. Accessed November 10, 2017. https://www.lastampa.it/cronaca/2014/03/26/news/la-vita-dei-bimbi-dell-aquila-1.35782160.

Annuziato, Sarah. 2014. "Knox Case Has Put the Italian Legal System on Trial in the US." *The Conversation*, January 30. Accessed November 10, 2020. https://theconversation.com/knox-case-has-put-the-italian-legal-system-on-trial-in-the-us-22606.

Antonini, Orlando. 2010. *I terremoti aquilani*. Todi: Tau Editrice.

Arena, John. 2012. *Driven from New Orleans: How Nonprofits Betray Public Housing and Promote Privatization*. Minneapolis: University of Minnesota Press.

Augé, Marc. 1995. *Non-Places: Introduction to an Anthropology of Supermodernity*. Translated by Johns Howe. London: Verso.

Austin, Diane E. 2006. "Coastal Exploitation, Land Loss, and Hurricanes: A Recipe for Disaster." *American Anthropologist* 108, no. 4: 671–691.

Auyero, Javier. 2000. "The Hyper-Shantytown: Neo-Liberal Violence(s) in the Argentine Slum." *Ethnography* 1, no. 1: 93–116.

Balchin, Paul N. 2008. *Urban Development in Renaissance Italy*. Chichester, UK: John Wiley & Sons.

Banfield, Edward. 1958. *The Moral Basis of a Backward Society*. New York: Free Press.

Bankoff, Greg. 2003. "Constructing Vulnerability: The Historical, Natural, and Social Generation of Flooding in Metropolitan Manila." *Disasters* 27, no. 3: 224–238.

Beha, Oliviero. 2008. *Il paziente italiano: da Berlusconi al berlusconismo passando per noi*. Rome: Avagliano.

Benadusi, Mara. 2016. "The Earth Will Tremble? Expert Knowledge Confronted after the 2009 L'Aquila Earthquake." *Archivio Antropologico Mediterraneo Online* 18, no. 2: 17–31.

Bianchi, Roberto. 2003. "Il ritorno della piazza. Per una storia dell'uso politico degli spazi pubblici tra Otto e Novecento." *Zapruder* 1: 30–48.

Blackburn, Carole. 2009. "Differentiating Indigenous Citizenship: Seeking Multiplicity in Rights, Identity, and Sovereignty in Canada." *American Ethnologist* 36, no. 1: 66–78.

Boatti, Giorgio. 2004. *La terra trema. Messina 28 dicembre 1908. I trenta secondi che cambiarono l'Italia, non gli italiani*. Milan: Mondadori.

Bobbio, Norberto. 2008. *Contro i nuovi dispotismi—Scritti sul berlusconismo*. Bari, IT: Dedalo.

Bock, Jan-Jonathan. 2017. "The Second Earthquake: How the Italian State Generated Hope and Uncertainty in Post-Disaster L'Aquila." *Journal of the Royal Anthropological Institute* 23, no. 1: 61–80.

Bode, Barbara. 1989. *No Bells to Toll: Destruction and Creation in the Andes.* New York: Scribner.

Boissevain, Jeremy. 1974. *Friends of Frieds: Networks, Manipulators, and Coalitions.* New York: St. Martin's.

Bolzoni, Attilio. 2014. "L'Aquila, così il cantiere più grande d'Europa ha partorito una città fantasma." *La Repubblica,* January 14. Accessed August 10, 2017. http://www.repubblica.it/cronaca/2014/01/14/news/l_aquila_tra_negozi_chiusi_e _palazzi_sventrati_il_cantiere_pi_grande_d_europa_ha_partorito_una_citt _fantasma-75873760/.

Bonaccorsi, Manuela. 2009. "Verbali Volant." *Left,* December 11.

Bono, Irene. 2010. "Oltre la «mala Protezione civile»: l'emergenza come stile di governo." *Meridiana* 65/66: 185–205.

Bordignon, Fabio, and Luigi Ceccarini. 2013. "Five Stars and a Cricket: Beppe Grillo Shakes Italian Politics." *South European Society and Politics* 18, no. 4: 427–449.

Bourdieu, Pierre. 2002. "The Force of Law: Toward a Sociology of the Juridical Field." In *Law and Anthropology,* edited by Martha Mundy. Burlington, VT: Ashgate.

Boyer, Dominic, and Alexei Yurchak. 2010. "American Stiob: Or, What Late-Socialist Aesthetics of Parody Reveal about Contemporary Political Culture in the West." *Cultural Anthropology* 25, no. 2: 179–221.

Boyer, Dominic. 2006. "Ostalgie and the Politics of the Future in East Germany." *Public Culture* 18, no. 2: 361–381.

———. 2013. "Simply the Best: Parody and Political Sincerity in Iceland." *American Ethnologist* 40, no. 2: 276–287.

Brandmayr, Federico. 2017. "How Social Scientists Make Causal Claims in Court: Evidence from the L'Aquila Trial." *Science, Technology & Human Values* 42, no. 3: 346–380.

Brint, Steven G. 1994. *In an Age of Experts: The Changing Role of Professionals in Politics and Public Life.* Princeton, NJ: Princeton University Press.

Brubaker, Rogers. 1992. *Citizenship and Nationhood in France and Germany.* Cambridge, MA: Harvard University Press.

Brucker, Gene. 2005. *Living on the Edge in Leonardo's Florence: Selected Essays.* Berkeley: University of California Press.

Bulsei, Gian-Luigi, and Alfio Mastropaolo, eds. 2011. *Oltre il terremoto. L'Aquila tra miracoli e scandali.* Rome: Viella.

Caciagli, Mario. 1977. *Democrazia Cristiana e potere nel Mezzogiorno.* Florence: Guaraldi.

Cafagna, Luciano. 1994. *Nord e Sud: non fare a pezzi l'unità d'Italia (I grilli)*. Venice: Marsilio.

Calandra, Lina M. 2012a. "Territorio e democrazia: considerazioni dal post-sisma aquilano." In *Sismografie. Ritornare a L'Aquila mille giorni dopo il sisma*, edited by Fabio Carnelli, Orlando Paris, and Francesco Tommasi. Rome: Edizione Effigi.

———. 2012b. *Territorio e democrazia. Un laboratorio di geo-grafia sociale nel doposisma aquilano*. L'Aquila: L'Una.

Calhoun, Craig. 2010. "The Idea of Emergency: Humanitarian Action and Global (Dis)Order." In *Contemporary States of Emergency: The Politics of Military and Humanitarian Intervention*, edited by Didier Fassin and Mariella Pandolfi, 20–53. New York: Zone Books.

Candea, Matei, and Laura Jeffery. 2006. "The Politics of Victimhood." *History and Anthropology* 17, no. 4: 287–296.

Canniffe, Eamonn. 2008. *The Politics of the Piazza: The History and Meaning of the Italian Square*. Aldershot, UK: Ashgate.

Caporale, Antonello. 2010. *Terremoti Spa. Dall'Irpinia all'Aquila. Così i politici sfruttano le disgrazie e dividono il paese*. Milan: Rizzoli.

Caporale, Giuseppe. 2012. "Bertolaso e il terremoto: 'Sia un'operazione mediatica'." *La Repubblica*, January 17. Accessed May 15, 2021. https://video.repubblica.it/le -inchieste/bertolaso-e-il-terremoto-sia-un-operazione-mediatica/85961/84350.

Cappelletto, Francesca. 2003. "Long-Term Memory of Extreme Events: From Autobiography to History." *The Journal of the Royal Anthropological Institute* 9, no. 2: 241–260.

Carnelli, Fabio, Orlando Paris, and Francesco Tommasi, eds. 2012. *Sismografie. Ritornare a L'Aquila mille giorni dopo il sisma*. Arcidosso: Edizioni Effigi.

Cartlidge, Edwin. 2012. "Aftershocks in the Courtroom." *Science* 338, no. 6104: 184–188.

Cassano, Franco. 2009. *Tre modi di vedere il sud*. Bologna: Il mulino.

Castles, Stephen, and Alastair Davidson. 2000. *Citizenship and Migration: Globalization and the Politics of Belonging*. New York: Routledge.

Cavalli, Enrico. 2003. *La grande Aquila: politica, territorio ed amministrazione all'Aquila tra le due guerre*. L'Aquila: Colacchi.

Cerasani, Emilio. 1986. *I terremoti registrati nella Marsica in Marruvium e S. Sabina. Memorie storiche di due civiltà*. Pratola Peligna, IT: Grafica Italiana.

———. 1990. *Storia dei terremoti in Abruzzo: aspetti umani, sociali, economici, tecnici, artistici e culturali*. Sulmona: Accademia Sulmonese degli Agghiacciati.

Cerasoli, Domenico. 2010. "De L'Aquila non resta che il nome. Racconto di un terremoto." *Meridiana* 65/66: 35–58.

Cervellati, Pier Luigi. 1991. *La città bella. Il recupero dell'ambiente urbano*. Bologna: Il Mulino.

Chairetakis, Anna. 1991. "The Past in the Present: Community Variation and Earthquake Recovery in the Sele Valley, Southern Italy, 1980–1989." PhD thesis, Department of Anthropology, Columbia University.

Charney, Igal. 2007. "The Politics of Design: Architecture, Tall Buildings and the Skyline of Central London." *Area* 39, no. 2: 195–205.

Chubb, Judith. 2002. "Three Earthquakes: Political Response, Reconstruction, and Institutions: Belice 1968, Friuli 1976, Campania 1980." In *Disastro! Disasters in Italy Since 1860: Culture, Politics, Society*, edited by John Dickie, John Foot, and Frank Snowden. New York: Palgrave Macmillan.

Cialente, Massimo. 2013. "Cialente su Vittorini: 'Credo non stia bene, andrebbe aiutato.'" 6aprile.it, March 2. Accessed July 22, 2017. http://www.6aprile.it /featured/2013/03/02/cialente-su-vittorini-credo-non-stia-bene-andrebbe -aiutato.html.

Ciccozzi, Antonello. 2010. "Aiuti e miracoli ai margini del terremoto de L'Aquila." *Meridiana* 65/66: 227–255.

———. 2011. "Catastrofe e C.A.S.E." In *Il terremoto dell'Aquila. Analisi e riflessioni sull'emergenza*, edited by Università degli Studi Dell'Aquila. L'Aquila: Edizione L'Una.

———. 2013. *Parola di Scienza: Il terremoto dell'Aquila e la Commissione Grandi Rischi. Un'analisi antropologica*. Rome: DeriveApprodi.

———. 2015. "«Com'era-dov'era». Tutela del patrimonio culturale e sicurezza sismica degli edifici all'Aquila." *Etnografia e ricerca qualitativa* 2: 259–276.

———. 2017. "Forms of Truth in the Trial Against the Commission for Major Risks: Anthropological Notes." *Archivio Antropologico Mediterraneo on line* 18, no. 2: 65–81.

Ciranna, Simonetta. 2003. "Segni di monumentalità nazionale nell'architettura abruzzese." In *L'architettura nelle città italiane del XX secolo*, edited by Vittorio Franchetti Pardo. Milan: Jaca Book.

Clark, Stuart. 2012. "From Galileo to the L'Aquila Earthquake: Italian Science on Trial." *The Guardian*, October 24. Accessed August 1, 2017. https://www .theguardian.com/science/across-the-universe/2012/oct/24/galileo-laquila -earthquake-italian-science-trial.

Clementi, Alessandro, and Elio Piroddi. 1986. *L'Aquila*. Rome/Bari: Laterza.

Clementi, Alessandro. 1979. *L'arte della lana in una città del Regno di Napoli (sec. XIV-XVI)*. L'Aquila: Japadre.

———. 1998. *Storia dell'Aquila. Dalle origini alla prima guerra mondiale*. Rome/ Bari: Laterza.

Collins, Harry, and Robert Evans. 2007. *Rethinking Expertise*. Chicago: University of Chicago Press.

Colten, Craig E. 2006a. *An Unnatural Metropolis: Wresting New Orleans from Nature*. Baton Rouge: Louisiana State University Press.

———. 2006b. "Vulnerability and Place: Flat Land and Uneven Risk in New Orleans." *American Anthropologist* 108, no. 4: 731–734.

Conley, John M., and William M. O'Barr. 1990. *Rules versus Relationships: The Ethnography of Legal Discourse*. Chicago: University of Chicago Press.

———. 1998. *Just Words: Law, Language, and Power*. Chicago: University of Chicago Press.

Cowan, Jane K. 1990. *Dance and the Body Politic in Northern Greece*. Princeton, NJ: Princeton University Press.

Dainotto, Roberto. 2003. "The Gubbio Papers: Historic Centers in the Age of the Economic Miracle." *Journal of Modern Italian Studies* 8, no. 1: 67–83.

Das, Veena. 2006. *Life and Worlds: Violence and the Descent into the Ordinary*. Berkeley: University of California Press.

Davies, Lizzy. 2012. "Jailing of Italian Seismologists Leaves Scientific Community in Shock." *The Guardian*, October 23. Accessed August 1, 2017. https://www .theguardian.com/world/2012/oct/23/jailing-italian-seismologists-scientific -community.

Davis, Ian, and David Alexander. 2016. *Recovery from Disaster*. Abingdon, VA: Routledge.

Davis, John. 1970. "Morals and Backwardness." *Comparative Studies in Society and History* 12, no. 3: 340–353.

Day, Michael. 2012. "Italian Scientists Jailed for Six Years after Failing to Issue Warnings Ahead of Deadly L'Aquila Earthquake." *The Independent*, October 22. Accessed August 1, 2017. http://www.independent.co.uk/news/world/europe /italian-scientists-jailed-for-six-years-after-failing-to-issue-warnings-ahead-of -deadly-laquila-earthquake-8221905.html.

De Waal, Alexander. 1997. *Famine Crimes: Politics & the Disaster Relief Industry in Africa*. Bloomington: Indiana University Press.

Del Negro, Giovanna. 2004. *The Passeggiata and Popular Culture in an Italian Town: Folklore and the Performance of Modernity*. Montreal: McGill-Queen's University Press.

Di Tanna, Giuliano. 2010. "'Il sisma? Stamattina ridevo a letto'." *Il Centro*, February 12. Accessed May 5, 2021. https://www.ilcentro.it/abruzzo/il-sisma-stamattina -ridevo-a-letto-1.411665.

Dickie, John. 2006. "Timing, Memory and Disaster: Patriotic Narratives in the Aftermath of the Messina-Reggio Calabria Earthquake, 28 December 1908." *Modern Italy* 11, no. 2: 147–166.

———. 2008. *Una catastrofe patriottica. 1908: il terremoto di Messina*. Translated by F. Galimberti. Roma/Bari: Laterza.

Diefendorf, Jeffry M. 1993. *In the Wake of War: The Reconstruction of German Cities after World War II*. New York: Oxford University Press.

Di Nicola, Primo. 2010. "L'Aquila aspetta il miracolo." *L'Espresso*, February 11. Accessed August 11, 2017. http://espresso.repubblica.it/palazzo/2010/02/11/news /l-aquila-aspetta-il-miracolo-1.18749?preview=true.

Dines, Nick. 2012. *Tuff City: Urban Change and Contested Space in Central Naples.* New York: Berghahn Books.

Dipartimento della Protezione Civile. 2011. "Commissione Nazionale dei Grandi Rischi." Accessed September 28, 2014. http://www.protezionecivile.gov.it/jcms /it/commissione_grandi_rischi.wp.

Di Stefano, Pietro. 2012. "Di Stefano bacchetta il New York Times. L'assessore comunale va all'attacco: non ci servono lezioni, dico no alle demolizioni ideologiche." *Il Centro*, December 8. Accessed July 20, 2017. http://www.ilcentro .it/l-aquila/di-stefano-bacchetta-il-new-york-times-1.1147042?utm_medium= migrazione.

Dollar, John. 2010. "The Man Who Predicted an Earthquake." *The Guardian*, April 5. Accessed August 1, 2017. https://www.theguardian.com/world/2010/apr/05 /laquila-earthquake-prediction-giampaolo-giuliani.

Donadio, Rachel. 2009. "Thousands Mourn Quake Victims at Funeral Mass." *New York Times*, April 10. Accessed August 10, 2017. http://www.nytimes.com/2009 /04/11/world/europe/11italy.html?_r=0.

Doughty, Paul L. 1999. "Plan and Pattern in Reaction to Earthquake: Peru, 1970–1998." In *The Angry Earth: Disaster in Anthropological Perspective*, edited by Susanna M. Hoffmann and Anthony Oliver-Smith. London: Routledge.

D'Souza, Frances. 1982. "Recovery Following the South Italian Earthquake, November 1980: Two Contrasting Examples." *Disasters* 6, no. 2: 101–109.

Dzenovska, Dace. 2018. "Emptiness and Its Futures: Staying and Leaving as Tactics of Life in Latvia." *Focaal* 80, no. 1: 16–29

Erbani, Francesco. 2010. *Il disastro: L'Aquila dopo il terremoto—le scelte e le colpe.* Rome: Laterza.

Erikson, Kai T. 1976. *Everything in its Path: Destruction of Community in the Buffalo Creek Flood.* New York: Simon and Schuster.

European Court of Auditors. 2013. Special Report No 24/2012—"The European Union Solidarity Fund's Response to the 2009 Abruzzi Earthquake: The Relevance and Cost of Operations." Luxembourg: Publications Office of the European Union.

Farinosi, Manuela, and Alessandra Micalizzi, eds. 2013. *NetQuake. Media digitali e disastri naturali. Dieci ricerche empiriche sul ruolo della rete nel terremoto dell'Aquila.* Milan: FranoAngeli.

Farmer, Sarah. 1999. *Martyred Village: Commemorating the 1944 Massacre in Oradour-sur-Glane.* Berkeley: University of California Press.

Fassin, Didier, and Mariella Pandolfi. 2010. "Introduction: Military and
    Humanitarian Government in the Age of Intervention." In *Contemporary States
    of Emergency: The Politics of Military and Humanitarian Interventions*, edited by
    Didier Fassin and Mariella Pandolfi. Brooklyn: Zone Books.
Faubion, James D. 1994. *Modern Greek Lessons: A Primer in Historical
    Constructivism.* Princeton, NJ: Princeton University Press.
Ferragina, Emanuele. 2009. "The Never-Ending Debate about The Moral
    Basis of a Backward Society: Banfield and 'Amoral Familism.'" *Journal of the
    Anthropological Society of Oxford* 1, no. 2.
Foot, John. 2003. *Modern Italy.* New York: Palgrave Macmillan.
Forgacs, David. 2013. "Looking for Italy's Public Sphere." *Journal of Modern Italian
    Studies* 18, no. 3: 348–361.
Forino, Giuseppe. 2015. "Disaster Recovery: Narrating the Resilience Process in
    the Reconstruction of L'Aquila (Italy)." *Geografisk Tidsskrift-Danish Journal of
    Geography* 115, no. 1: 1–13.
Fortun, Kim. 2001. *Advocacy after Bhopal: Environmentalism, Disaster, New Global
    Orders.* Chicago: University of Chicago Press.
Fox News. 2012. "Italian Court Convicts 7 Scientists for Failing to Predict
    Earthquake," October 22. Accessed August 1, 2017. http://www.foxnews.com
    /science/2012/10/22/italian-court-convicts-7-scientists-for-failing-to-predict
    -earthquake/.
Frisch, Georg Josef. 2010a. *L'Aquila. Non si uccide così anche una città?* Naples: Clean.
———. 2010b. "Un altro terremoto. L'impatto urbanistico del progetto C.a.s.e."
    Meridiana 65/66: 59–84.
Gearin, Mary. 2012. "Italian Scientists Convicted for Failing to Predict Quake."
    ABC News, October 22. Accessed August 1, 2017. http://www.abc.net.au/news
    /2012-10-23/italian-scientists-convicted-over-earthquake-warning/4328046.
Gellner, Ernest, and John Waterbury, eds. 1977. *Patrons and Clients in
    Mediterranean Societies.* London: Duckworth.
Ginsborg, Paul. 2001. *Italy and Its Discontents: Family, Society, State.* New York:
    Palgrave Macmillan.
———. 2004. *Silvio Berlusconi: Television, Power and Patrimony.* London: Verso.
———. 2013. "Civil Society in Contemporary Italy: Theory, History and Practice."
    Journal of Modern Italian Studies 18, no. 3: 283–295.
Glick Schiller, Nina. 2005. "Transborder Citizenship: An Outcome of Legal
    Pluralism Within Transnational Social Fields." In *Mobile People, Mobile
    Law. Expanding Legal Relations in a Contracting World*, edited by Franz von
    Benda-Beckman, Kebbit von Benda-Beckman, and Anne Griffiths. London:
    Ashgate.
Goffman, Erving. 2007 [1961]. *Asylums: Essays on the Social Situation of Mental
    Patients and Other Inmates.* New Brunswick, NJ: Aldine Transaction.

Gribaudi, Gabriella. 1996. "Images of the South." In *Italian Cultural Studies*, edited by David Forgacs and Robert Lumley, 72–87. Oxford: Oxford University Press.

Guarnizo, Luis Eduardo. 2001. "On the Political Participation of Transnational Migrants: Old Practies and New Trends." In *E Pluribus Unum? Contemporary and Historical Perspectives on Immigrant Political Incorporation*, edited by Gary Gerstle and John Mollenkopf. New York: Russel Sage Foundation.

Guyer, Jane. 2007. "Prophecy and the Near Future: Thoughts on Macroeconomic, Evangelical, and Punctuated Time." *American Ethnologist* 34, no. 3: 409–421.

Hajek, Andrea. 2013. "Learning from L'Aquila: Grassroots Mobilization in Post-Earthquake Emilia-Romagna." *Journal of Modern Italian Studies* 18, no. 5: 627–643.

Hamber, Brandon, and Richard A. Wilson. 2002. "Symbolic Closure through Memory, Reparation and Revenge in Post-Conflict Societies." *Journal of Human Rights* 1, no. 1: 35–53.

Hammar, Tomas. 1990. *Democracy and the Nation State*. London: Routledge.

Harrell-Bond, Barbara. 1993. "Creating Marginalised Dependent Minorities: Relief Programs for Refugees in Europe." *Refugee Studies Program Newsletter* 15: 14–17.

Hastrup, Frida. 2011. *Weathering the World. Recovery in the Wake of the Tsunami in a Tamil Fishing Village*. New York: Berghahn Books.

Hayner, Priscilla. 2002. *Unspeakable Truths: Transitional Justice and the Challenge of Truth Commissions*. New York: Routledge.

Henry, Doug. 2005. "Anthropological Contributions to the Study of Disasters." In *Disciplines, Disasters and Emergency Management: The Convergence and Divergence of Concepts, Issues and Trends From the Research Literature*, edited by David A. Mcentire. Emittsburg, MD: Federal Emergency Management Agency.

Herscher, Andrew. 2010. *Violence Taking Place: The Architecture of the Kosovo Conflict*. Stanford: Stanford University Press.

Herzfeld, Michael. 1991. *A Place in History: Social and Monumental Time in a Cretan Town*. Princeton, NJ: Princeton University Press.

———. 1992. *The Social Production of Indifference: Exploring the Symbolic Roots of Western Bureaucracy*. Chicago: University of Chicago Press.

———. 1997. *Cultural Intimacy: Social Poetics in the Nation-State*. Abingdon: Routledge.

———. 2001. "Irony and Power: Toward a Politics of Mockery in Greece." In *Irony in Action: Anthropology, Practice, and the Moral Imagination*, edited by James W. Fernandez and Mary Taylor Huber. Chicago: University of Chicago Press.

———. 2009. *Evicted from Eternity: The Restructuring of Modern Rome*. Chicago: University of Chicago Press.

———. 2013. "The European Crisis and Cultural Intimacy." *Studies in Ethnicity and Nationalism* 13, no. 3: 491–497.

Hoffman, Susanna, and Anthony Oliver-Smith, eds. 1999. *The Angry Earth: Disaster in Anthropological Perspective*. Abingdon: Routledge.

———. 2002. *Catastrophe and Culture: The Anthropology of Disaster.* Santa Fe: School of American Research Press.

Holston, James, ed. 1999. *Cities and Citizenship.* Durham, NC: Duke University Press.

Hooper, John. 2009. "Silvio Berlusconi Keeps His Promise to the Earthquake Victims of L'Aquila." *The Guardian,* November 27. Accessed August 11, 2017. https://www.theguardian.com/world/2009/nov/27/italy-earthquake -berlusconi-promise-tents.

Howard, Marc Morjé. 2002. "The Weakness of Postcommunist Civil Society." *Journal of Democracy* 13, no. 1: 157–169.

Humphrey, Caroline. 2002. *The Unmaking of Soviet Life.* Ithaca, NY: Cornell University Press.

Il Centro. 2013. "Paura in Garfagnana, Gabrielli: frutto avvelenato dell'Aquila,' February 1. Accessed May 15, 2021. https://www.ilcentro.it/l-aquila/paura-in -garfagnana-gabrielli-frutto-avvelenato-dell-aquila-1.1167731.

Imperiale, Angelo Jonas, and Frank Vanclay. 2016. "Experiencing Local Community Resilience in Action: Learning from Post-Disaster Communities." *Journal of Rural Studies* 47: 204–219.

Jackson, Michael. 2005. "Storytelling Events, Violence, and the Appearance of the Past." *Anthropological Quarterly* 78, no. 2: 355–375.

———. 2007. *Excursions.* Durham, NC: Duke University Press.

———. 2011. *Life within Limits.* Durham, NC: Duke University Press.

Jacobs, Jane. 1961. *The Death and Life of Great American Cities.* New York: Random House.

James, Erica Caple. 2011. "Haiti, Insecurity, and the Politics of Asylum." *Medical Anthropology Quarterly* 25, no. 3: 357–376.

Jameson, Frederic. 1991. *Postmodernism, or, the Cultural Logic of Late Capitalism.* Durham, NC: Duke University Press.

Jansen, Stef. 2015. *Yearnings in the Meantime: "Normal Lives" and the State in a Sarajevo Apartment Complex.* New York: Berghahn Books.

Jencks, Charles. 2005. *The Iconic Building: The Power of Enigma.* London: Frances Lincoln.

Johnson, Cedric, ed. 2011. *The Neoliberal Deludge: Hurricane Katrina, Late Capitalism, and the Remaking of New Orleans.* Minneapolis: University of Minnesota Press.

Kendall, Bridget. 2009. "Italy's Minimalist G8 Summit." BBC. Accessed August 10, 2017. http://news.bbc.co.uk/1/hi/world/europe/8145847.stm.

Kertzer, David I. 2007. "Banfield, i suoi critici e la cultura." *Contemporanea* 10, no. 4: 701–709.

Kibread, Gaim. 1993. "The Myth of Dependency Among Camp Refugees in Somalia: 1979–1989." *Journal of Refugee Studies* 6, no. 4: 321–349.

Kimmelman, Michael. 2012. "In Italian Ruins, New York Lessons." *New York Times*, November 30. Accessed July 20, 2017. http://www.nytimes.com/2012/12 /01/arts/design/in-laquila-italy-lessons-for-rebuilding-from-storm.html?_r=0.

Klein, Naomi. 2000. *No Logo: Taking Aim at the Brand Bullies*. Toronto: Knopf Canada.

———. 2007. *The Shock Doctrine*. London: Penguin.

Klemek, Christopher. 2011. *The Transatlantic Collapse of Urban Renewal: Postwar Urbanism from New York to Berlin*. Chicago: University of Chicago Press.

Klingmann, Anna. 2007. *Brandscapes: Architecture in the Experience Economy*. Cambridge, MA: MIT Press.

Knight, Daniel. 2015. "Wit and Greece's Economic Crisis: Ironic Slogans, Food, and Antiausterity Sentiments." *American Ethnologist* 42, no. 2: 230–246.

Knorr Cetina, Karin. 1981. *The Manufacture of Knowledge: An Essay on the Constructivist and Contextual Nature of Science*. Oxford: Pergamon.

———. 1999. *Epistemic Cultures: How the Sciences Make Knowledge*. Cambridge, MA: Harvard University Press.

Kwon, Heonik. 2006. *After the Massacre: Commemoration and Consolation in Ha My and My Lai*. Berkeley: University of California Press.

———. 2008. *Ghosts of War in Vietnam*. Cambridge: Cambridge University Press.

Kymlicka, Will, and Wayne Norman. 1994. "Return of the Citizen: A Survey of Recent Work on Citizenship Theory." *Ethics* 104, no. 2: 352–381.

Lambek, Michael, and Paul Antze. 1996. "Introduction: Forecasting Memory." In *Tense Past: Cultural Essays in Trauma and Memory*, edited by Michael Lambek and Paul Antze. London: Routledge.

La Repubblica. 2009. "Ecco le leggi che hanno aiutato Berlusconi," November 23. Accessed August 10, 2017. http://www.repubblica.it/2009/11/sezioni/politica /giustizia-18/scheda-leggi/scheda-leggi.html.

Lazarus-Black, Mindie. 2001. "Law and the Pragmatics of Inclusion: Governing Domestic Violence in Trinidad and Tobago." *American Ethnologist* 28, no. 2: 388–416.

Leone, Pina. 2012. "La mobilitazione cittadina del 2010." In *Territorio e democrazia—Un laboratorio di geografia sociale nel doposisma aquilano*, edited by Lina M. Calandra, 375. L'Aquila: L'Una.

Leshner, Alan I. 2010. "Open Letter." AAAS, June 29. Accessed March 20, 2021. https://www. https://www.aaas.org/sites/default/files/s3fs-public/10_06 _29earthquakelettertopresidentnapolitano.pdf.

Liguori, Paolo. 2009. *Il terremoto della ricchezza. Inchiesta sull'Irpiniagate*. Milan: Ugo Mursia.

Lopez, Luigi. 1988. *L'Aquila: le memorie, i monumenti, il dialetto: guida alla città*. L'Aquila: G. Tazzi.

Low, Setha M. 1999. "Spatializing Culture: The Social Production and Social
   Construction of Public Space in Costa Rica." In *Theorizing the City: The New
   Urban Anthropology Reader*, edited by Setha M. Low, 111–137. Piscataway, NJ:
   Rutgers University Press.

Lucarelli, Carlo. 2009. *G8: Cronaca di una battaglia*. Torino: Einaudi.

Lumley, Robert, and Jonathan Morris. 1997. *The New History of the Italian South—
   The Mezzogiorno Revisited*. Exeter: Exeter University Press.

Mammarella, Luigi. 1990. *L'Abruzzo ballerino. Cronologia dei terremoti in Abruzzo
   dall'epoca romana al 1915*. L'Aquila: Adelmo Polla Editore.

Mancini, Paolo. 2013. "The Italian Public Sphere: A Case of Dramatized
   Polarization." *Journal of Modern Italian Studies* 18, no. 3: 335–347.

Mandel, Ruth. 2008. *Cosmopolitan Anxieties: Turkish Challenges to Citizenship and
   Belonging in Germany*. Durham, NC: Duke University Press.

Marconi, Francesco. 2009. "L'Aquila: terremoto del 1703, una catastrofe ignorata."
   InStoria. Accessed August 24, 2013. http://www.instoria.it/home/aquila
   _terremoto_1703.htm.

Martin, Keir. 2013. *The Death of the Big Men and the Rise of the Big Shots: Custom
   and Conflict in East New Britain*. New York: Berghahn Books.

Martinotti, Guido. 2013. "Empty *Piazze*. The Waning of Urban Civism in Italian
   Politics." *Journal of Modern Italian Studies* 18, no. 3: 322–334.

Marzocchi, Warner. 2012. "Putting Science on Trial." *Physics World* (December): 18–19.

Mastropaolo, Alfio. 2005. *La mucca pazza della democrazia. Nuove destre,
   populismo, antipolitica*. Turin: Boringhieri.

———. 2010. "Dello scandalo." *Meridiana* 65/66: 9–34.

Matteucci, Piera. 2012. "Gabrielli: 'Emiliani meglio di abruzzesi,' E Cialente attacca
   il governo." *La Repubblica*, October 16. Accessed August 10, 2017. http://www
   .repubblica.it/cronaca/2012/10/16/news/gabrielli_emiliani_hanno_reagito_meglio
   _di_abruzzesi_la_differenza_non_la_fa_la_quantit_di_denaro-44627704/.

McDonogh, Gary. 1999. "Discourses of the City: Policy and Response in Post-
   Transitional Barcelona." In *Theorizing the City: The New Urban Anthropology Reader*,
   edited by Setha M. Low, 342–376. Piscataway, NJ: Rutgers University Press.

McNeill, Donald. 1999. *Urban Change and the European Left: Tales from the New
   Barcelona*. London: Routledge.

Mela, Alfredo. 2010. "Emergenza e ricostruzione dopo il terremoto: la resilienza
   comunitaria e gli interventi di sostegno." *Meridiana* 65/66: 85–99.

Mishler, William, and Richard Rose. 2002. "Learning and Re-Learning Regime
   Support: The Dynamics of Post-Communist Regimes." *European Journal of
   Political Research* 41, no. 1: 5–36.

Miyazaki, Hirokazu. 2004. *The Method of Hope: Anthropology, Philosophy, and
   Fijian Knowledge*. Stanford: Stanford University Press.

————. 2006. "Economy of Dreams: Hopes in Global Capitalism and Its Critique."
  Cultural Anthropology 21, no. 2: 147–172.
Moe, Nelson. 2002. *The View from Vesuvius: Italian Culture and the Southern
  Question, Studies on the History of Society and Culture.* Berkeley: University of
  California Press.
Molé, Noelle J. 2011. *Labor Disorders in Neoliberal Italy: Mobbing, Well-Being, and
  the Workplace.* Bloomington: Indiana University Press.
————. 2013. "Trusted Puppets, Tarnished Politicians: Humor and Cynicism in
  Berlusconi's Italy." *American Ethnologist* 40, no. 20: 288–299.
Moore, Henrietta, and Nicholas J. Long. 2012. "Introduction: Sociality's New
  Directions." In *Sociality: New Directions*, edited by Henrietta Moore and
  Nicholas J. Long. Oxford: Berghahn Books.
Moresco, Antonio. 2012. "Il progetto—Un cammino a piedi per ricucire con i nostri
  passi l'Italia: 5 maggio–5 luglio 2012." Repubblica Nomade. Accessed July 27, 2017.
  https://camminacammina.wordpress.com/imprese-passate/stella-ditalia/stella
  -ditalia-il-progetto/.
Muehlebach, Andrea. 2012. *The Moral Neoliberal: Welfare and Citizenship in Italy.*
  Chicago: University of Chicago Press.
Naito, Daisuke, Ryan Sayre, Heather Swanson, and Satsuki Takahashi, eds. 2014. *To
  See Once More the Stars: Living in a Post-Fukushima World.* Nampa, ID: Pacific.
Nature. 2012. "Shock and Law." October 23. Accessed August 1, 2017. http://www
  .nature.com/news/shock-and-law-1.11643.
Navaro-Yashin, Yael. 2002. *Faces of the State: Secularism and Public Life in Turkey.*
  Princeton, NJ: Princeton University Press.
————. 2012. *The Make-Believe Space: Affective Geography in a Postwar Polity.*
  Durham, NC: Duke University Press.
Nussbaum, Martha. 2013. *Political Emotions: Why Love Matters for Justice.* Cambridge,
  MA: Harvard University Press.
Oliver-Smith, Anthony, and Gregory Button. 2008. "Family Resemblances
  between Disasters and Development-Induced Displacement: Hurricane Katrina
  as a Comparative Case Study." In *Capitalizing on Catastrophe: Neoliberal
  Strategies in Disaster Reconstruction*, edited by Nandini Gunewardena and Mark
  Schuller. Walnut Creek, CA: Alta Mira.
Oliver-Smith, Anthony. 1992. *The Martyred City: Death and Rebirth in the Peruvian
  Andes.* Prospect Heights, NY: Waveland.
————. 1996. "Disasters and Natural Hazards." *Annual Review of Anthropology* 25:
  303–328.
Ong, Aihwa. 1996. "Cultural Citizenship as Subject-Making: Immigrants Negotiate
  Racial and Cultural Boundaries in the United States." *Current Anthropology* 37,
  no. 5: 737–751.

————. 1999. *Flexible Citizenship: The Cultural Logics of Transnationality.* Durham, NC: Duke University Press.

Ophir, Adi. 2010. "The Politics of Catastrophization: Emergency and Exception." In *Contemporary States of Emergency: The Politics of Military and Humanitarian Interventions,* edited by Didier Fassin and Mariella Pandolfi. New York: Zone Books.

Orsina, Giovanna. 2014. *Berlusconism and Italy: A Historical Interpretation.* Basingstoke, UK: Palgrave Macmillan.

Özerdem, Alpaslan, and Gianni Rufini. 2013. "L'Aquila's Reconstruction Challenges: Has Italy Learned From Its Previous Earthquake Disasters?" *Disasters* 37, no. 1.

Pachenkov, Oleg. 2011. "Every City Has the Flea Market It Deserves: The Phenomenon of Urban Flea Markets in St. Petersburg." In *Urban Spaces after Socialism: Ethnographies of Public Places in Eurasian Cities,* edited by Tspylma Darieva, Wolfgang Kaschuba, and Melanie Krebs. Chicago: University of Chicago Press.

Pardee, Jessica Warner. 2014. *Surviving Katrina: The Experiences of Low-Income African American Women.* Boulder, CO: First Forum, Lynne Riener.

Parisse, Giustino. 2013. "Il terremoto e l'ipocrisia del Prefetto." *Il Centro,* January 20. Accessed July 22, 2017. http://www.ilcentro.it/abruzzo/il-terremoto-e-l -ipocrisia-del-prefetto-1.1163499.

Parrinello, Giacomo. 2015. *Fault Lines: Earthquakes and Urbanism in Modern Italy.* New York: Berghahn Books.

Partridge, Damani. 2012. *Hypersexuality and Headscarves: Race, Sex, and Citizenship in the New Germany, New Anthropologies of Europe.* Bloomington: Indiana University Press.

Patterson, Denis. 1999. *Law and Truth.* Oxford: Oxford University Press.

Pellizzetti, Pierfranco. 2009. *Fenomenologia di Berlusconi.* Rome: Manifestolibri.

Petrei, Fabrizia. 2012. "Democrazia e comunicazione pubblica nel post-sisma: verso quale partecipazione all'Aquila?" In *Sismografie. Ritornare a L'Aquila mille giorni dopo il sisma,* edited by Fabio Carnelli, Orlando Paris, and Francesco Tommasi, 41–48. Rome: Edizione Effigi.

Petryna, Adriana. 2002. *Life Exposed: Biological Citizens after Chernobyl.* Princeton, NJ: Princeton University Press.

Petterson, John, Laura Stanley, Edward Glazier, and James Philipp. 2006. "A Preliminary Assessment of Social and Economic Impacts Associated with Hurricane Katrina." *American Anthropologist* 108, no. 4: 643–670.

Pipyrou, Stavroula. 2014. "*Cutting* Bella Figura: *Irony, Crisis, and Secondhand Clothes in South Italy.*" *American Ethnologist* 41, no. 3: 532–546.

————. 2016a. *The Grecanici of Southern Italy: Governance, Violence, and Minority Politics.* Philadelphia: University of Pennsylvania Press.

———. 2016b. "Adrift in Time: Lived and Silenced Pasts in Calabria, South Italy." *History and Anthropology* 27, no. 1: 45–59.

Pitt-Rivers, Julian Alfred. 1971. *The People of the Sierra*. Chicago: University of Chicago Press.

Pitzalis, Silvia. 2016. *Politiche del Disastro—Poteri e contropoteri nel terremoto emiliano*. Verona, IT: ombre corte.

Platt, Rutherford H. 1999. *Disasters and Democracy: The Politics of Extreme Natural Events*. Washington, DC: Island.

Pleyers, Geoffrey. 2010. *Alter-Globalization: Becoming Actors in the Global Age*. Cambridge: Polity.

Poniatowska, Elena. 1995. *Nothing, Nobody: The Voices of the Mexico City Earthquake*. Translated by Aurora Camacho de Schmidt. Philadelphia: Temple University Press.

Ponzini, Davide, and Michele Nastasi. 2011. *Starchitecture: scene, attori e spettacoli nelle città contemporanee*. Turin: Allemandi.

Popham, Peter. 2009a. "Berlusconi Turns Adversity to Political Advantage After Quake; the Italian Leader's Energetic Reaction to the Disaster Has Been a PR Triumph." *The Independent*. Accessed August 10, 2017. http://www.independent .co.uk/news/world/europe/berlusconi-turns-adversity-to-political-advantage -after-quake-1666868.html.

———. 2009b. "Italy's Requiem for Earthquake Victims: As the Mass Funerals Were Held in L'Aquila, a Nation Stopped, Mourned and Wept for Those That Lost Their Lives in the Disaster." *The Independent*. Accessed August 10, 2017. http://www.independent.co.uk/news/world/europe/italys-requiem-for -earthquake-victims-1667295.html.

Poppi, Cesare. 1983. "'We Are Mountain People': Tradition and Ethnicity in the Ladin Carnival of the Val di Fassa (Northern Italy)." PhD thesis, Department of Social Anthropology, University of Cambridge.

Prats, Jordi. 2012. "The L'Aquila Earthquake: Science or Risk on Trial?" *Significance* 9, no. 6: 13–16.

Pratt, Jeff. 1986. *The Walled City: A Study of Social Change and Conservative Ideologies in Tuscany*. Göttingen: Rader.

Putnam, Robert. 2000. *Bowling Alone: The Collapse and Revival of American Community*. New York: Simon & Schuster.

Redattore Sociale. 2013. "L'Aquila quattro anni dopo. Almeno 20 mila persone senza lavoro," April 4. Accessed August 10, 2017. http://www.redattoresociale .it/Notiziario/Articolo/430055/L-Aquila-quattro-anni-dopo-Almeno-20-mila -persone-senza-lavoro.

Reed-Danahay, Deborah, and Caroline B. Brettel, eds. 2008. *Citizenship, Political Engagement, and Belonging: Immigrants in Europe and the United States*. New Brunswick, NJ: Rutgers University Press.

Revelli, Marco. 2013. "A Fragile Political Sphere." *Journal of Modern Italian Studies* 18, no. 3: 296–308.

Ricevuto, Matteo. 2014. "L'Aquila 5 anni dopo/I morti di serie A e quelli di serie B." Globalist, March 15. Accessed March 20, 2021. https://www.globalist.it/world/2016 /05/08/l-aquila-5-anni-dopo-i-morti-di-serie-a-e-quelli-di-serie-b-55700.html.

Ringel, Felix. 2012. "Towards Anarchist Futures? Creative Presentism, Vanguard Practices and Anthropological Hopes." *Critique of Anthropology* 32, no. 2: 173–188.

————. 2018. *Back to the Postindustrial Future: An Ethnography of Germany's Fastest-Shrinking City*. New York: Berghahn Books.

Rosaldo, Renato. 1994. "Cultural Citizenship in San Jose, California." *PoLAR* 17, no. 2: 57–63.

Ross, Fiona C. 2003. *Bearing Witness: Women and the Truth and Reconciliation Commission in South Africa*. London: Pluto Books.

Rossetti, Carlo. 1994. "Constitutionalism and Clientelism in Italy." In *Democracy, Clientelism, and Civil Society*, edited by Luis Roniger and Ayse Günes-Ayata. Boulder, CO: Lynne Rienner.

Rossi, Ino. 1993. *Community Reconstruction After an Earthquake: Dialectical Sociology in Action*. Westport, CT: Praeger.

Rubini, Aleardo. 2011. *I terremoti in Abruzzo. Cronaca, storia, arte, leggenda*. Villamagna: Tinari.

Russo, Giovanni, and Corrado Stajano. 1981. *Terremoto: le due Italie sulle macerie del Sud, volontari e vittime, camorristi e disoccupati, notabili e razzisti, borghesi e contadini, emigranti e senzatetto*. Milan: Garzanti.

Rutheiser, Charles. 1999. "Making Place in the Nonplace Urban Realm: Notes on the Revitalization of Downtown Atlanta." In *Theorizing the City: The New Urban Anthropology Reader*, edited by Setha M. Low, 317–341. Piscataway, NJ: Rutgers University Press.

Salvadorini, Ranieri. 2013. "Il terremoto nell'anima." *Mente—Il mensile di psicologia e neuroscienze* 100: 24–33.

Santili, Berardino. 2014. "Il suicidio di Rocco Pollice: L'Aquila che non pensa a ricostruire le menti." AbruzzoWeb, January 17. Accessed August 11, 2017. http:// www.abruzzoweb.it/contenuti/il-suicidio-di-rocco-pollice--laquila-che-non -pensa--a-ricostruire-le-menti/537157-327/.

Santoro, Giuliano. 2012. *Un grillo qualunque—Il Movimento 5 Stelle e il populismo digitale nella crisi dei partiti italiani*. Rome: Castelvecchi.

Sarat, Austin. 2002. "Vengeance, Victims, and the Identities of Law." In *Law and Anthropology*, edited by Martha Mundy. Burlington, VT: Ashgate.

Schneider, Jane, ed. 1998. *Italy's "Southern Question":Orientalism in One Country*. Oxford: Berg.

Schubert, Dirk, ed. 2016. *Contemporary Perspectives on Jane Jacobs: Reassessing the Impacts of an Urban Visionary*. London: Routledge.

Schwartz, Shalom H., and Anat Bardi. 1997. "Influences of Adaptation to Communist Rule on Value Priorities in Eastern Europe." *Political Psychology* 18, no. 2: 385–410.

Sebastiani, Marco. 2010. Preface, "L'Aquila anno zero." In *L'Aquila anno zero*, edited by Marco D'Antonio. Rome: DED'A.

Setta, Sandro. 2005. *L'uomo qualunque, 1944–1948*. Bari: Editori Laterza.

Settembre, Roberto. 2014. *Gridavano e piangevano. La tortura in Italia: ciò che ci insegna Bolzaneto*. Torino: Einaudi.

Sheppard, Imanni. 2011. *Health, Healing and Hurricane Katrina: A Critical Analysis of Psychosomatic Illness in Survivors*. San Diego: Cognella.

Signorelli, Amalia. 1983. *Chi può e chi aspetta: Giovani e clientelismo in un'area interna del Mezzogiorno*. Naples: Liguori.

Silverman, Sydel. 1968. "Agricultural Organization and Social Structure, and Values in Italy: Amoral Familism Reconsidered." *American Anthropologist* 70, no. 1: 1–20.

———. 1975. *Three Bells of Civilization: The Life of an Italian Hill Town*. New York: Columbia University Press.

Simpson, Edward. 2013. *The Political Biography of an Earthquake: Aftermath and Amnesia in Gujarat, India*. London: Hurst.

Siu, Lok. 2005. *Memories of a Future Home: Diasporic Citizenship of Chinese in Panama*. Stanford: Stanford University Press.

Skultans, Vieda. 1998. *Testimony of Lives: Narrative and Memory in post-Soviet Latvia*. London: Routledge.

Solnit, Rebecca. 2010. *A Paradise Built in Hell—The Extraordinary Communities That Arise in Disaster*. New York: Penguin.

Spanu, Michele. 2016. "La Maddalena: dopo il mancato G8 è la capitale delle incompiute." *Sardinia Post*, February 27. Accessed August 11, 2017. http://www .sardiniapost.it/cronaca/la-scheda-la-maddalena-dopo-il-mancato-g8-e-la -capitale-delle-incompiute.

Squires, Nick, and Gordon Rayner. 2009. "Italian Earthquake: Expert's Warnings Were Dismissed as Scaremongering." *The Daily Telegraph*, April 6. Accessed August 1, 2017. http://www.telegraph.co.uk/news/worldnews/europe/italy/5114139 /Italian-earthquake-experts-warnings-were-dismissed-as-scaremongering.html.

Stajano, Corado. 1979. *Africo*. Turin: Einaudi.

Steinberg, Ted. 2006. *Acts of God: The Unnatural History of Natural Disasters in America*. Oxford: Oxford University Press.

Stephens, Sharon. 2002. "Bounding Uncertainty: The Post-Chernobyl Culture of Radiation Experts." In *Catastrophe and Culture: The Anthropology of Disaster*, edited by Susanna M. Hoffman and Anthony Oliver-Smith. Santa Fe: School of American Research Press.

Stewart, Angus. 1995. "Two Conceptions of Citizenship." *The British Journal of Sociology* 46, no. 1: 63–78.

Sudjic, Deyan. 2006. *The Edifice Complex: How the Rich and Powerful Shape the World*. London: Penguin.

Tafuri, Manfredo. 1992. *Ricerca del Rinascimento: principi, città, architetti, Saggi*. Torino: Giulio Einaudi.

Tak, Herman. 1988. "Changing Campanilismo: Localism and the Use of Nicknames in a Tuscan Mountain Village." *Ethnologia Europaea* XVIII: 149–160.

———. 1990. "Longing for Local Identity: Intervillage Relations in an Italian Mountain Area." *Anthropological Quarterly* 63, no. 2: 90–100.

———. 2000. *Feste in Italia meridionale. Rituali e trasformazioni in una storia locale*. Potenza: Edizioni Ermes.

Tarlo, Emma. 2007. "Hijab in London: Metamorphosis, Resonance and Effects." *Journal of Material Culture* 12, no. 2: 131–156.

3e32.2013. "Cialente, l'unica mente fragile sei tu. Solidarietà a Vittorini e ai parenti delle vittime," March 4. Accessed May 12, 2021. http://www.abruzzo24ore.tv /news/Cialente-l-unica-mente-fragile-sei-tu-Solidarieta-a-Vittorini-e-ai-parenti -delle-vittime/113779.htm.

Torres, Gabriel. 1997. *The Force of Irony: Power in the Everyday Life of Mexican Tomato Workers*. Oxford: Berg.

Tribunale di L'Aquila. 2013. Motivazione. Sezione Penale: n.253/10 R.G.N.R, n. 1497/10 R.G.G.I.P, n. 448/11 R.D.Dib., n. 380/12 R. Sent. L'Aquila: Tribunale di L'Aquila.

Turner, Bryan. 1992. "Outline of a Theory of Citizenship." In *Dimensions of Radical Democracy: Pluralism, Citizenship and Community*, edited by Chantal Mouffe, 33–62. London: Verso.

Vaughan, Megan. 1987. *The Story of an African Famine: Gender and Famine in Twentieth-Century Malawi*. Cambridge: Cambridge University Press.

Ventura, Francesco. 1984. "The Long-Term Effects of the 1980 Earthquake on the Villages of Southern Italy." *Disasters* 8, no. 1: 9–11.

Verdery, Katherine. 1996. *What Was Socialism, and What Comes Next?* Princeton, NJ: Princeton University Press.

———. 1999. *The Political Lives of Dead Bodies: Reburial and Postsocialist Change, The Harriman Lectures*. New York: Columbia University Press.

Vertovec, Steven. 1998. "Multicultural Policies and Modes of Citizenship in European Cities." *International Social Science Journal* 50, no. 156: 187–199.

Vertovec, Steven, and Susanne Wessendorf, eds. 2010. *The Multiculturalism Backlash*. Abingdon: Routledge.

Vittorini, Vincenzo. 2013. "Comune L'Aquila: Servono gli straordinari, e cialente si mette part-time per la pensione." 6aprile.it, March 1. Accessed July 22, 2017.

http://www.6aprile.it/featured/2013/03/01/comune-laquila-servono-gli
-straordinari-e-cialente-si-mette-part-time-per-la-pensione.html.

Vivant, Elsa. 2011. "Who Brands Whom? The Role of Local Authorities in the Branching of Art Museums." *The Town Planning Review* 82, no. 1: 99–115.

Watkin, David. 2005. *A History of Western Architecture.* New York: Watson-Guptill Publications.

Wilson, Richard A. 2001. *The Politics of Truth and Reconciliation in South Africa: Legitimizing the Post-Apartheid State.* Cambridge: Cambridge University Press.

Wright, Beverly. 2011. "Race, Place, and the Environment in the Aftermath of Katrina." *Anthropology of Work Review* 32, no. 1: 4–8.

Yeo, Michael. 2014. "Fault Lines at the Interface of Science and Policy: Interpretative Responses to the Trial of Scientists in L'Aquila." *Earth-Science Reviews* 139: 406–419.

Yoneyama, Lisa. 1999. *Hiroshima Traces: Time, Space, and the Dialectics of Memory.* Berkeley: University of California Press.

Yurchak, Alexei. 1997. "The Cynical Reason of Late Socialism: Power, Pretense and the *Anekdot.*" *Public Culture* 9: 161–188.

———. 2003. "Soviet Hegemony of Form: Everything Was Forever, Until It Was No More." *Comparative Studies in Society and History* 45, no. 3: 480–510.

Zinn, Dorothy Louise. 2001. *La Raccomandazione. Clientelismo vecchio e nuovo.* Translated by Caterina Dominijanni. Rome: Donzelli Editore.

INDEX

Abbado, Claudio, 125–26, 129
ABC News, 195
Abruzzo, 2, 11
Accumoli, 12
Africo, 28
agency: in Aquilani's recollections of
disaster-relief operation, 51–54, 56, 57–59,
60–61, 68; debates about reconstruction
and restoration and, 110–12; Major Risks
Commission trial and, 194; wheelbarrow
protest (2010) and, 41–42, 61–65, 74, 80,
93, 103, 112. *See also* politics and political
agency
Alessia (L'Aquila resident), 66–67
Alexander, David, 219
Alfredo (L'Aquila resident), 92–93
Allison, Anne, 139
Amatrice, 12
Amedeo (L'Aquila resident), 131–32, 133, 134
American Association for the Advancement
of Science (AAAS), 196
amoral familism, 27–28
Anna (L'Aquila resident), 56–57
Antonio (L'Aquila resident), 163
Apennine Mountains, 11, 12–13
Appello per L'Aquila: municipal elections
(2012) and, 129–30, 149–54, 158, 160, *161*,
164–66, 228; municipal elections (2017)
and, 231

Ascoli Piceno, 12
Assemblea Cittadina, 121, 139
A-TV (local television station), 168, 183–84
Auditorium del Parco, 112, 125–36, 129, 138
Augé, Marc, 141n17
authoritarian leadership, 40
Avezzano, 12–13

Banfield, Edward, 27
Barberi, Franco, 198
Barca, Fabrizio, 87, 121
Barcelona, 118
Belice earthquake (1968), 42
Berlusconi, Silvio: Aquilani's views of, 146,
149; *Draquila* (documentary film) and,
65–67; emergency relief operation in
L'Aquila and, 3, 15–17, 61–62; G8 summit
(Genoa, July 20–22, 2001) and, 45–46;
G8 summit (L'Aquila, July 8–10, 2009)
and, 17–19, 45, 46–48, 61; international
perceptions of, 44–47, 48–49; media
coverage and, 3, 42–51, 226; Progetto Case
and, 16–17, 19; resignation (2011) of, 21
berlusconismo, 4, 26, 227
Bertolaso, Guido, 15–16, 43, 46, 62, 149,
207–9. *See also* Major Risks Commission
(Commissione Grandi Rischi)
Bilbao, 125
Billi, Marco, 200, 208–10, 214

JAN-JONATHAN BOCK received his PhD in Social Anthropology from the University of Cambridge. He is editor (with Sharon Macdonald) of *Refugees Welcome? Difference and Diversity in a Changing Germany* and (with John Fahy and Samuel Everett) of *Emergent Religious Pluralisms*. Jan directs the Business Council for Democracy (BC4D) for the Hertie Foundation, Germany.